Law and Ethics in Intensive Care

Law and Ethics in Intensive Care

Edited by

Christopher Danbury
Christopher Newdick
Andrew Lawson
Carl Waldmann

OXFORD
UNIVERSITY PRESS

Great Clarendon Street, Oxford OX2 6DP

Oxford University Press is a department of the University of Oxford.
It furthers the University's objective of excellence in research, scholarship,
and education by publishing worldwide in

Oxford New York

Auckland Cape Town Dar es Salaam Hong Kong Karachi
Kuala Lumpur Madrid Melbourne Mexico City Nairobi
New Delhi Shanghai Taipei Toronto

With offices in

Argentina Austria Brazil Chile Czech Republic France Greece
Guatemala Hungary Italy Japan Poland Portugal Singapore
South Korea Switzerland Thailand Turkey Ukraine Vietnam

Oxford is a registered trade mark of Oxford University Press
in the UK and in certain other countries

Published in the United States
by Oxford University Press Inc., New York

British Library Cataloguing in Publication Data

Data available

Library of Congress Cataloging in Publication Data

Data available

Typeset in Minion by Glyph International, Bangalore, India
Printed in Great Britain
on acid-free paper by
The MPG Books Group, Bodmin and King's Lynn

ISBN 978–0–19–956203–9

10 9 8 7 6 5 4 3 2 1

Oxford University Press makes no representation, express or implied, that the drug
dosages in this book are correct. Readers must therefore always check the product
information and clinical procedures with the most up-to-date published product
information and data sheets provided by the manufacturers and the most recent codes of
conduct and safety regulations. The authors and the publishers do not accept responsibility
or legal liability for any errors in the text or for the misuse or misapplication of material in
this work. Except where otherwise stated, drug dosages and recommendations are for the
non-pregnant adult who is not breastfeeding.

Preface

The practice of intensive care is being transformed. Demographic changes mean that more of us live to a good age and will require intensive care later in our lives. Pharmaceutical and medical technologies have introduced a range of treatments, which for many are life-saving, but for others have less significant impact and leave them in a fragile and uncertain condition. Patients and their relatives have seen their rights in this area transformed, so that the old paternalistic approaches of the past have been replaced with a duty to be open, to discuss, and to negotiate. And, of course, there is the pressure of NHS governance and the need to manage the risk of litigation if things go wrong.

The great American jurist, Charles Warren, once said that the law floats on a sea of ethics. Modern critical care medicine too provokes multiple ethical and legal problems, which make it even more difficult to know who and when to admit to intensive care, at what stage should invasive management be withdrawn, and who should decide. These profound dilemmas, made more complicated in a setting of scarce resources, mandate an understanding of relevant contemporary laws and the ethical principles that underpin our actions. This collection of articles on ethical and legal aspects of intensive care medicine is published at a crucial time both in the evolution of critical care medicine but also with respect to the way society is responding to health care challenges.

The book addresses a variety of ethical controversies in the United Kingdom relevant to our speciality. Although there inevitable overlap, we have divided the book into a series of sections as follows: Part A addresses issues of competency and autonomy and includes chapters by Bell on 'Consent for Intensive Care: Public and Political Expectations vs. Conceptual and Practical Hurdles', Bryden on 'Adults Who Lack

Capacity to Consent', and Newdick and Danbury on 'the Best Interests of Babies and Children'. Part B focuses on issues between doctor and patient, with chapters by McLean and Morgan on 'Taking it or Leaving It: Demanding and Refusing Treatment in Intensive Care', Biggs on 'Dying to Know: Legal and Ethical Issues Surrounding Death and Do Not Resuscitate Orders', Lawson on 'Diagnosing Death', and Woodcock on 'Research in Intensive Care'. Finally, Part C considers the challenges of managing the intensive care unit, with contributions from Pittaway and Peacock on 'NHS Governance of Critical Care', Newdick and Danbury on 'Reverse Triage? Managing Scarce Resources', Coggon on 'Doing What's Best: Organ Donation and Intensive Care', and Waldmann, Soni, and Lawson on 'Conflicts of Interest'.

Although not comprehensive, we have developed key issues of interests to intensivists, and the chapter authors have been selected for their reputation and passion for the subject. We hope that there is something useful for everybody in this book.

CD, CN, AL, CW

Contents

Part C **Management-focused issues**

Contributors

Dr Dominic Bell
Consultant in Intensive Care/
Anaesthesia,
The General Infirmary at Leeds,
UK

Professor Hazel Biggs
Professor of Medical Law,
School of Law,
University of Southampton,
UK

Dr Margaret Branthwaite
Retired Barrister,
Formerly Consultant in
Anaesthesia, Intensive Care and
Respiratory Medicine,
Royal Brompton Hospital,
UK

Dr Daniele C Bryden
Consultant in Intensive Care
Medicine and Anaesthesia,
Sheffield Teaching Hospitals
NHS Trust,
UK

Dr John Coggon
British Academy Postdoctoral
Fellow, School of Law,
University of Manchester,
UK

Dr Christopher Danbury
Consultant in Intensive Care
Medicine and Anaesthetics,
Royal Berkshire Hospital,
UK

Dr Andrew Lawson
Honorary Senior Lecturer,
Medical Ethics, Imperial College
Post Graduate Student,
Worcester College, Oxford,
UK

Professor S. A. M. McLean
International Bar Association,
Chair of Law and Ethics in
Medicine,
School of Law,
University of Glasgow,
UK

Dr Derek Morgan
Professor of Medical Law and
Jurisprudence,
School of Law,
University of Sheffield,
UK

Professor Christopher Newdick
School of Law,
The University of Reading,
UK

Nicholas A Peacock
Barrister,
Hailsham Chambers,
UK

David Pittaway QC
Barrister,
Hailsham Chambers,
UK

Dr Neil Soni
Consultant in Intensive Care
and Anaesthetics,
Chelsea and Westminster
Hospital,
UK

Dr Carl Waldmann
Consultant Intensive Care and
Anaesthesia,
Royal Berkshire Hospital,
UK

Dr Thomas E Woodcock
Consultant in Intensive Care
and Anaesthetics,
Southampton University
NHS Trust,
UK

Introduction

An introduction to ethical models

Andrew Lawson

... imagine that you are charged with building the edifice of human destiny, the ultimate aim of which is to bring people happiness to give them peace and contentment at last, but that in order to achieve this it is essential and unavoidable to torture just one speck of creation, that same little child beating her chest with her little fists, and imagine that this edifice has to be erected on her unexpiated tears. Would you agree to be the architect under those conditions? Tell me honestly!

Dostoevsky; The Brothers Karamazov (Vol 1, Pt 2, Bk 5, Ch 4)

What is ethics?

Dostoevsky asks a fundamental moral question above. Do the consequences of our actions count, or does the suffering of the little child outweigh any benefits? We might add whether the rights of the child are important or whether to torture a little child is not what a good person might do.

Ethics, or moral philosophy, is a branch of philosophy concerned with norms and values, rights and wrongs, and what ought or what not ought to be done. In other words, coming after reflection, argument and analysis, to a sense of what one ought to do under given sets of circumstances. A branch of ethics that concerns health and or life sciences has been called medical ethics (in the United Kingdom) or bioethics (in the United States).

Medical practice has long reflected on the relationship between the physician and the patient in its broadest sense, from Socrates to the present day. Such reflections principally concerned the moral obligations of physicians in preventing disease and treating the sick and injured. In a sense, the values that underpinned medical practice were assumed to be obvious and the recitation of the Hippocratic oath upon qualification was deemed to suffice. Attitudes change however, and the revelation that physicians had been involved in unethical experimentation, and other atrocities, upon humans in Nazi Germany during World War II seems to have been a turning point in questioning the assumption of the good of the physician. The Nuremburg Code on research ethics in 1946 represents a milestone in this shift of attitudes.

By the 1960s, these assumptions were increasingly questioned, in part as technological advances such as artificial ventilation, transplantation, and dialysis changed the scope of medicine, leading to the necessity for novel decisions to be made. An example still debated is when might it be right to withdraw artificial ventilation, and would that be the same as not starting it? Initially such questions fell within the purview of philosophers, lawyers, and religious organizations but by the 1970s, ethical think tanks and the academic study of these were rising. Medical ethics (or bioethics) has become the study and critical analysis of the ethical issues that arise in the interrelationships between law, medicine, life sciences, theology, and biotechnology.

Before proceeding to describe ethical models, it is worth considering some common reactions to the idea of 'medical ethics' as a distinct entity.

Ethics and religion

For many, the default position when faced with a difficult ethical problem in practice was to ask the hospital, or local chaplain or priest. For many religious believers, the answers to ethical problems are to be found in sacred texts such as the Bible or the Koran and in the various commentaries and discussions that have flowed from them. There is often an assumed link between popular conceptions of morality and religion, equating moral principles with divine revelation. Notwithstanding the plurality of religions present in western societies or the fact that reliance on religious tenets will involve applying such principles to situations unheard of or undreamt of when the religion was first promulgated, there remains a fundamental problem. This was first formulated by Plato in the Euthyphro. Is the good good because God commands it, or does God command it because it is good? If the former is true, then morality is mere obedience to an arbitrary will. If the latter is true then morality is independent of the will of God, so recourse to knowledge of the divine, at least in ethics, is redundant. We might agree that rape and murder are 'wrong'. What if a God were to say they are right? Would that make them right, if so would it be somewhat arbitrary and not supported by reason?

Ethics and the law

It would be convenient if we could look to the law as a source for our ethical needs. Clearly the law is important and the practice of health care takes place within a framework of laws and regulations relevant to the particular jurisdiction. However, the fact that something is legal does not necessarily imply that it is morally permissible, nor is the converse true. If an act is illegal, it may be morally permissible. The apartheid laws in South Africa and the anti-Jewish penal codes in Germany in the 1930s are example of 'laws' which we might consider to be unethical. Abortion was made legal in the UK in 1967; does this mean it was morally wrong before the law changed but not afterwards? There is a distinction and the American jurist Earl Warren put the relationship succinctly in 1964:

> In civilized life, law floats in a sea of ethics. Each is indispensable to civilization. Without law, we should be at the mercy of the least scrupulous; without ethics, law could not exist.

Common sense and subjectivity

One of the common critiques of medical ethics is that the problems that are discussed can be dealt with a bit of common sense. Training as a health care provider and applying common sense is all you need, not studying moral theory. There is an element of truth to this, for in day-to-day practice doctors and nurse have for generations worked in an ethical manner. Notwithstanding the various 'evil' doctors and nurses in history; for the most part, the training and self selection of people in the caring professions ensures a high level of 'ethical conduct', and simply learning moral theory does not make one more ethical than learning the 10 Commandments makes one a Christian. However, we are more often now presented with problems which common sense cannot solve. In the event of a pandemic flu, how will we decide whom to ventilate, would it be morally correct (if illegal) to assist the death of a suffering patient at their request, and what is the difference between withholding and withdrawing treatment. These problems are not commonsensical and entail more moral debate to resolve them.

The problem of subjectivity often arises in discussions on medical ethics, the idea that all ethical arguments are reduced to subjective disputes over wrong and right and hence ethical discourse can get you nowhere. There are a number of problems with this approach. Taken to its conclusion, that all actions are morally subjective and therefore not amenable to any kind of objective analysis, leaves us in nihilistic world where there are no prohibitions or sanctions and all actions; killing new-born babies or killing people to harvest their organs without their consent become morally equal. This thread that seems at variance with most societal norms. We may agree that there is disagreement but the fact that there is disagreement does not throw light on the validity, or lack thereof, of any argument. The lack of consensus on a matter, for example evolution, does not mean there is no objective truth to be found or that it is worthwhile looking for it.

Another argument against formal medical ethics has been that while medicine, and science in general, is characterized by the existence of an objective truth, ethical discourse is not amenable to such 'truths'. However a cursory look at what are considered to be established truths in medicine and science often reveals profound disagreement. The usage of 'evidence-based medicine' is an accepted practice and one might say a cultural norm in western societies, but there exists a body of thought that challenges such orthodoxy. Similar conflict exists in various branches of pure science.

Ethical terms

Ethics (or moral philosophy) is broadly divided into normative and non-normative. Normative ethics involves the general inquiry into which models or norms should we use as a guide to analysing conduct or concepts, the 'should' of ethics. Non-normative ethics involves the investigation of moral behaviours and belief and the analysis of the language and methodology of reasoning in ethics, the 'is' in ethics.

Some authors have also coined the term 'common morality' as a bedrock from which to start ethical discourse, the common morality being that set of moral norms that binds people together as some sort of sociological glue. In a sense, the existence of a 'common morality' is a defence against the criticism of subjectivity in ethics. If we all share a common morality or ethics then it is not all subjective.

Ethical models

Broadly speaking, ethics is divided into four basic theories of right and wrong actions. Utilitarianism, deontological, or rights-based theories (Kantianism), virtue ethics (into which we may include feminist ethics), and the four principles approach. The four principles approach, which is the most commonly taught model in medical schools, is based arround the concepts (or principles) of justice, beneficence, non-malfeasance, and autonomy. It is perhaps the pre-eminent theoretical model used in the health sciences. Virtue ethics takes its roots in the ancient Greek philosophies of Aristotle and Plato. Virtue ethicists believe that the rightness or wrongness of an action is embedded in the character of the individual. The deontological approach has its roots in Kantianism. In this approach, the agent must act rationally and consistently to be moral. Finally utilitarianism is a moral theory, which essentially looks at the consequences of an act. The morality of an act is crystallized by the consequences, this sort of analysis is exemplified by the usage of outcome measures for populations such as in vaccination.

Utilitarianism

While academic philosophers and ethicists will define many sub-types of utilitarianism for the purposes of generalization, utilitarianism can be defined as a consequentialist philosophy whereby actions are held to be right or wrong by virtue of their consequences. It has its roots in the writings of Jeremy Bentham and John Stuart Mill and is fundamentally based on the 'fact' that suffering is evil and happiness is good. Extending this into the moral sphere allows us to judge action on the basis of these simple alternatives and avoids conflicting principles and the conflict of absolutes.

It is, when applied to health care, an impersonal theory in that any act is assessed as to its overall effect upon persons in general, not for any one particular person. Acts are considered right when they 'maximize net welfare'. The rightness of an act (or health care intervention) is crystallized in terms of the welfare of the persons, or population, concerned. The sum of the positive and negative effects are aggregated. Thus for any given health care intervention, the overall balance of benefit over harm is what is assessed by a consequentialist analysis.

Health care planning, strategic decisions over resource allocation, and decisions as to how to allocate resources in pandemics or emergency situations are good examples of where consequentialist analysis is pursued in contemporary health care. The health economic analyses of NICE using such tools as the quality adjusted life year (QALY) and vaccination programs also have a consequentialst, aggregating basis to them. The herd immunity produced by vaccination may not necessarily benefit a specific person, nor might an identifiable person benefit from a treatment recommended by NICE, but in both cases the health gains to the population are maximized.

Utilitarianism has hallways suffered from the problem of consequentialist conception of morality and virtue that any means (as in the unexpiated tears of the child) can be used to justify a good enough end. To use a controversial issue, if autism were actually caused by the MMR vaccine in a small number of children then the net benefits to the population would justify this harm to them when viewed through a consequentailst lens. This seems to be almost counter-intuitive, conflicting in some way with our common morality.

Original consequentialist philosophy stressed the importance of 'happiness' or pleasure. And it was only to be applied to sentient beings. This poses the difficult question as to how we measure happiness, if indeed we can measure it, and to what extent unconscious humans, animals, or the developing human (embryo or foetus) fall within the scope of our consequentialist radar.

Modern utilitarians have attempted to combine deontological theories with utilitarianism, as well as attempting to accommodate goods other than happiness or pleasure such as equality and fairness in an effort to acknowledge its shortcomings. Utilitarianism can also be seen as too demanding, and to a certain extent as diminishing individual responsibility. For each action or decision, an agent makes a calculation of net benefit to determine whether the consequence produces an overall increase in happiness of all concerned, at that point and in the future. This is an aspect of the theory that is too demanding for the individual—the calculation of the effect of an act or decision upon everybody involved now and in the future. The theory was advanced at a time when concepts of chaos theory were unknown and the permutations would seem to be infinite. To use a well-known metaphor, if a butterfly flapping its wings can trigger a series of events leading to a hurricane how can I, with any accuracy, analyse my decision to save the life of x vs. y? Imagine a field of dominoes laid out in random patterns, how could you predict which will fall when a single domino is pushed over?

A utilitarian would also state that I, having pushed the first domino over, must have responsibility for all the other falling dominoes. This may be true of the dominoes but human beings are not dominoes and make decisions as to how to act. The utilitarian removes their responsibility for their actions because their 'falling' is a consequence of the first domino falling. As Benn points out, 'the results of assigning responsibility so promiscuously is that no one is really responsible for anything'.

Utilitarianism implies that people should give up what they have at all times to benefit others who are in greater need. This is not consistent with social mores now or in the past. In advocating the approach that all should behave in such a manner it devalues those who do so, as it does not distinguish between obligatory actions and supererogatory actions. The demand to maximize happiness, however defined, would have implications for how can we define the geographical limitations of our obligations. We would be obliged to forego intensive care in the United Kingdom until those resources had been used to bring the level of health care in developing countries up to our basic standard. A laudable aim, but not practical in a political or sociological sense.

Deontology and Kant

Deontological moral theories are, broadly speaking, in opposition to consequentialst theories in that the morality of an action is a function of the act itself rather than the consequences. Moral rightness consists of acting rationally and consistently, independent of empirical or other motives.

Emmanuel Kant, an eighteenth-century Prussian philosopher, is seen as a father of modern deontology. He believed that humans had autonomy of will and could by acting rationally in accordance with a 'supreme moral law' ensure the rightness of their actions. He formulated the 'categorical imperative' that stated that we should always treat rational humanity as an end in itself and never merely as a means to an end. He stressed that we should only act on principles that we would wish to become universal laws, and stressed the independent moral worth of a person. Kant rejected the concept of moral philosophy as being tested as an empirical science, relying on an a priori method. The basic moral standards are a constitutive feature of people acting in a moral fashion not because of any commitment to authority, tradition or common sense, the come before, a priori, all else.

Kantianism has been criticized for being too absolute; it was unequivocal that the supreme moral laws applied without exception. Thus to lie, even to save a life, would be a moral wrong. The absolutist stance also gave no weight to concepts such as being good, caring or helping others, and seems out of keeping with our 'common morality'.

More recently W D Ross in the early twentieth century refined deontological concepts stating:

> The moral order ... is just as much part of the fundamental nature of the universe (and ... of any possible universe in which there are moral agents at all) as is the spatial or numerical structure expressed in the axioms of geometry or arithmetic.

He described seven prima facie duties:

- Fidelity—Fulfilling promises (implicit and explicit)
- Reparation—Making up for wrongful acts

- Gratitude—Repaying for past favours
- Non-maleficence—A duty to not injure others
- Justice—Promoting the distribution of happiness
- Beneficence—A duty to improve the condition of others
- Self-improvement.

These duties were self-evident and should prevail in any moral consideration. He also thought that in any given situation one of the duties would evidently become the weightiest and overrule the others, becoming an absolute obligation. Some of these duties re-appear in the four principles approach. Ross's list has been criticized for being unsystematic and illogical, and not being able to determine what our actual moral obligations might be in particular situations. The accuracy of the list has also been questioned. His reply was that it was accurate as far as it goes, that there was no reason to assume that our moral obligations would be the same in all circumstances.

Despite criticisms of lists and the absolutist nature of deontology, it has strong contemporary resonance. The general medical council has a list of 'duties of a doctor'.

- Make the care of your patient your first concern.
- Protect and promote the health of patients and the public.
- Provide a good standard of practice and care.
- Treat patients as individuals and respect their dignity.
- Work in partnership with patients.
- Be honest and open and act with integrity.

Virtue ethics

Virtue ethics has its roots in ancient Greece in the teachings of Plato and Aristotle. Plato discussed four key virtues: wisdom, courage, temperance, and justice. Aristotle considered that people are better able to regulate their emotions and reason when they acquire good habits of character. Virtue ethicists thus think that right and wrong cannot be defined in terms of pre-set moral principles or rules. The distinction between right and wrong is made by being sensitive to situations in a moral sense or expressing fundamentally good or admirable character traits. In virtue ethics, the motives and character of the agent are what counts. They help us reach morally correct decisions when we are faced with difficult choices.

As a principle for developing good moral character, being virtuous is appealing as a means of solving difficult ethical problems though it seems to have some disadvantages. How do we determine what is the 'right' sort of character and how does just having the right sort of character ensure a correct decision? Similarly how do we distinguish or rank differing virtues? Perhaps as an ethical model it says more about the psychology of morality than the nature of moral truth.

The four principles

Beauchamp and Childress first unveiled the four principles approach to medical ethics in 1979. Since that time they have become very popular and have become the standard model for medical ethical discourse and teaching in UK medical schools. The four principles are general guides to judgement and have been described as mid-level principles mediating between high-level moral theory and low-level common morality.

Autonomy

Respect for autonomy is the principle of respect for decision-making capacities of autonomous persons allowing them to make reasoned informed choices. Autonomy can be divided into autonomy of thought, intention, and action. Respect for autonomy has developed into a professional obligation, which is both a negative obligation, in which we must not constrain autonomous choice, and a positive obligation where we must ensure that patients are able to be autonomous as much as is possible. This entails proper disclosure of information relevant to the decision-making process and actively looking to promote autonomy by ensuring understanding. In the context of illness, it is probable that there is some degree of impairment of autonomy. In the critical care setting, all aspects of autonomy may be significantly impaired. A properly sedated patient should have no autonomy of thought or will but may have some of action.

Beneficence

Health care professionals have a moral obligation to act in such a way as to benefit their patients. This principle of beneficence includes all actions taken to the benefit of others. Unlike simple acts of kindness or altruism, which while desirable, could not be seen as obligatory, beneficence in medicine is. This general obligation is seen in preventative medicine and in public health programs, which would not be characterized as optional. Health care professionals thus have voluntarily taken on an obligation; it is debateable whether such obligations to benefit others necessarily exist outside of health care. Good Samaritan acts are not obligatory.

This principle of beneficence has its limitations though. How much risk is obligatory for a doctor or nurse to take when treating a patient? Those HCPs in the armed forces have voluntarily taken on a different level of risk. In the event of a pandemic infectious disease, it is arguable how much risk doctors and nurses are obliged to take.

Beneficence also has to be tempered with other factors. An autonomous patient has a right to refuse or decline a treatment even if it is thought to be in his or her best interests, the respect for individual autonomy trumps beneficence in this example. Beneficence has also to be tempered by non-maleficience and justice.

Non-maleficience

The principle of non-harming is also central to medicine. However it is true that all treatment has the potential to do harm. Invasive monitoring on the ITU involves a risk of complication and will cause some discomfort or pain as will any surgical procedure. The harm caused needs to be proportional to the benefit.

Justice

Considerations of justice also need to be considered. Justice in this context is concerned with the fair distribution of health resources. Institutions such as NICE using health economic tools as mentioned above attempt to distribute the health budget. Doctors often feel that this 'distributive justice' impacts on the relationship between them and the patients under their care, arguing that their obligations are to their patients and that the responsibility for allocation of resources does not function at the bedside. However, marginally beneficial intensive care may be justifiably limited on the basis of societal consensus that its cost is too high in relation to the value of its outcome. The American Thoracic Society Bioethics Task Force stated in 1997 that 'extraordinary expenditures of resources for marginal gains unfairly compromise the availability of a basic minimum level of health care services for all'. Such issues have great relevance in the context of dealing with pandemics.

The four principles approach has proved very popular and is amenable to using in many differing situations and forms a workable template in practice. However, they do have limitations. It is difficult to see how one orders the principles in complex situations and how one settles conflicts between principles. In much common discourse, solutions to ethical problems have been reduced to a simple recitation of the four principles without consideration of the abstract concept of what the principles actually mean, as if a solution can be simply achieved just by invoking the principles. Clearly interpretation of them in the context of a problem is desirable. However, notwithstanding any criticisms, the success of the four principles approach is testament to their utility.

Which model and when?

From a practical point of view, no one model can provide a solution to all ethical dilemmas and it would be surprising if it were so. Kantianism seems to grate against human psychology, utilitarianism may be too demanding, virtue ethics a bit fuzzy, and the four principles may seem a little too simplistic. They all have their shortcomings. We may though make a broad distinction between macro-ethical problems such as resource allocation across society and choices as to what treatment is best for a given disease and the micro-ethics of dealing with patients on an individual level.

Health care in general has a strong utilitarian basis as described above. Optimizing which treatment for sepsis involves pooling data and producing a population-based recommendation. That recommendation may not be valid for an individual, indeed we cannot be certain that any treatment will work definitely for a given individual, but we know we can maximize the outcome for a group. At the micro level, while a degree of maximizing outcome occurs, the relationship between the HCP and the patient is more about being 'a good person' and doing the right thing for him or her. It is perhaps at this level that the four principles come into their own.

Medical ethics helps us crystallize complex issues, and the varying models give us the tools to describe our analyses and decision-making process.

References

1 Kuchel T, Williams E, Beytagh F (1976). In Memoriam. Earl Warren. Chief Justice of the United States. *California Law Review*, **64**(1): 2–13.
2 Veatch R (2003). Is There a Common Morality? *Kennedy Institute of Ethics Journal*, **13**(3): 189–192.
3 Benn P (1998). *Ethics*. London: UCL Press, 81.
4 Ross W D (1951). *Foundations of ethics: the Gifford lectures delivered in the University of Aberdeen, 1935–1936*. Oxford, Clarendon.
5 Ibid p. 26.
6 www.gmc-uk.org/guidance/
7 Beauchamp P, Childress J (2001). *2001 Principles of Biomedical Ethics*. New York, Oxford University Press.
8 ATS Bioethics Task Force (1997). Fair Allocation of Intensive Care Unit Resources. *Am J Respir Crit Care Med*, **156**: 1282–1301.

Evolution of health care law

Margaret Branthwaite

Registration and regulation of medical practitioners

Medical practitioners share the common public duty to conform to the laws of the jurisdiction within which they practice. In addition, they are required to *apply* the law in areas such as public health, mental health, and drug prescribing and are *subject to* laws that regulate the conduct of the profession. The Medical Act 1858, replaced by the Medical Act 1983, established the basis for medical registration and permitted the profession itself to accept responsibility for regulating the conduct of individual practitioners. This position has gradually changed, reflecting in part a growing emphasis on the rights of individuals and an increased willingness to challenge authority, but also in response to a number of well-publicized medical scandals involving practitioners not always acting in the best interests of their patients and methods of professional self-regulation which have been found wanting.[1-3]

A flurry of statutory enactments has extended and modified the powers of the General Medical Council (GMC), changed the composition and size of the council, established an over-arching supervisory body, the Council for Healthcare Regulatory Excellence, and paved the way for the introduction of a system of regular revalidation and relicensing for all practising doctors. A National Clinical Assessment Authority has been established to investigate and advise on the performance of practitioners where cause for concern has been raised, and the Commission for Healthcare Audit and Inspection is empowered to investigate standards of care in both public and private medical services. Medical disciplinary procedures have changed too, with lowering from the criminal to the civil standard of proof, and a requirement that GMC Council members do not sit on any adjudication committee, so preventing any perception of a dual role as both prosecutor and judge. This plethora of new legislation has resulted in a widespread feeling of insecurity within a profession, which, in the past, had confidence in its own authority and anticipated its decisions would be supported by the courts and public alike. The loss of self-confidence resulting from the more stringent regulatory framework has been exacerbated by the simultaneous growth in legal actions challenging clinical practice.

Claims arising from clinical negligence: Procedural reform

A number of factors combined during the second half of the twentieth century to generate a rapid rise in both the number and cost of claims against health care professionals and services. These included an increasingly assertive public, state funding of most health care, more complex, high-risk procedures, the availability of Legal Aid to finance claims, and the high cost of long-term care for those with serious disability resulting from an adverse clinical event. Liability for the defence and settlement of claims was often shared between a medical defence organization representing the interests of an individual practitioner and a hospital authority with vicarious liability for all other employees. This created a potential for conflict which was not only financial but also procedural because practitioners feared that an economically expedient settlement might damage their professional reputation. Resolution came in 1990 when the liability of National Health Service (NHS) Hospital Trusts was extended to medical staff, albeit with concern among the profession that expediency rather than justice might prevail. By contrast, private practitioners, and general practitioners within the NHS, retain individual liability.

The standard of care required of a practitioner at English law is determined by judicial appraisal of medical opinion. In 1957, in *Bolam v Friern Hospital Management Committee*,[4] it was held that a doctor is not to be deemed negligent if acting in accordance with the opinion of a responsible body of medical practitioners skilled and practised in that art. A similar test was enunciated in Scotland in 1955.[5] The *Bolam* test was refined in 1998 by a need to demonstrate that expert opinion is 'reasonable', is based on a consideration of risks and benefits, and is capable of withstanding logical analysis.[6] Even with this refinement, the test for breach of duty itself leaves room for contention but successful claimants must also be able to show that the breach of duty, rather than the natural history of the disease or recognized hazards of a high-risk procedure, was responsible for injury.[7] If, as is often the case, negligence contributes to but is not solely responsible for an injury, claimants can recover in proportion to the degree of negligent causation, and full recovery may be allowed if the magnitude of the contribution of negligence to the injury suffered genuinely cannot be determined. Conversely, claims founded on loss of a chance of a good recovery when treatment has been negligently withheld do not succeed if the claimant would have had less than a 50 percent chance of recovery even with treatment,[8] a rigid position endorsed by the House of Lords in 2005.[9]

Thus both limbs of the test for negligence—breach of duty and causation of foreseeable injury—are notoriously difficult to establish in claims arising from clinical practice. Just resolution, whether by negotiation between the parties or determination by the court, can only be achieved if expert opinion is independent, objective and unbiased. Unfortunately, experts appointed and paid by the parties have not always fulfilled these conditions. Adversarial confrontation was the norm and neither the courts nor the NHS had control of the conduct of individual cases. Lord Woolf's report into Civil Justice in England and Wales[10] identified clinical negligence as an area where legal procedure was failing most seriously. His criticisms were wide-ranging and involved clinicians and their representatives as well as claimants.

Some consistency of approach was achieved in 1995 with the establishment of the National Health Service Litigation Authority to handle claims against NHS Trusts. Subsequently it restricted the handling of clinical negligence claims to specifically designated and experienced legal firms. The rules governing the grant of Legal Aid were made more stringent in 2000 and clinical negligence claims funded by Legal Aid could thereafter only be handled by specifically authorized firms. New Civil Procedure Rules, introduced in 1999 and based upon recommendations in Lord Woolf's report,[10] set out specific procedures to be followed in the management of clinical negligence claims and encourage the use of less adversarial methods of resolution such as mediation. An obligatory pre-action procedure involving early disclosure of expert opinion has allowed many cases to settle without formal litigation. Conduct of cases that fail to resolve at the pre-action stage has been transferred to the court, which has wide-ranging powers to define time limits, appoint experts, restrict their numbers, and order meetings of experts to define and refine the areas of disagreement between the parties. All experts are now required to acknowledge that their primary duty is to the court and must override any obligation to the party providing instructions. These developments have facilitated swifter and less contentious resolution of claims.

The National Health Service Redress Act 2006 seeks to simplify the investigation and just settlement of claims of lower value, although a potential for bias remains in that the Trust itself is responsible for investigating the claim against it. Dissatisfaction with health care can also result in a complaint rather than a claim for damages, and a uniform system for handling complaints against NHS services was established in 1996 and revised in 2004. The powers of the Health Service Commissioner or Ombudsman have been extended to include clinical as well as administrative concerns. Health authorities are also required to establish a Patient Advocacy and Liaison Service to provide information and support to patients dissatisfied with or unclear about their entitlements, and the Health and Social Care Act of 2001 creates a duty to consult and involve the public in health care planning.

Deference to autonomy

The traditional view that 'doctor knows best' prevailed for many years but has been eroded over time. The evolution of the law on consent is a good illustration. Valid consent to medical intervention requires the voluntary decision of a patient with mental capacity who is provided with a sufficiency of information. In a much discussed and far from unanimous decision,[11] the House of Lords held in 1985 that the *Bolam* principle applied to the giving of information as well as to the provision of clinical services. In other words, sufficiency of information was that deemed to be so by a responsible body of medical opinion. By 1994 this view was under attack, with Lord Woolf declaring that failure to warn of the risk of impotence after repair of rectal prolapse in a young man was neither reasonable nor responsible, despite contemporaneous expert evidence to the contrary.[12] In a later case[13] Lord Woolf went further by advocating incorporation of the 'reasonable patient' test, as used in the United States and Canada, into English law. Current recommendations and revised consent forms for use in NHS hospitals reflect this change. More detailed disclosure is now deemed necessary, based upon consideration of the magnitude and risk of potential complications, and any specific features of individual patients which would enhance their significance to that person. Forms used to record consent are intended to evidence that appropriate information has been provided by a practitioner of suitable experience and understood by the patient.

A claim for negligence founded on failure to provide sufficient information must show not only that the information given *was* insufficient but also that had the claimant known fully the risks involved, consent would have been withheld. At one time, this was a difficult legal hurdle to surmount but a series of cases, culminating in a decision in the House of Lords in 2004[14] indicate that the courts now accept a claimant need only evidence what alternative option or timescale would have been pursued. Failure sufficiently to warn was held to be a breach of the patient's right to autonomy.

Deference to patient autonomy has also been reflected in legal endorsement of the right of competent adult patients to withhold consent to treatment, even life-sustaining treatment, providing they are acting voluntarily.[15] Subsequent caselaw,[16] endorsed by the statutory provisions of the Mental Capacity Act 2005, sets out criteria to define what constitutes capacity to make such a decision. The Mental Capacity Act also makes provision for the patient's views to be respected in the event of future incapacity, either by means of an advance decision or by endowing another with lasting power of attorney, a role extended by the Act to include decisions about medical treatment. These are primarily rights for avoiding unwanted treatment. There is no legal basis for patients to insist upon a particular form of treatment,[17] and advance directives requesting treatment, even if the patient is by then in a persistent vegetative state, need not necessarily be respected. However, if what the patient requests lies within the boundaries of responsible medical opinion, albeit is not something the practitioner is prepared to undertake, there is a professional duty to refer the patient elsewhere.[18]

Role of law in the resolution of ethical disputes

Establishing principles and policy

The factors that led to the increase in litigation against clinical staff and services have also spawned controversial social and ethical conflicts. Areas generating particular concern have been the regulation of reproduction[19] and treatment at the beginning and end of life.[20,21] Two types of conflict can be identified: questions of principle as to the legality of an individual treatment or procedure, and matters arising from conflict between patient or patient's representative and clinical teams. Matters of principle can be established through a test case, often appealed through the higher courts to the House of Lords to ensure that any principle enunciated has the highest authority. Alternatively, statutory legislation is enacted in response to an innovative medical situation, for example, the Human Tissue Act 2004 and Human Fertilisation and Embryology Act 1990.

In one of the earliest cases, an eminent gynaecologist was prosecuted for procuring the abortion of a 14-year-old victim of gang rape.[22] His acquittal, on a legal technicality, spawned a wider debate which took place against the background knowledge of illegal abortion which was practised widely, unregulated, and dangerous. Concern for upholding moral values was challenged by proponents of individual choice but eventually the voice of the majority prevailed with the passage in 1967 of the Abortion Act. The debate continues however, especially as evidence has accumulated of the capacity of the foetus to experience pain and possibly emotion. Both the principle and the detail of this legislation have been challenged. The topic is particularly contentious because there is the potential for conflict between the parents, between the interests of the mother and the unborn child, and between the freedom of choice of an individual and the interests of society as a whole.

These include not only conflict between the advocates of autonomy and those who consider there are over-arching moral, possibly religious considerations that prohibit the practice, but also the potential impact on the moral values and behaviour of a society in which abortion is sanctioned. It is in these circumstances that the law can be used to arbitrate. But this does not imply that either the judiciary or the legislature have exceptional ethical insight or moral values. It merely means that the law—however created—is deemed by society to define the boundaries of acceptable behaviour: to regulate rather than to resolve and to define what is permitted, as distinct from what is 'right' or 'wrong'.

Assisted dying is another example where there is potential conflict between the interests of the individual and those of society as a whole. Test cases challenging prohibition of voluntary euthanasia or assisted suicide[23] and attempts to introduce regulatory legislation[24] have failed. And yet, as with abortion, the demand is there as manifest by the number of UK citizens who have travelled abroad to seek an assisted death in more liberal jurisdictions. Evidence from such jurisdictions does not support the contention of risk to society as a whole or to individual vulnerable members within it.[25]

Resolving conflict arising from the treatment of individuals

Neither the traditional nor the modern versions of the Hippocratic Oath[26] offer sufficiently detailed guidance to resolve many of these concerns but a more practical framework exists in the ethical principles promulgated by Beauchamp and Childress,[27] which define the duties of practitioners as beneficence, non-maleficence, respect for autonomy, and equity. But what constitutes 'beneficence' or 'non-maleficence' can be a matter of opinion, especially when innovative treatments pose new questions, individually and for society.

Cases involving the management of persons lacking mental capacity have been prominent among those presented for individual determination—whether of the legality of a proposed procedure or the resolution of conflict between the parties. As a result, the courts have introduced and developed the concept of 'best interests',[28] which has since been codified in the Mental Capacity Act 2005. The term is difficult to define but is no less meaningful as a result, any more than is the more medically familiar concept of 'normality'. Best interests were considered at length in 2001 in the matter of S (Adult Patient: sterilisation)[29] when Thorpe LJ stated that 'in deciding what is best for the disabled patient the judge must have regard to the patient's welfare as the paramount consideration. That embraces issues far wider than the medical. Indeed it would be undesirable and probably impossible to set bounds to what is relevant to a welfare determination'. In the same case, Butler-Sloss P added that 'the principle of the "best interests" of the patient as applied by the court extends beyond the considerations governing the propriety and advisability of medical treatment developed in the Bolam case .... the judicial decision will incorporate broader ethical, social, moral and welfare considerations'. In a later case,[30] Hedley J commented that 'the infinite variety of the human condition never ceases to surprise and it is that fact that defeats any attempt to be more precise in the definition of best interest'. At best then the *Bolam* test can provide options as to what constitutes best interests but it is open to the court to take into account other factors, including the opinions, albeit neither the wishes nor religious convictions, of carers and family.[31]

When disputes have arisen, it is important to distinguish between those in which the applicant seeks a declaration of what treatment or policy constitutes 'best interests', from matters in which procedural deficiencies have led to conflict. In a matter which reached the European Court of Human Rights (ECHR) in 2004,[32] there was conflict between the parents of a mentally disabled minor and hospital staff about life-prolonging treatment. The ECHR criticized the trust for failing to seek determination by the courts in a matter involving the human rights of a minor and his family whereas in an earlier hearing, the Court of Appeal[33] reaffirmed that it is inappropriate for an English court to declare, as a matter of law, what a hospital should or should not do. The risks and limitations of attempts to impose clinical decision by the courts were explored and clarified in 2005 when the Court of Appeal cautioned against the making of open-ended declarations involving damaged or gravely ill children.[34] 'It is not the function of the court to oversee the treatment plan for a gravely ill child. That function is for the doctors, in consultation with the child's parents. Judges take decision on the basis of particular factual sub-strata. The court's function is to make a particular decision on a particular issue. It is not the function of the court to be used as a general advice centre'.

This limitation of the role of the courts in resolving ethical conflict in the management of medical cases has been reflected in subsequent caselaw, which illustrates that the court's role is permissive, not prescriptive. In *Simms v Simms*,[35] an application was made for a declaration that it would be lawful to administer an experimental treatment for variant Creutzfeld-Jakob disease not recommended by any authority in the United Kingdom. A consultant neurosurgeon was willing to provide the treatment but was not supported by any local colleagues or authorities. The court expressed the hope that the Department of Health would investigate alternative centres which might be willing to provide the treatment and, in the event, both patients were referred to a centre in Northern Ireland. An even more interventionist approach was apparent when a consensual application was made for permission to withdraw hydration and nutrition from a patient in persistent vegetative state.[36] The Official Solicitor was appointed to represent the interests of the patient and, having researched the topic, identified a number of case reports claiming improved conscious level after the administration of Zopiclone, a drug usually used to sedate. Expert opinion was obtained to the effect the drug would do no harm if the patient was truly in a persistent vegetative state but that if there was any response, then the diagnosis was invalid. In the light of this advice and contrary to the wishes of the family, the court ruled that the drug should be tried before hydration and nutrition were withdrawn.

An apparent rebuttal of medical opinion by the courts was manifest in the case of a conscious child with severe spinal muscular atrophy.[37] The hospital trust applied for a declaration that it would be lawful and in the child's best interests to withdraw mechanical ventilation and allow the child to die. The parents made a cross-application for an order requiring the hospital to carry out tracheostomy to facilitate continued treatment. Despite the large body of medical opinion in favour of cessation of treatment, Holman J dismissed all the applications and went further by stating his personal opinion was that it was positively in the child's best interest to remain alive. The essential elements in his argument were as follows:

+ There is a strong but rebuttable presumption in favour of life.

+ The function of the court is solely to determine 'best interests'.

+ Best interests go far beyond purely medical concerns, are a matter for individual determination, based upon evidence from those involved with the care of the child, including the parents whose opinions, as distinct from their wishes, are relevant to the analysis.

+ It is not for the court to determine questions of ethics—even if the Trust's application were granted, the decision whether or not actually to discontinue treatment was a matter for the clinical staff and parents.

This decision created a flurry of medical criticism,[38–40] fears being expressed that the courts can now dictate medical treatment and might require measures that no responsible practitioner would provide. These fears are unfounded—Holman J was careful to reject the application to order a tracheostomy (although this was subsequently undertaken consensually) and, in considering what constituted the child's best interests, restricted himself only to selecting among five treatment options which had been identified for him by the joint report of four external medical experts.

Allocation of resources

The fourth ethical principle enunciated by Beauchamp and Childress[27]—equity, or equitable provision according to need—can also be contentious but has spawned far less litigation. The role of the law was established in Re B[41] when the Court of Appeal declared it was not the function of the courts to make decisions concerning the effectiveness of treatment nor to determine the allocation of scarce resources. Subsequently The National Institute for Health and Clinical Excellence (NICE) was established to provide guidance on public health, health technologies, and clinical practice. NICE evaluates new treatments and makes recommendations on the basis of an incremental cost effectiveness ratio per quality adjusted life year (QALY). Treatments where the ratio is £20,000 or less per QALY are more likely to be recommended than those of £30,000 or more, but NICE recommendations are guidelines, not binding authority, and so allow for 'exceptional circumstances'. The process used by NICE to reach its decisions has been subject to legal challenge,[42] and there have also been successful applications for judicial review of decisions based on both NICE recommendations and other NHS directives. However these have usually been founded on procedural grounds such as acting irrationally or in reliance on irrelevant factors.[43,44]

Impact of Human Rights Act 1998

The United Kingdom was an original signatory to the Articles of the 1950 European Convention for the Protection of Human Rights and Fundamental Freedoms but the Articles were not incorporated into English domestic law until the Human Rights Act 1998 came into force in 2000. Despite expectations to the contrary, the effect of this legislative change on medical caselaw has been limited. Applications claiming contravention of one or more of the rights have succeeded in the context of detention under mental health legislation and disciplinary proceedings against medical practitioners. Existing English law on decisions at the end of life has been upheld[23,45] although Article 6, the right to private and family life, was deemed to be transgressed by a nonconsensual Do Not Resuscitate order.[32]

Article 2, the right to life, does not impose an obligation on the NHS to provide medical care in all cases where life might otherwise be endangered.[46] Furthermore, the positive obligation of Article 2 to protect life is not breached by simple negligence on the part of NHS personnel which results in death.[47] However, any death occurring while in the care of the state should still be subject to effective and independent investigation. If there is any suspicion of criminality in a health care related death[48] or death occurs while a subject is detained by the State, for example in custody or under the terms of mental health legislation, the rights under Article 2 are engaged and there is a more stringent obligation on the state to initiate an effective, independent and public investigation into the circumstances[49,50] However, a properly conducted inquest is one of a number of ways in which this investigative function can be discharged. The term 'properly conducted inquest' in this context means that the interpretation of 'how' the deceased died must now be taken to mean not only 'by what means' but also 'in what circumstances'.

Finally it is worth noting that virtually all the developments cited in this chapter have taken place from the middle of the twentieth century onwards. It remains to be seen whether this pace of change will be sustained.

References

References to Statute and Statutory Instruments are not cited individually. They can be accessed at www.opsi.gov.uk and www.hmso.gov.uk

1 Learning from Bristol: report of the public inquiry into children's heart surgery at the Bristol Royal Infirmary 1984–1995. Command Paper CM 5207; 2001.

. 2 The Report of the Royal Liverpool Children's Inquiry (2001). Report on the removal, retention and disposal of human organs and tissues at Alder Hey Children's Hospital. www.rlcinquiry.org.uk

3 The Shipman Inquiry, Fifth Report. Safeguarding Patients: Lessons from the Past – Proposals for the Future. December 2004 Command Paper Cm 6394.

4 *Bolam v Friern Hospital Management Committee* [1957] 1 WLR 583.

5 *Hunter v Hanley* [1955] S.C. 200.

6 *Bolitho v City and Hackney HA* [1998] AC 232.

7 *Wilsher v Wessex AHA* [1988] AC 1074.

8 *Hotson v East Berks AHA* [1987] AC 750.

9 *Gregg v Scott* [2005] UKHL 2.

10 Access to Justice (1996). Final report by The Right Honourable the Lord Woolf MR to the Lord Chancellor on the civil justice system in England and Wales. The Stationery Office, London.

11 *Sidaway v Royal Bethlem* and Maudsley Hospital [1985] AC 871.

12 *Smith v Tunbridge Wells HA* [1994] 5 Med LR 334.

13 *Pearce v United Bristol Healthcare NHS Trust* [1998] EWCA Civ 865.

14 *Chester v Afshar* [2004] UKHL 41.

15 *Re T* (Adult: refusal of treatment) [1992] EWCA (Civ) 18;4 All ER 649.

16 *Re C* (Refusal of medical treatment) [1994] 1 All ER 819.

17 *R (Burke) v GMC* and Ors [2005] EWCA Civ 1003.

18 General Medical Council 2006. *Good Medical Practice*: s 8.

19 *Gillick v West Norfolk and Wisbech Area Health Authority* [1986] AC 112.

20 *Airedale Hospital Trustees v Bland* [1992] UKHL 5.

21 *Re A* (Minors) (Conjoined Twins: Separations) [2000] EWCA Civ 254.

22 *R v Bourne* [1939] 1 KB 687.

23 *Pretty v Director Of Public Prosecutions & Anor* [2001] EWHC Admin 788
European Court ruling: *Pretty v United Kingdom* [2002] ECHR 427.

24 Select committee report into Assisted Dying for the Terminally Ill Bill (4 April
2005) http://www.publications.parliament.uk/pa/ld/ldasdy.htm

25 Battin MP, van der Heide A, Ganzini et al. (2007). Legal physician-assisted dying
in Oregon and the Netherlands: evidence concerning the impact on patients in
'vulnerable' groups. *J Med Ethics*, **33**: 591–597 and see htt p://www.oregon.gov/
DHS/ph/pas/index/shtml

26 Loefler I (2002). Why the Hippocratic ideals are dead. *BMJ*, **324**: 1463.

27 Beauchamp TL, Childress JF. (2001). *Principles of Biomedical Ethics*, 5th ed. Oxford
University Press, Oxford.

28 *F v W Berkshire HA* [1990] 2 AC 1.

29 *Re S* (Adult Patient: Sterilisation) [2000] 3 WLR 1288.

30 *Portsmouth NHS Hospitals Trust v Wyatt & Wyatt* [2004] EWHC 2247 Fam.

31 *An NHS Trust v A and SA* [2005] EWCA (Civ) 1145.

32 *Glass v UK* (ECHR – Application No 61827/00); [2004] Lloyd's Rep Med 433.

33 *R v Portsmouth Hospital NHS Trust* [1999] EWCA Civ 1914.

34 *Wyatt & Wyatt v Portsmouth Hospitals NHS Trust* [2005] EWCA Civ 1181.

35 *Simms v Simms & Anor; A v A* (a child) & Anor [2002] EWHC 2734 Fam.

36 Dyer C (2006). Judge over-rules family's wish that patient should be allowed to
die. *BMJ*, **333**: 1089 (and see *BMJ*, 2007; **334**: 176)l.

37 *An NHS Trust v MB and Mr and Mrs B* [2006] EWHC 507 (Fam).

38 Danbury C, Newdick C (2006). Withdrawal of treatment in critical care: who
decides? *J Int Care Soc*, **7**(2): 23–24.

39 Tibballs J (2007). Legal basis for ethical withholding and withdrawing of life-
sustaining medical treatment from infants and children. *J Paed & Child Health*,
43: 230–6.

40 Isaacs D, Kilham HA, Jacobe S et al. (2008). Gaining consent for publication in
difficult cases involving children. *BMJ*, **337**: a1231.

41 *R v Cambridge Health Authority ex parte B* [1995] EWCA Civ 49.

42 *R (Eisai Ltd) v The National Institute for Health and Clinical Excellence* [2007]
EWCA Civ 438.

43 *R (Fisher) v N Derbyshire Health Authority* [1997] EWHC Admin 675.

44 *R (Rogers) v Swindon NHS Primary Care Trust and Secretary of State for Health*
[2006] EWCA (Civ) 392.

45 *NHS Trust A v Mrs M; NHS Trust B v Mrs H* [2001] Lloyd's Rep Med 28.

46 *A National Health Service Trust v D & Ors* [2000] Lloyd's Rep Med 411.

47 *R (Goodson) v HM Coroner for Bedfordshire and Luton & Anor* [2004] EWHC 2931 Admin.

48 *R (Khan) v Secretary of State for Health* [2003] EWCA Civ 1129.

49 *R (Takoushis) v HM Coroner for Inner North London & Ors* [2005] EWCA Civ 1440.

50 *Savage v S Essex Partnership NHS Foundation Trust* [2007] EWCA Civ 1375.

Part A

Issues of competence and autonomy

Chapter 1

Consent for intensive care: Public and political expectations vs. conceptual and practical hurdles

M D Dominic Bell

Introduction

Intensive care is a complex subject, predictably intangible and difficult to understand for the general public, or indeed for many other disciplines of medical practice. The simple origins of this specialty within ventilatory support for paralysis, or as a continuation of resuscitation or peri-operative care, have served to define our practice as an extension of treatment initiated by other medical specialties rather than a discrete intervention appropriate for proactive patient choice. The overall style of earlier intensive care provision, with mainly non-standardized care, delivered by part-time practitioners, limited post-discharge treatment or audit of outcomes, and patient ownership resting with the parent specialty, served to maintain this position, with little public scrutiny of the process.

Recent years have, however, seen independent specialty status, formalized training and accreditation, and an increasingly standardized process of care as the evidence base for effective treatments expands with robust research and consensus guidelines. The philosophy of intensive care has also changed over this timeframe, with greater emphasis on early identification of the at-risk patient within the broader hospital, timely implementation of treatments to modify critical illness, and the accompanying opportunity for proactive engagement of parent specialty, patient, and next of kin prior to the point of decompensation. With a more defined treatment strategy, greater knowledge of outcomes, and the opportunity for earlier discussion with the patient, it could reasonably be expected that this process parallel all other medical interventions, with informed consent directing the process of care.

Historically, the concept of consent is founded in common law as an essential process to distinguish surgical activity from actionable assault, but has become progressively refined to represent the profession's ethical rather than strictly legal duty to respect the autonomy, or right to self-determination, of the patient. This transition from medical paternalism has paralleled the universal rise of broader human rights, but has been particularly fuelled within the UK by scandals involving the withholding of information from patients on the outcomes from cardiac surgery[1] and post-mortem procedure.[2] New legislation such as the Human Tissue Act 2004[3] has been borne out of the subsequent public and political dissatisfaction, placing great emphasis on the comprehensiveness of information and full understanding of what is involved. The standard now demanded by the courts is not what the health care professional believes is reasonable to disclose or their perspective on the significance of any risk, but what the individual patient may interpret as significant.[4] These standards are further emphasized in recommendations from defence societies, government, and professional bodies.[5,6]

While the concept of informed consent has never been formally enshrined in statute within the UK therefore, there is an expectation that information will be provided in an understandable format on what is proposed and the associated risks and benefits, with a similar level of detail on alternatives including doing nothing. There should be enough time for the patient to reflect on what is suggested, with the opportunity for further questions, and freedom from any pressure or coercion to comply with the practitioner's favoured strategy. Consent furthermore should be a dynamic process with constant re-evaluation of the above issues rather than a presumption of ongoing consent simply based on continuing compliance.

A major barrier to conformity with these principles is that significant numbers of intensive care patients have already lost capacity, a fundamental prerequisite for consent, at the point of presentation and never regain this during the length of their critical illness. There are, however, opportunities for early proactive engagement in patients with chronic disease that is likely to present with life-threatening deterioration or complications, in other patients early on in the admission process where progression is predictable, and particularly in patients about to undergo major surgery with a foreseeable requirement for post-operative intensive care.

It should also be noted that even for those patients whose capacity has been compromised by illness or medication, but where subsequent health care choices have to be undertaken, attempts should be made to promote capacity and subsequent autonomous decision-making. This obligation is unequivocally spelt out within the Mental Capacity Act 2005,[7] which further emphasizes how lack of capacity is limited to a specific decision at a specific point in time rather than a continuing feature, which would prevent any consideration of choice on any subject at any time. Even with severe brain injury or dysfunction, such as dementia, the default position should be that health-care professionals seek to determine capacity for decision-making and promote this where possible.

Given the above defined recommendations from the relevant authorities, the emphasis is therefore on seeking fully informed consent for all aspects of intensive care provision, mirroring every other health-care intervention. While this approach would meet legal requirements, the feasibility of such an undertaking has to be assessed in the first instance, and the more fundamental question of whether patients wish for such a system in relation to critical illness and end of life care, or prefer a style based more on 'benign paternalism', needs to be secondarily considered.

Feasibility of informed consent within critical care

In addressing the first of these challenges, the feasibility of informed consent for intensive care revolves around a series of questions:

1 Can the basic process of care be defined, and further refined for specific categories of illness?

2 How are outcomes defined and calculated?

   a survival of critical illness

   b survival to leave hospital

   c longer-term survival

   d dependence on medical intervention throughout these stages

   e survival vs. health status

   f quality of life throughout these stages.

3 How do age, background comorbidity, and triggering pathology influence the above issues?

4 Can understanding be achieved of the ancillary facets of intensive care such as dependency, loss of privacy, threat to personal dignity, compromised capacity, or the mental and physical effort of weaning and rehabilitation?

5 Can there be rational judgement on when the potentially temporary burdens of living during critical illness outweigh the prospects of longer-term recovery, and when this should therefore limit further life-sustaining medical treatment?

This series of questions not unreasonably generates reservations as to whether it is possible to specify the clinical course of the patient during the intensive care pathway and set out the components of care that the patient might wish to partake of or decline at different stages of that pathway, and whether it is possible to carry out this exercise without compromising the normal process of coordinated care. An obvious unwanted consequence for all involved, of any attempt to prescribe the clinical pathway, would be the potential future restriction on a flexible approach to care depending on the patient's response to primary treatments, which is in essence the philosophy of intensive care.

The relatively recent and ultimately simplistic attempts to engage patients on proactive decision-making on resuscitation[8] is illustrative of this problem, namely that a complex decision with significant ramifications cannot and should not be reduced to a simple 'yes' or 'no'. Resuscitation manoeuvres should also be placed in the context of earlier life-sustaining medical treatment on which the patient should definitely have an opinion, since this is likely to be determinative on both the incidence of a cardiac arrest and the likely outcome.

These identified questions and further hurdles will be addressed below.

Can the process of intensive care be defined?

Intensive care is less a specific treatment for a defined pathology, and more a complex amalgam of multi-system support, the need for which has been dictated by decompensation of the patient. This in turn may be due to the magnitude of the triggering pathology in a previously healthy individual, such as polytrauma or meningococcal septicaemia, may reflect underlying comorbidity such as respiratory or immune disease, or some combination such as major surgery in the presence of established cardio-respiratory pathology. Optimization of the patient in these circumstances requires treatments such as sedation which have no therapeutic value other than facilitating necessary interventions as ventilation, alongside invasive monitoring and multiple radiological and laboratory investigations. In many cases, intensive care is less of a treatment and more an assessment of a patient's physiological reserve for withstanding medical or surgical illness by ongoing evaluation of their response to the various support strategies.

This difficulty in defining the principles of intensive care is amplified by the range of approaches between and even within units on virtually every aspect of management from choice of monitoring modality to criteria for prescribing expensive treatments such as activated protein C. Although there is an expanding evidence base for certain approaches and consensus guidelines with international convergence, such as the *Surviving Sepsis Campaign*[9] or transfusion thresholds,[10] current national research demonstrates how basic questions such as the optimal timing for a tracheostomy remain unanswered.[11]

The overall package of intensive care becomes even harder to define for the purposes of consent when considering the multidisciplinary input into direct delivery of care, involving medical, nursing, and physiotherapy staff, all with independent codes of practice and all with different implications in relation to consent. While the medical components of care have been discussed above, nursing interventions cover diverse aspects relevant to privacy, independence, and dignity, such as personal hygiene and bowel care, while physiotherapy may involve encouragement of the patient in activities for which there is little enthusiasm or even absolute resistance, such as passive stretching, mobilization, and spontaneous ventilatory effort independent of mechanical support.

If therefore, intensive care cannot be readily defined as a medical treatment, because of fundamental conceptual aspects coupled with significant variation in the approach to critical illness, and management involves a range of health-care professionals each with a different impact on a patient's autonomy and personal integrity, the starting requirement for consent, in which the proposed treatment is described, is rendered problematical.

Can the indications for intensive care be defined?

Although intensive care is routinely perceived by the lay public as synonymous with being on a 'life-support machine', it is apparent that there are a spectrum of indications for ICU admission from the planned slow emergence from anaesthesia after major surgery to the continuation of the resuscitation process after decompensation of the patient following trauma, medical illness, or surgery. When one considers furthermore that critical care should be as much a pre-emptive process as reactive rescue care, patients at a low level of illness severity and the probability of not needing an escalation of support may be moved into such an environment for a higher intensity of monitoring associated with just basic aspects of care. By definition, this process needs to be flexible and responsive, and is often based on the subjective opinion of an experienced clinician as much as objective measures of physiological derangement such as Modified Early Warning Score (MEWS),[12] creating difficulty with translation into a specific template for the purposes of consent.

Furthermore, intensive care is a process of patient management rather than a geographical location, and logistical issues may at times dictate that the critically ill patient requiring multi-system support will have this delivered in a non-designated area, and at times the patient with a lower severity of illness may be monitored in an ICU bed, in the absence of step-down availability. It would be too simplistic therefore and inappropriately restrictive of future choice to have absolute restrictions on admission to intensive care, as a geographical resource, as a component of proactive consent.

Can the prognosis from and the goals of intensive care be defined?

When considering the spectrum of indications for admission to intensive care as set out above, it would be reasonable, for the purposes of informed decision-making, to map these against crude estimates for prognosis, invasiveness of support, length of stay, the physical and mental burdens of weaning from support, the impact on subsequent overall health status and future dependency on health-care and medical interventions.

The most fundamental barrier to such decision-making lies in the lack of prognostic accuracy, since there are very few conditions, such as brainstem death, which unequivocally allow practitioners to adopt an absolute position on outcome. Even if accurate survival figures were available, it is questionable whether a individual could or would make a choice to either partake of or decline intensive care between a range of predicted mortality from very high to very low, since survival is an all or none phenomenon, rather than relative. Systems have been devised to improve predictive accuracy and facilitate informed choice[13] and one would naturally incorporate factors such as age, comorbidity, and the reversibility of the triggering pathology into the prognosis and decision-making, particularly if an individual scored highly across multiple fields, but it can be seen that these aspects, which inevitably lack precision for the individual patient, can rarely be determinative.

It could be considered reasonable therefore to eliminate these factors from the decision-making and to base prognosis on the patient's response to escalation of care, recognizing the inherent difficulty of incorporating a deferred decision into the process of consent, which conceptually is founded on more precise and binding decision-making at the time the patient has capacity.

Are there issues beyond survival which are integral to consent and can these be determined?

Not only is the prognosis for survival elusive for the individual patient for a particular set of circumstances, such that an actual trial of intensive care would be required for greater accuracy, but it is apparent that prognosis alone should not direct decision-making. The likelihood of survival requires triangulation with the burden and length of intensive care, and the quality of life in the event of survival.

The concept of 'burden' is, however, both very individual and complex, since it covers not only pain and discomfort, but loss of autonomy and privacy, embarrassment at dependence on others for personal hygiene, innate objection to aspects of care such as catheterization, fear of mental disturbance, any of which may skew a proactive decision when an individual is enjoying full health. It would be essential therefore to emphasize that many of these aspects are temporary and modifiable by medication to relieve discomfort, anxiety or distress, and may actually be welcomed during critical illness as relief from the primary impact of that condition, a consideration that may not be apparent until that point in time. The experienced practitioner will thus have observed the patient with irreversible end-stage lung disease for whom all parties have consensually agreed on limiting support to non-invasive ventilation, but who then requests that intubation be reconsidered in the face of profound dyspnoea. It can be questioned therefore how any individual could proactively assess the burdens of intensive care, or the burdens of rejecting invasive support, and generate a binding directive on this basis.

Quality of life in the event of survival is another highly subjective dimension, incorporating medically assessed markers such as organ dysfunction, neurological disability, and any predictable need for hospitalization or ongoing medical intervention, but more critically, considering the impact of these on the individual patient, their family and relevant others. The patient would need to consider therefore aspects such as dependence on others, limitations in capacity for exercise or physical activity, restrictions on employment, social and leisure activity, the future viability of relationships, or any aspect which was of specific relevance and importance for that individual, and attempt to give these factors a more objective weighting when reaching an informed decision.

It is quite apparent that the overwhelming majority of individuals accommodate and adapt to significant illness and accompanying disability without considering an absence of value to their life, and it can be questioned therefore whether patients should be forced to make a decision proactively that may be skewed by their own and indeed their doctor's misconceptions as to the impact of disability, and consequently restrict their future access to life-sustaining medical treatment. It is acknowledged that there is very little data on longer term outcomes from intensive care, with conflicting conclusions, certain studies suggesting greater levels of satisfaction amongst survivors than may have been predicted,[14] but with others questioning health-related quality of life.[15] It is also apparent that focused medical and psychological support programmes following discharge have the capacity to positively modify aspects of any recovery,[16] but provision of such care is currently under-resourced and relatively random. In the face of inconsistent results and variability in access to appropriate treatment, it is difficult to imply to individual patients that this information should direct their decision.

A fundamental barrier to proactive consent is created therefore by the observation that the elements essential to an informed choice; prognosis, the burdens of intensive care and quality of life in the event of survival, can only be determined more objectively by initiation of intensive care, a process which then prevents an informed choice by removing or significantly compromising an individual's capacity, and on this basis, making a truly informed choice again appears rarely possible.

Barriers to balanced communication on aspects of care

With lack of precision on key decision-making factors, one could argue that clinicians attempting proactive decision-making should simply present information to the patient on the process of care, and simplify choice to refusal of intensive care, or admission to intensive care with continuation of active treatment until absolute identification of medical futility. Although specific and isolated cases demonstrate how patients may have very consistent and fixed views on quality of life both prior and subsequent to intensive care, without the need for any such information on prognosis and treatment options, and prefer withdrawal of active support and death to the continuation of LSMT,[17] most practitioners would predictably feel uncomfortable offering such stark choices rather than balanced support, and this strategy while theoretically facilitating patient choice in certain cases, would not generally serve patient, professional, unit or the public well.

In the face of uncertainty, a 'trial' of intensive care appears a pragmatic solution, but if subsequent decision-making on the grounds of prognosis, the burdens of care, and quality of life in the event of survival cannot be based on pre-treatment discussion because the patient cannot take an informed view, and is subsequently left therefore to health care professionals and others once the process has been initiated, the process of consent is once again invalidated.

It is very difficult furthermore to present such complex information in a manner that can be understood both intellectually and emotionally, and is free from influence.

Most lay individuals would have difficulty understanding and processing detail on the complex components of care and the principles behind normalization of physiological systems, which theoretically is the most emotionally neutral aspect of the information. Even the description of these aspects has however the capacity to induce fear over the invasiveness, dependency, and loss of autonomy, which may then compromise rational decision-making.

The communication of prognosis represents an even greater challenge, since simple issues such as whether this is described negatively, as in the risk of dying rather than the probability of survival, are likely to influence the response. It is known, for example, that mothers presented with a 20% risk of a child with Down's syndrome are more likely to opt for amniocentesis than the group informed of an 80% chance of a normal child.[18] When the subject matter extends to debate on the burdens of intensive care and the quality of life in the event of survival, it is apparent the topics are becoming more opinion based and the overt emphasis on the negative aspects of care may be construed by the patient as an attempt to discourage uptake.

In these circumstances, there is the risk of the patient pursuing active care despite significant side effects and very little chance of survival, in the belief that the position of the health care professionals is driven by resource limitations or discrimination against certain categories of patient on the grounds of disability, rather than genuinely warning the patient and promoting an informed choice. One illustration of this is the higher likelihood of black American women opting for highly toxic chemotherapy with little chance of ensuring survival, based on the belief that the provision of information on this specific issue is designed to discourage them, being founded in persistent discrimination.[19]

While one would not expect such prejudice on the grounds of race or colour within contemporary intensive care, it is apparent that misconceptions or strongly held beliefs with regard to outcome from critical illness are present within the medical profession. There was a commonly held view that survival from an AIDS-defining illness requiring intensive care was so poor that admission was not indicated, until such time that outcome studies revealed otherwise.[20] Most practitioners will acknowledge that nihilism over haematological malignancy or a repeat admission for exacerbation of COPD will historically have skewed decision-making away from active support for these categories of patient.

The additional consideration which generates an uncomfortable element of decision-making and is relevant to how information is given is the fact that intensive care is ultimately a limited geographical resource, and practitioners are routinely forced to consider which patients have the greatest chance of benefiting. While this should be based on clinical criteria without any discrimination or consideration of an individual's worth to society, there are occasions, such as refusal of the decompensated Jehovah's Witness who is refusing all blood products, which might be construed by others as discrimination on religious grounds.

It is important to acknowledge therefore that factors other than the patient's best interests may influence communication with the patient or their next of kin, such as resource limitations or the practitioner's preconceptions, and even in the absence of these issues, the dialogue may unduly influence a decision, either because emphasis is placed on negative aspects, or religious and cultural views are not recognized or accommodated, generating a request for all active support despite clear evidence of futility, based on a belief that discrimination is driving decision-making.

There are significant barriers therefore to provision of understandable information on the process and complexity of intensive care, which raise additional questions as to whether proactive consent can ever be achieved. A further problem is generated because theoretically a patient should not be forced to refuse or sign up to the package of care that is the standard for the individual unit, but should be able to access a style of care, which approximates to their own values and beliefs. If, however, the process of care becomes fragmented with certain aspects of care declined, delivery of the overall goals may be significantly compromised, in addition to the obvious practical problems in providing piecemeal care. If furthermore, intensive care is reduced to a definable package, dictated by consent, there would inevitably be restrictions on refining techniques and introducing new technology, or trialling new treatment options in the face of a poor response to first-line treatment. The question has to be asked therefore whether the patient can and should be allowed any autonomy regarding particular facets of intensive care.

Aspects of care that benefit others

Certain aspects of care are not directed specifically at individual patient benefit, but reflect either an obligation to utilize the resource effectively and efficiently, or broader professional goals such as audit and research. It is questionable whether these factors which either bring no individual benefit or actually compromise patient well-being can be considered an integral component of the package which in effect the patient consents to when agreeing to intensive care. For example, if the policy of an ICU is to transfer the most stable and least dependent patient out when demand exceeds availability, is the prospective patient in any position to refuse this option proactively and can a lack of objection at the outset be viewed as adequate consent when the need arises for such transfer? Similarly if research or the education of medical students is the norm for a specific unit, is it possible for a patient to prospectively opt out without harbouring concerns that commitment to their care will be compromised, and therefore feeling under obligation to consent?

Other related issues include organ donation and post-mortem examinations, which cause a high level of angst among next of kin in the usual circumstances of facing difficult decisions without any true inkling of the patient's position on these matters.

While clearly it would assist both practitioners and next of kin in subsequent discussions if the patient's opinion was known, there are potential harms of induced anxiety if the patient, in an already vulnerable state, considers either that a 'positive' response to donation may skew the process of care away from making every effort to preserve life and more towards the potential recipient, or regarding a post-mortem, that death is the likely outcome.

Capacity—elusive and potentially harmful

A further problem in the pursuit of consent is created by the varying and unpredictable levels of capacity at different stages of a critical illness, since consent is intended to be a dynamic process with the opportunity for revision at any stage, and theoretically moments of competence should be used to confirm or cancel the patient's previously expressed position, or establish their position if a previous determination has not been reached.

The reality is that capacity is invariably compromised in these circumstances, creating the burden of the decision-making process for the patient while simultaneously questioning the validity of that decision-making and undermining the value of the exercise. Although the Mental Capacity Act 2005 specifies the continuous assessment of capacity and the need to promote capacity whenever this is compromised, the usual scenario within intensive care is that a genuinely capacitous state is rarely reached, and harms can be created by efforts to ensure this by generating discomfort and distress, which themselves compromise capacity, if analgesia and sedation are withdrawn solely to assess capacity. If therefore, there are significant barriers to achieving informed consent prior to or within the early stages of a critical illness before capacity is compromised, and this becomes even less attainable once the critical illness is established, how can the principle of respect for autonomy be practically applied?

Patient's views and wishes

This raises the more fundamental question of whether consent as a process for life-sustaining medical treatment (LSMT) is something that patients really wish to engage in proactively. In those jurisdictions where advance directives have a formal status, only a small percentage of the population have completed such an order, believing this to be restrictive on future choices by either failing to anticipate advances in medical care or indeed changes of the patient's perceptions once acute illness supervened. In these circumstances, patients expressed a preference for benign medical paternalism, which accommodated the opinion of the next of kin as representative of the patient's values and beliefs. [21] It is important therefore to distinguish acceptable variants of benign medical paternalism from the discredited examples, which were intended to protect patients and relatives from distressing details. This approach generated significant public distrust in the medical profession in the aftermath of the Alder Hey retained organs scandal and was instrumental in change to the determination of a patient's resuscitation status, with the current expectation that the patient be given the ultimate authority.

This does of course raise the issue of whether the patient is better served by being invited as a consumer to make a choice on a complex subject of which predictably they would have limited knowledge, in the circumstances of hospitalization and illness, which carry the hazard of compromising rational decision-making, with potential automatic exclusion of medical advice. The benign medical paternalism, which is seemingly sought by patients incorporates the therapeutic value of taking decisions when requested to, assisting decision-making with advice and recommendations when similarly requested, without compromising an individual's need for control in certain key areas. This construct accommodates a full spectrum of patient's wishes, from the individual who wishes to make their own informed choice, to those who wish not to be given information on treatment options and who prefer medical guidance. While appearing at first visit to be contrary to contemporary ethical principles, it clearly seeks to determine the patient's wishes with regards to levels of patient–practitioner responsibility for decision-making, and retains the service facet of the doctor–patient relationship, with value and reassurance for patient as well as practitioner and public. It would be regrettable if the majority of the population were disadvantaged by imperatives driven by worthy principles but enforced by a small minority who simplistically demand that the position of the patient is determinative.

The status of the next-of-kin in decision-making

A further confounding factor in whatever approach is taken towards consent is the status of the next of kin in decision-making once the patient loses capacity. While most members of the public would be confident that their values and beliefs would be accurately represented by their next of kin, their authority is limited to providing information on these aspects, unless formally empowered with a lasting power of attorney for personal welfare (LPAPW) with specified responsibility regarding LSMT. Although government directives and professional guidelines specify the involvement of the next of kin in decision-making for the incompetent patient, their ability to direct care will therefore be limited. The ideal scenario for patient care in these circumstances is an absolute consensus position from intensive care team, parent specialty and next of kin, and in the majority of cases this is achieved without placing any responsibility for decision-making on the next of kin, a position which should be avoided. Transferring responsibility onto the next of kin for a decision in an area where their expertise is limited, and where their emotional involvement could inappropriately compromise objectivity, carries the risk of longer term guilt or resentment towards health care staff if they believe themselves responsible for either limiting LSMT prematurely, or alternatively, forcing the burden of protracted ineffective support on the patient. The converse of this is when the opinion of the next of kin as to the appropriate course of action is ignored, and if patients have no faith in medical decision-making or the concept of benign medical paternalism, there is little alternative to a highly specific advance directive or appointment of a LPAPW in ensuring that one's wishes are both explicit and determinative.

Pragmatic solutions

In the face of the abovementioned problems, it would be understandable if intensive care staff considered proactive consent too elusive a concept and reverted to a historical model whereby patients were admitted under the parent specialty as a continuum of acute care, with little anticipatory engagement by the intensive care team. The reality is however that intensive care carries a high mortality and with the exception of those patients who demonstrate a spiral of deterioration refractory to all treatment strategies, decisions will have to be taken on the continuation of active support when it becomes apparent for whatever reason that the goals of intensive care are not attainable.

In these circumstances, all relevant parties are protected if the decision-making is as informed as possible by the patient's values and beliefs with regard to dependency on medical support, tolerable quality of life in the event of survival, and position on what constitutes a good death. It appears inescapable therefore that when circumstances suggest a high likelihood of requiring intensive care, that these issues should be explored and formally documented. It should also be apparent that even when survival is the more likely outcome, intensive care is invasive and associated with significant physical and psychological burdens, potentially over a protracted period. For this to be justifiable, there has to be strong evidence that this approximates to the patient's wishes. It is also clear that failing to proactively engage the patient causes broader individual and societal harms. If the patient is not made aware of the seriousness of their condition before the point of decompensation, they are denied the opportunity to plan for dying, and if patients are denied the opportunity to decline admission to intensive care, then not only is this cohort of patients inappropriately managed with little respect for autonomy, but a hardship is imposed on the public by unwarranted expense and a restriction on access to a scarce resource for those patients more capable of benefiting.

This exercise has to be undertaken therefore, and although much of the primary information and opinion gathering can be undertaken by the parent specialty, it requires a member of the intensive care team to facilitate an informed discussion on the benefits and risks of intensive care. This approach is in line with the principles of consent for other medical and surgical activity, where it is anticipated that the practitioner undertaking the consent process is someone capable of delivering the proposed care or intervention. The opportunity for early engagement of patient and family outside the geographical confines of the ICU already exists, via the platform of outreach critical care, at the point when Early Warning Scores trigger assessments at ward level. This evaluation can reasonably progress beyond recommending strategies to rectify physiological derangement and asking, 'does this patient require an ICU admission?', to 'will this patient benefit from an ICU admission?' and 'does this patient want an ICU admission?' Such an assessment requires a determination on capacity in the first instance, followed by an appraisal of the impact of comorbidity and medical interventions on background quality of life, focusing where appropriate on when these factors would make life intolerable and when therefore the patient would not wish to undergo LSMT. Even if a decision is taken to escalate care, it is important to have this information as an objective point of reference should complications develop which would take the patient across the specified threshold and into the 'intolerable burden of living' territory. This condition demands that a patient's higher neurological function is intact such that he or she is aware of their condition and thereby suffers, a situation that most intensive care patients are protected from. Ultimately this assessment has then to be undertaken by others, thereby once more compromising principles of consent or placing an undue burden on the next of kin to provide a 'substituted judgement', but this is at least assisted by an earlier exploration with the patient.

An additional concern of the public is profound neurological disability, which even if not associated with suffering, represents loss of identity and dignity, and constitutes a burden to others, such that many individuals would not wish to be maintained with LSMT if there was no chance of a meaningful recovery from their perspective. These aspects should certainly be discussed if proposed interventions such as intra-cranial surgery or major vascular procedures carry a risk of neurological insult.

Having explored the above areas, it would then be reasonable to determine how active a participant in health care decision-making the patient wished to be. Respect for autonomy does not translate into sim-ply providing information and expecting the patient to decide, but offering a range of options including making a choice with limited information or asking the doctor to make recommendations based on knowledge of the disease, potential treatments, and the health status and values of the patient. Respect for autonomy may also include accommodating the patient's wishes that no decisions be made at that point in time, but in the event of requiring intensive care at some future point and not fulfilling the criteria for capacity, that decisions be taken between medical staff and next of kin.

Meeting the expectations of patients, given this range of attitude and wishes, is clearly problematical, but requires detailed information on the process of care, outcomes, the staff involved, decision-making for the incompetent adult, the role of the next of kin, sharing of informa-tion, research etc. for those patients who wish to make as informed a decision as possible. It can be anticipated that most patients would only wish for overview information on these issues rather than highly specific detail, and it is possible therefore to have basic informa-tion booklets with the option of secondary pamphlets on aspects that would be of particular interest to the patient, such as transfusion or a tracheostomy.

It is also important to distinguish between the main categories of patient who would predictably approach these difficult questions dif-ferently. Those patients who carry a high risk of decompensation in association with elective surgery should theoretically be better placed to address these questions rationally without the adverse influence of ill health, and a determination of their wishes on key issues can reasonably be pursued. It has to be considered however that extensive discussion on the limitations and harms of intensive care may not be ideal mental preparation for major surgery from the patient's perspective.

Patients whose background pathology will predictably require intensive care at some future stage if life is to be sustained, such as advanced respiratory disease or neurodegenerative disorders, should also be engaged as soon as feasible, given the predictably worse outcome within this cohort of patients compared to 'elective' admissions.

Patients who are admitted acutely and are on the verge of decompensation at the point an ICU assessment is requested, are likely to be less capable of and willing to undergo a demanding series of questions on quality of life and values and beliefs, and staff should therefore be mindful of pursuing otherwise ideal goals. In these circumstances, engagement of the next of kin is essential, acknowledging that at a time of significant distress it will predictably be difficult to consolidate information on illness, prognosis, process of care, and the limitations on their authority for decision-making.

It can also be anticipated that next of kin will not always be in agreement with the medical overview and recommendations, particularly if this favours a limitation on active support. This may be due to understandable factors such as an unwillingness to take responsibility for such a significant decision within a relatively pressurized timeframe, or a genuinely held belief that the patient's quality of life was acceptable despite major disability. Other drivers for a contrary position include guilt over their previous commitment to care and support of the patient, religious views on the sanctity of life, or a belief that the medical position is driven by discrimination on the grounds of age, lifestyle or religion, or that resource allocation is a primary concern. In these circumstances, although the emphasis has to be on protecting the patient from the harms of interventions, which will be futile from either a physiological perspective or because they will not restore an acceptable quality of life, the patient's best interests are rarely promoted by conflict between health care team and next of kin. Maintaining communication, exploring the drivers behind an individual's position, empathizing with their circumstances, and allowing time and space and making concessions are important strategies in maintaining both dialogue and mutual respect, which in turn are fundamental to concepts of consent. Although recognizing that in extreme circumstances an application to the courts might be essential to resolve an impasse, which is generating obvious patient harms, a process which pits the relative authority of health care professionals and legal system against the next of kin who by definition are in a vulnerable position, intuitively runs contrary to broad principles of consent.

An aspect of intensive care responsibilities that is often overlooked in these discussions with either patient or next of kin relates to end-of-life procedures when ICU admission is not considered or when a later decision is taken to withdraw active support when the goals of intensive care have not been realized. The public are only too aware of how even UK doctors feel that they have to end their lives overseas in pursuit of a good death[22] and would predictably wish for reassurance that any discomfort or distress associated with dying would be managed competently and confidently without fear of professional repercussions. It is apparent that there is a range of practice in this area[23] and a restrictive approach borne out of the practitioner's personal beliefs should engender greater public concern than benign paternalism. Unit policy and practice on these issues should therefore be unambiguous and accessible, with the overall benefit of protecting all parties. This responsibility to promote and provide a 'good death' when this is inevitable, equally extends to those patients who are refused or who decline ICU admission, since this is an integral part of the overall responsibility and the decision-making process, particularly when palliative care may not be able to accommodate the patient within a reasonable timeframe.

There may therefore be many facets to consent and many barriers to approaching an ideal model, but policies need to be formulated to meet the needs of particular institutions and to demonstrate that the principles of legislation such as the Mental Capacity Act are being adhered to. The process of patient engagement on these issues needs documentation to confirm compliance with all directives, but more importantly as an objective point of reference on the patient's quality of life, values and beliefs, which will shape medical decision-making once the patient has lost capacity and the goals of intensive care are not achievable.

Conclusions

Consent, the cornerstone of contemporary medical practice, is a challenging concept when considering the complexities of intensive care. To achieve the maximum good for all parties, this political and professional imperative has to go beyond simple provision of information, patient choice and documentation of process. The majority of patients requiring intensive care may be better served by broad discussion on their values and goals, an ongoing evaluation of their response to escalating interventions and cares, and delayed decision-making informed by these aspects, predictably when the patient has lost capacity. Whilst this approach may be criticized as paternalism, however benign, it appears preferable to early forced patient choice, which superficially would conform with political directives, but which carries the risk of simplistic decisions that then restrict future choice. If we are to offer options as an essential feature of consent, these should arguably include that of allowing the health care team to take decisions once the patient loses capacity, in the light of their response to treatment.

These approaches may be viewed however as contravening current standards of consent by individuals or organizations unfamiliar with the complexities of intensive care, and the whole subject needs broad professional and public debate therefore if we are to achieve maximal patient and public good, limit practitioner vulnerabilities, and enhance the status of our specialty by demonstrating a reasoned and reasonable strategy in this challenging area.

References

1 The Bristol Royal Infirmary Inquiry. London: Central Office of Information, 2001.
2 Redfern M (2001). The Royal Liverpool Children's Inquiry Report. London: The Stationery Office.
3 http://www.hta.gov.uk/about_hta/human_tissue_act.cfm
4 *Chester v Afshar* [2004] HL 41. http://www.publications.parliament.uk/pa/ld200304/ldjudgmt/jd041014/cheste-1.htm
5 HSC 2001/023: Good practice in consent: achieving the NHS Plan commitment to patient-centred consent practice. Department of Health London 2001.http://www.dh.gov.uk/en/Publicationsandstatistics/Lettersandcirculars/Healthservicecirculars/DH_4003736.

6 Consent: patients and doctors making decisions together. General Medical Council 2008.

7 http://www.opsi.gov.uk/acts/acts2005/ukpga_20050009_en_1

8 HSC 2000/028. Resuscitation Policy. Department of Health London 2000.

9 http://www.survivingsepsis.org/implement/resources/guidelines

10 http://www.cochrane.org/reviews/en/ab002042.html

11 http://www.tracman.org.uk/

12 Subbe CP, Kruger M, Rutherford P, Gemmel L (2001). Validation of a modified Early Warning Score in medical admissions. *Q J Med* **94**: 521–526.

13 Knaus WA, Harrell FE Jr, Lynn J, et al. (1995) The SUPPORT prognostic model. Objective estimates of survival for seriously ill hospitalized adults. Study to understand prognoses and preferences for outcomes and risks of treatments. *Ann Intern Med* **122(3)**: 191–203.

14 Eddleston JM, White P, Guthrie E (2000). Survival, morbidity, and quality of life after discharge from intensive care. *Critical Care Med.* **28(7)**: 2293–2299.

15 Hofhuis JG, Spronk PE, van Stel HF, et al. (2008). The impact of critical illness on perceived health related quality of life during ICU treatment, hospital stay, and after hospital discharge; a long term follow-up study. *Chest* **133**: 377–385.

16 Cuthbertson BH, Rattray J, Johnston M, et al. (2007) A pragmatic randomised, controlled trial of intensive care follow up programmes in improving longer-term outcomes from critical illness: the PRACTICAL study. *BMC Health Serv Res* **7**: 116.

17 *Ms B v An NHS Hospital Trust* [2002] EWHC 429 (Fam)

18 McNeil BJ, Pauker SG, Sox HC, Tversky A (1982). On elicitation of preferences for alternative therapies. *N Engl J Med* **306**: 1259–1262.

19 Lerner BH (2001). *The Breast Cancer Wars. Hope, Fear And The Pursuit of a Cure in Twentieth-Century America.* Oxford University Press, New York.

20 Bhagwanjee S et al. (1997). Does HIV status influence the outcome of patients admitted to a surgical intensive care unit? A prospective double blind study *BMJ* **314**: 1077–1084.

21 Perkins HS (2007). Controlling death: the false promise of advance directives. *Ann Intern Med* **147**: 51–57.

22 Obituaries (2006). Anne Turner [editorial]. *BMJ* **332**: 306.

23 Poulton B, Ridley S, Mackenzie-Ross R, Rizvi S (2005). Variation in end-of-life decision-making between critical care consultants. *Anaesthesia* **60**: 1101–1105.

Chapter 2

Adults who lack capacity to consent

Daniele C Bryden

Introduction to incapacity

Consent is a fundamental principle of medical ethics that recognizes an individual's right to autonomy and self-determination. Differing views as to the nature of autonomy exist from one of simple independence of decision-making to that of autonomy encompassing a need to incorporate additional values such as an ability to form goals based on initial desires and wishes.[1]

There is a common law presumption of competence, and both English and Scottish laws protect the right of a patient to give or withhold consent irrespective of their reasoning behind the decision, but the patient must demonstrate an ability to display rational thinking, supporting a more complex view of autonomy.[2] All health professionals must therefore provide sufficient information to patients to enable them to attempt to make a rational decision. Morally however, this is probably insufficient, since the patient must also understand the clinician's proposal, and this is outside the health professional's control. However the law is concerned principally in the manner of disclosure so that the information is given in a way that is capable of being understood. Consent is a process of information exchange between the health professional and the patient that allows a patient to exercise their right to autonomy. As such, it is equally valid for a patient to refuse that information provided he/she is aware of their entitlement to it, although the Code of Practice for the Adults with Incapacity (Scotland) Act counsels professionals to watch out for undue influence from others on a patient and their decisions regarding consent and refusals of information.[3] Intensive care practice is often structured with a time frame where consent can truly be considered to be a process, and where many patients for various reasons do not retain capacity.

This chapter considers how these issues apply to critical care practice and how considerations in cases of incompetence such as the 'best interests' and 'substituted judgements' tests are considered. It will also examine any possible changes that the advent of the Mental Capacity Act 2005 may have on this area.

Development of best interests test

It is a general common law principle that unauthorized contact between individuals is criminal assault, unless it falls under one of the recognized exceptions vitiated by consent and discussed by the House of Lords in *R v Brown*.[4] Moreover unauthorized touching could also constitute the civil tort (or equivalent civil delict in Scotland) of battery/trespass. In the case of Ms B, who continued to receive life-sustaining ventilation despite her wishes to the contrary, she was awarded nominal damages for the tort, recognizing that 'there is a serious danger of a benevolent paternalism which does not embrace recognition of the personal autonomy of the severely disabled patient'.[5] For the law to uphold these principles in the face of a severely ill/injured patient needing life-saving treatment on intensive care would be nonsense, and non-consensual treatment is considered lawful, provided the treatment is deemed necessary and in the patient's best interests.[6]

In order for a proposed course of action to meet the necessity requirement, it must be necessary to perform the treatment without consent,[7] and not just a matter of convenience to do so without waiting for the patient to recover capacity, e.g. the intensive care patient who has an acute airway problem requiring intubation and mechanical ventilation. If it is reasonably possible to delay any treatment until the patient becomes competent, then that should be considered regardless of whether there may be an additional medical benefit to the patient.[8] This might apply to the incidental finding of an additional medical condition that is not life-threatening and does not affect the course of the patient's treatment on the ICU, e.g. the presence of an ovarian cyst seen on CT scan images of the abdomen performed to assess the extent of pelvic trauma. In *Williamson v East London HA*, a patient underwent a mastectomy without consent having agreed only to the removal of a leaking breast implant.[9] The court found for the patient as although the operation would have been necessary at some point, she had not had this possibility discussed with her and would not have given her consent at that point had it been discussed with her. The authors of Mason and McCall Smith's textbook on medical law and ethics counsel health care staff to try to obtain information from any family member or friend if a patient is unconscious 'to discover any anticipatory choice on the part of the patient or other details which might affect a clinical decision'.[10] The difficulty for critical care professionals is that there are often intercurrent conditions in our patient population such as pain, hypoxia, sepsis, etc., which can often bring into doubt the competence of an adult to consent to or refuse treatment. Physical pain and emotional distress have been identified as vitiating factors in negating the ability of a pregnant woman to weigh up adequately the considerations necessary in her refusal to undergo a forceps delivery.[11] In such cases, the gravity and potential for such treatments to be literally life-saving suggest that less evidence is needed to rebut any presumption of competence. 'The graver the consequences of the decision, the commensurately greater the level of competence is required to take the decision'.[12]

The second condition of 'best interests' is harder to define categorically as it is inevitably a normative standard. In *Re F*, concerning a proposal to sterilize a mentally handicapped woman deemed incapable of making a competent decision regarding the procedure, Lord Goff recognized the problems for professionals working in more acute areas, and suggested that 'the doctor must act in accordance with a responsible and competent body of relevant professional opinion, on the principles set down in *Bolam v Friern* Hospital Management Committee'.[13] Therefore, until the Mental Capacity Act 2005, it was left to professional medical opinion to determine what was in the patient's best interests with accusations of paternalism, and confusion over the narrowness or breadth of 'best interests'. Subsequent examinations of the test in cases like Bland[14] and Re MB[15] have considered best interests to be much wider considerations than the purely medical: Butler- Sloss LJ's view summarizes this as 'best interests encompasses medical, emotional and all other welfare issues',[16] however the 'Bolam' test is not always sufficient to judge best interests[17] and the ultimate decision will rest with the courts.[18]

The problems with the best interests test and its subsequent examination by bodies such as the Law Commission, which recommended a similarly wide view, led to the creation of the Mental Capacity Act 2005 and the creation of a statutory definition of 'best interests' for an incapacitated individual. Section 2 of the Act defines incapacity thus: 'a person lacks capacity in relation to a matter if at the material time he is unable to make a decision for himself in relation to the matter because of an impairment of, or a disturbance in the functioning of, the mind or brain'. Along with the Section 3 (1) requirements to understand the relevant information, retain it, use it as part of the decision-making process and communicate the decision, it clarifies some of these difficulties for critical care professionals who must regularly make decisions regarding the wisdom of initiating treatment of incompetent adults. It can be less clear, however, how health care professionals should utilize the 'best interests' test when treatments are already established.

Substituted judgement test

In contrast, the substituted judgement test is more widely used for considerations of treatment of the incompetent patient in the United States. It tries to second guess what a patient would have chosen in a particular set of circumstances in contrast to the best interests test, which uses information to try to decide what on balance is best for that patient. At first glance, it would seem to be a more subjective assessment and less paternalistic than the best interests test. However, it is often the case that an incompetent patient on an ICU cannot express any sort of choice and has rarely had previous experience of the proposed treatment requiring a decision, e.g. tracheostomy to facilitate weaning. In effect, the ICU doctor would look to a third party, whether relative or other colleague with previous clinical responsibility for the patient, to substitute the patient's decision. Therefore in practice, the third party is using their *own* judgement to second guess that of the patient's. This is subject to heavy criticism as flawed and 'in the absence of real evidence equivalent to guesswork'.[19] Of interest to ICU physicians is that the test has been applied to the case of Nancy Cruzan in the United States, where an application was sought to remove artificial nutrition and hydration from her while she existed in a permanent vegetative state. The court did demand the need for evidence that not continuing to exist in a vegetative state was consistent with Nancy's wishes, and this was able to be provided from both her friends and parents. The U.S. courts appear to have adopted a position that in using the substituted judgement test, the presumption is to adopting continuation of life-preserving treatment as a default position, as this causes less harm to the incompetent individual.

As commentators like McLean have noted, use of a substituted judgement test is often very difficult to apply and equally as open to abuse as the best interests test. Harm may equally well come from being kept alive in a state with no prospect of recovery or in such a way that assumes that the individual would not have had any interests in how they were cared for or without considering the possibility that parties who are consulted will have their own interests in the outcome. 'Close family members may have a strong feeling that they do not wish to witness the continuation of the life of a loved one which they regard as hopeless, there is no automatic assurance that the view of close family members will necessarily be the same as the patient's would have been had she been confronted with the prospect of her situation'.[20]

Overlap of best interests and substituted judgement

While not accepted by UK courts as an alternative test to the best interests test, it is inevitable that some consideration is given to the postulated wishes of the incompetent patient. At issue, however, is often the degree to which emphasis is given to these 'estimated wishes'. At a basic level, health care practitioners working within critical care environments routinely attempt to establish a patient's views on their treatments and likely future health desires as part of good practice standards. However, this is only in relation to the extent of any treatment that is consistent with professional judgement and not as a way of enforcing treatment that is not considered medically appropriate (see R (on the application of Burke) v General medical Council, [2006] Q.B. 273).

UK courts have not, to date, formally adopted a substituted judgement test either in place of or parallel to the best interests test, but there is evidence that when an individual is incompetent, consideration is given to what is thought to be their likely wishes. In Re J[21] Lord Donaldson cited a Canadian case, Re Superintendent of Family and Child Service and Dawson,[22] as useful in guiding the application of the best interests test in the incompetent patient by considering what their wishes would have been. It is unfortunate that both of these cases concern children who have never been in a position to express any wishes, and so there is no case law to suggest that the courts would adopt this approach in the case of an incapacitated adult.

It is arguable that in practice there may be very little difference between the best interests and substituted judgement test when considering an incompetent patient. Since as part of the statutory definition of 'best interests' the Mental Capacity Act 2005 requires consultation with individuals in the absence of an Advance Directive, it is likely these individuals may either have a good idea of the incompetent person's wishes, or have been given specific instructions. In both situations therefore, consultation using best interests guidance is arguably a more formalized version of the substituted judgement test, particularly within ICU practice in the United Kingdom where it is an almost universal practice to obtain information from relatives/carers as to any known prior wishes expressed by the patient.

Temporary incapacity

Treatment decisions

On an ICU, it is more usual to encounter patients who are incompetent due to illness, drugs, or hypoxia, among others, than to come across those who can be demonstrated to be competent to the satisfaction and confidence of those caring for them. It is not unusual therefore for health care professionals to arguably adopt a 'default' presumption of incompetence rather than to assume the position of competence required by ethics and the Mental Capacity Act 2005. Much of the case law concerning incompetence relates to patients who have a relatively long-term lack of capacity, e.g. learning disability where the issue is one of whether the individual is competent to make a particular decision, e.g. regarding sterilization. However, in the critical care population, lack of capacity is less open to dispute, e.g. unconsciousness, but may be temporary and the issues relate to the appropriateness of any decision in those circumstances where capacity may be regained at a later point or is never likely to be regained at all. In addition, as discussed, many situations occur, e.g. a need to perform tracheostomy to facilitate weaning, where contemporaneous consent is not possible.

There is no automatic proxy consent for another person.[23] Although it is not uncommon and is generally considered good practice to inform a patient's next of kin of any plans to perform surgery, this does not constitute a process of consent. Such conversations may be very useful in informing the doctor's decision, but such a decision is made under the doctrine of necessity, and it is inappropriate to ask relatives to sign a 'consent' form. Similarly, forms that are used to document such decisions are not consent forms, but rather a means to record that the procedure is being carried out under the aegis of this doctrine and to allow staff to formally record and consider the necessity of any treatment at such a point. *Bolton Hospitals NHS Trust v O* confirmed that when a patient is incompetent, it is appropriate to use reasonable force to provide treatment if that treatment is in their best interests.[24] While this may seem very paternalistic, the assumption is that the intervention is probably necessary to allow the patient to recover to such a point where he/she can form their own decision, e.g. holding an oxygen mask on a confused patient. The introduction from 1 April 2009 of the Deprivation of Liberty Safeguards allied to the Mental Capacity Act should not have a significant effect on such considerations. Since the introduction of the Mental Capacity Act, there is a limited provision under Section 9 for prior authorization of an individual to have a lasting power of attorney with certain limited authority to make health care decisions, although these do not extend to preventing life-sustaining treatments unless this has been specifically specified.

Other decisions

There are, however, instances when a patient may be rendered temporarily incapacitated on an ICU, where there are requests from police officers to perform tests or take samples to facilitate a criminal investigation. This can often lead to confusion among health care staff as to the conflicts between the need to protect patient confidentiality and the requirements of the law when a patient is incapacitated.

The Human Tissue Act 2004 concerns requests for DNA samples and identifies any removal of human tissue without consent (including blood and skin cells) as an offence unless the action falls within a list of excepted purposes such as to facilitate the functions of a coroner or to investigate or prosecute a crime.

Doctors have an ethical duty to protect patient confidentiality, but this may come into conflict with a requirement on us, as for any member of society, not to impede a criminal investigation. It is not uncommon for staff to be caring for a patient who has been involved in a road traffic collision and there may be genuine police concerns that drugs or alcohol were involved in the event. Under these circumstances, introducing a time delay to wait for the patient to regain capacity may result in the loss of important evidence. The Police Reform Act 2002 allows for samples to be taken without waiting for recovery of capacity, although testing of the specimen is not allowed until the patient recovers capacity and having been informed by the police officer that a sample has been taken, gives agreement for the sample to be used in this way. Health care professionals are in a position to object to the sample being taken, but only if the sampling process hinders patient care. If the specimen is not necessary for the patient's care, but the Police reform Act requires it, it would be better if time allows to get someone appropriately trained to take the sample but not involved in patient care eg a police surgeon, or another staff member if possible to avoid this conflict of interest.

Other forms of testing, e.g. HIV testing may be part of specific professional guidance from the bodies like the GMC, which recommends non consensual testing if it is in the patient's best interests to do so.

Permanent incapacity from unconsciousness

However, some patients may never recover consciousness and so entering into a process of consent is impossible, and there is no utility from delays in treatment providing the treatment can be shown to be in their best interests. There can, of course, be considerable difficulty in determining where those best interests may lie.

This is exemplified by the case of Anthony Bland, a young man who had been left in a permanent vegetative state following a hypoxic cerebral injury he sustained during the Hillsborough stadium crowd disaster.[25] It is of relevance to critical care practice in terms of the discussions surrounding the best interests test.

Anthony Bland's life was sustained in part by artificial enteral feeding and both Mr Bland's family and the medical team caring for him were of the view that it was inappropriate to continue feeding him in this manner. Airedale NHS Trust therefore sought a declaration that they could lawfully discontinue this feeding, which was challenged by the Official Solicitor as a proposed course of action amounting to unlawful killing. The first instance decision included a judgement from Sir Stephen Brown that withdrawal of feeding was consistent with Anthony's best interests having 'no therapeutic, medical or other benefit in continuing to maintain his ventilation, nutrition and hydration by artificial means'. The same test was supported by the Court of Appeal, with an extension of reasoning to include consideration of the 'constant invasions and humiliations' his body was subjected to from the treatment, the effects this would have on previous memories of him, and the 'prolonged ordeal imposed on all members of his family' and also to an altruistic notion that 'finite resources are better devoted to enhancing life than simply averting death'.

The House of Lords view of the application of the best interests test in Bland's case was controversial in that it was held 'the proposed conduct is not in the best interests of Anthony Bland, for he has no best interests of any kind'.[26] In their Lordships view, it is meaningless to apply the best interests test to the permanently unconscious, and continuation or withdrawal of further treatment should not be decided using the test. Rather they took the view that the best interests test should be reversed and consideration given to the utility of continuing with treatment that artificially prolongs life with an obligation on medical staff to stop further treatment: 'If there comes a stage where the responsible doctor comes to the reasonable conclusion (which accords with the views of a responsible body of medical opinion) that further continuance of an intrusive life support system is not in the best interests of the patient, he can no longer lawfully continue that life support system: to do so would constitute the crime of battery and the tort of trespass to the person'.[27] This is not an isolated decision, since the Inner House of the Court of Session in Scotland took the same view, that in cases of permanent unconsciousness, the correct application of the best interests test was a negative one, and that there could be no interest in being kept alive by artificial means.[28]

What then of cases where there are differences in medical opinion? In the case of Bland, Lord Browne-Wilkinson took the view that the application to the courts to discontinue life-prolonging treatment would be supported if there was a reasonable body of medical opinion, and that this was not negated by the presence of an opposing medical viewpoint: 'the courts only concern will be to be satisfied that the doctors' decision to discontinue is in accordance with a respectable body of medical opinion that it is reasonable'.[29]

This would appear to be legal support for a paternalistic view of medical care, which does not make full use of the best interests test, whether because as some have argued the view that permanent unconsciousness can have only a negative application of the best interests test is not making full use of the test,[30] or rather that the test in such cases should be replaced by the substituted judgement test as being ethically preferable.[31]

Determining best interests post Mental Capacity Act 2005

This reasoning has not been reconsidered yet at a higher court level in light of the Mental Capacity Act 2005 although It has been considered by Dame Butler-Sloss in the light of the Human Rights Act 1998 and is not held to be a contravention of an Article 2 Right to life.[32] Denzil Lush (Senior Judge of the Court of Protection) has argued that the MCA has moved the best interests test nearer to the substituted judgement test as there is an obligation for health professionals to consult.[33]

Similarly, by using the language of Bolam in the House of Lords, there is a suggestion that actions like withdrawals of treatment must be supportable by peer professional opinion. While there was no obligation in Lord Browne-Wilkinson's judgement to obtain peer opinion, it would seem reasonable that doctors within critical care who consult and canvass additional opinions will be in a better position to support decisions as to withdrawals of treatment in the unconscious patient when the options are continuing treatment with no prospect of making the patient fit enough to recover capacity or to withdraw treatment that is needlessly prolonging life.

Treatment which is of no direct benefit

There are difficulties in relation to the incompetent adult receiving treatment on ICU, which has no direct bearing on the course of their present condition. In the case of Stephen Blood, a man who died after receiving treatment on ICU for meningitis, the issue was in relation to treatment he received on the ICU to obtain sperm samples prior to his death, when his consent for the procedure was impossible to obtain. Subsequent use of the sperm was contrary to the requirement to have written permission from the donor as stipulated in the Human Fertilisation and Embryology Act 1990. Although his wife Diane argued that such treatment would have been consistent with his wishes to have children, she was not a disinterested party in the outcome of any decisions regarding the sperm samples. This was subject to a review and widespread consultation by Professor Sheila McLean.[34] In temporarily unconscious patients, gamete removal was only justified if the individual's fertility was likely to be affected and it was not consistent with their best interests to delay gamete removal until contemporaneous consent could be given, but rather to allow them to have the ability to choose whether or not to parent. There was, however, a clear lack of certainty as to whether in the permanently unconscious the best interests test would be applicable, and the only benefit which can accrue is one to a third party, namely the remaining partner (and possibly to any potential child).[35]

In light of the Bland judgement and the legal view that in cases of permanent unconsciousness, there can only really be a negative application of the best interests test, if an individual becomes unconscious with no prospect of recovery, it may be logical to make decisions regarding medical treatments by reference to parties whose interests may be bound up in such decisions, e.g. the relatives. Despite the requirements of the Mental Capacity Act 2005, many ICU professionals would be uncomfortable with any greater strengthening of third party views since in some cases of severe neurological injury, the process of reaching decisions regarding poor prospects of recovery is a gradual one, and it would in practical terms be very hard to identify a point at which the individual ceases to have any best interests and medical professionals should instead shift their considerations to third party interests. Many would rather be comfortable with the dissenting legal view expressed by Justice Stevens in the Nancy Cruzan case that her interests did not disappear with her loss of consciousness as she will have 'an interest in how she will be thought of after her death by those whose opinions mattered to her'.[36] This is akin to the Court of Appeal view of Anthony Bland's best interests, where it was clearly established that he had never considered such a situation and there could be no assessment of his wishes regarding his continuing existence in the PVS state. If this were the case, treatment withdrawal would be legally supported as consistent with a patient's interests to be remembered in a certain way or being treated in a manner consistent with their previous dignity. Both of these are views that are already held by many health care professionals, who believe that their current actions are consistent with such patterns of behaviour and thinking. However, this is not a policy of the courts or expressed in statute which merely require that we operate with reference to third party views in determining where a patient's best interests lie, but is unclear what if any interests such patients may still retain.

Summary

All adults are presumed to be competent and for medical treatment there is a general requirement to obtain consent. In a critical care setting, the necessity for life saving treatments and the presence of intercurrent medical conditions means that it may be easier to rebut any presumption of competence on the part of the patient to refuse life saving treatment but this cannot be assumed. Actions taken in patients lacking capacity should only be in the best interests of the patient and limited to what is deemed necessary at the time.

Prior to the introduction of the Mental Capacity Act 2005, the standard was that judged by a responsible and competent body of fellow professionals. The Act has formalised best interests along with a clearer definition of the requirements for capacity which brings greater clarification for critical care staff.

Problems remain in implementing the best interests test and the emphasis given to what the person's wishes are 'thought' to be in the absence of any clear prior knowledge. Although the MCA requires consultation with individuals close to the patient who may have an idea what these wishes are, unless they have been granted a lasting power of attorney to make decisions concerning life saving treatment, these only inform and do not wholly determine medical decision making. Unlike in the USA, we do not have formal legal recognition of substituted judgements of an incapacitated person's wishes.

In difficult cases involving treatment administration and withdrawal, critical care professionals are in a better position to make robust, defensible decisions if they consult fellow professionals as well as the immediate next of kin/independent mental capacity advocate they are required to. Under such circumstances, an individual patient's 'best interests' may involve many factors than the purely medical.

References

1 Dworkin G (1988). *The Theory and Practice of Autonomy*, Cambridge University Press, Cambridge.
2 *Re T (Adult: Refusal of Treatment)* 4 All ER 649.
3 Adults with Incapacity (Scotland) Act 2000.
4 *R v Brown* [1994] 1 AC 212.
5 *B v NHS Hospital Trust* [2002] 2 All ER 449.
6 *Re F* (mental patient: sterilisation) [1990] 2 AC 1 per Goff LJ.
7 *Marshall v Curry* [1933] 3 DLR 260.
8 *Murray v McMurchy* [1949] 2 DLR 442.
9 *Willamson v East London and City Health Authority* (1997) 41 BMLR 85.

10 Mason JK, Laurie GT (2006). Non-consensual treatment, *Law and Medical Ethics*, Oxford University Press, Oxford, p.353.

11 *Norfolk and Norwich Healthcare (NHS) Trust v W* 34 BMLR 16.

12 *Re MB (Medical Treatment)* [1997] 2 FLR 426.

13 *Re F (mental patient: sterilisation)* [1990] 2 AC 1.

14 *Airedale NHS Trust v Bland* [1993] AC 789 (CA)

15 *Re MB (Medical treatment)* 12 BMLR 64.

16 *Re A (Medical treatment: Male sterilisation)* [2000] 1 FCR 193.

17 *R v Doctor M* [2003] 1 FLR 667.

18 *Simms v Simms* [2003] 2 WLR 1465.

19 McLean, SAM (1997). Consent and the Law: review of the current provisions in the Human Fertilisation and Embryology Act 1990 for the UK Health ministers. *Human Reproduction update*; 3(6): 593–621.

20 Per Chief Justice Rehnguist cited in Gunther and Sullivan (1997). *Constitutional Law*, 13th ed. The Foundation Press, Westbury, NY, p. 605.

21 *Re J (a minor) (wardship: medical treatment)* [1991] Fam 33.

22 *Re Superintendent of Family and Child Service and Dawson* (1983) 145 DLR (3d) 610.

23 *Re T (adult: refusal of medical treatment)* [1992] 4 All ER 649.

24 *Bolton Hospitals NHS Trust v O* [2003] 1 FLR 824.

25 *Airedale NHS Trust v Bland* [1993] 1 All ER 821, (1993) 12 BMLR 64.

26 *Airedale NHS Trust v Bland* [1993] 1 All ER 821, (1993) 12 BMLR 64 per Lord Mustill at p. 141.

27 *Airedale NHS Trust v Bland* [1993] 1 All ER 821, (1993) 12 BMLR 64 per Lord Browne-Wilkison, p. 129.

28 Law Hospital *NHS Trust v Lord Advocate* 1996 SCLR 491–519.

29 *Airedale NHS Trust v Bland* [1993] 1 All ER 821, (1993) 12 BMLR 64 per Lord Browne-Wilkinson, p. 130.

30 Fenwick AJ (1998). Applying best interests to persistent vegetative state: a principled distortion? *Journal of Medical Ethics* 24: 86–92.

31 Mason JK, Laurie GT (1996). The management of the persistent vegetative state in the British Isles. *Juridical Review*, 263–283.

32 *NHS Trust A v M* and *NHS Trust B v H* 58 BMLR 87.

33 Lush, D. How effective has the MCA 2005 been in practice? Temple Head Annual Lecture, 19 March 2009, accessed on 2 March 2010 at www.temple-head.org.uk.

34 McLean SAM. Review of the Common Law Provisions relating to the Removal of Gametes and of the Consent Provisions in the Human Fertilisation and Embryology Act, July 1990.

35 *Ibid.* London: Department of Health, 1998 at para 1.9.

36 *Cruzan v Director*, Missouri Dept of Health (1990) 110 S Ct 2841, pp. 2885–2886.

Chapter 3

The best interests of babies and children

Christopher Newdick and
Christopher Danbury

The Royal College of Paediatrics and Child Health estimates that

> withdrawal of treatment in paediatric intensive care units accounts for between
> 43% and 72% of deaths in the UK and other countries... In the management of
> children with chronic conditions outside intensive care similar decisions are
> also made but much fewer data are available. At least 12 in 10,000 children are
> living with a life-threatening condition in this country. Many of these children
> receive palliative care at home where choices to withhold invasive and intensive
> interventions are made regularly.[1]

Within this group, with respect to neonatal mortality (death within the
first 28 days after birth), the most common causes of death arise in premature babies born before 37 weeks of gestational age (1.3 per 1,000 live
births), babies with congenital malformations (0.7 per 1,000 live births),
babies who die due to a catastrophic event during labour and delivery
(0.3 per 1,000 live births), and babies with infection (0.3 per 1,000 live
births).[2] These statistics demonstrate the difficulty in deciding whether
to strive to preserve the lives of babies born in these circumstances.[2] The
question is discussed in guidance from the Royal College of Paediatrics
and Child Health. It distinguishes five situations in which judgement
may have to be made as to whether life-prolonging treatment should be
administered. The first two situations may provoke least controversy,
i.e. when the child is (a) brain dead and (b) in a permanent vegetative
state (although differences of diagnosis may still exist).[3]

However, the latter three categories involve greater scope for
judgement and, inescapably, the opportunity for greater disagreement
between clinicians and relatives.[4] They are: (c) where there is 'no

chance' of recovery, i.e. 'treatment simply delays death without significant alleviation of suffering', (d) where there is 'no purpose' in treatment, i.e. 'the patient may be able to survive treatment [but] the degree
of physical and mental impairment will be so great that it is unreasonable
to expect them to suffer it', and (e) where the life is 'unbearable,' i.e.
'further treatment is more than can be borne.'[5] Inevitably, we may disagree whether a child satisfies any of these criteria, or to which category
they really belong.[6] Clearly, these principles and challenges are applicable
to the wider paediatric population and are not confined to neonates.

As there are fewer than 30 paediatric ICUs in the United Kingdom,[7]
it is likely that the first senior intensive care doctor responding to a
critically ill child will be an adult intensive care physician in a District
General Hospital. The patient is likely to be either a usually fit/healthy
child who is acutely unwell, or often, a chronically ill child, who has had
an acute deterioration. How then to respond? Problems arise in these
cases when there is conflict between clinician and parent. It is possible
to construct a 2 × 2 matrix summarizing the situation:

	Doctors wish to treat child	doctors do not wish to treat child
Parents, and or child wish treatment for the child	No conflict	Conflict
Parents, and or child, do not wish treatment for the child	Conflict	No conflict

Where there is no conflict, the desired option will occur. The issue
revolves around resolving conflict. The second situation is perceived by
clinicians as being harder, but the same principles apply. With a child
who is chronically ill, the parents (and child) often become more familiar with the child's specific condition than the general paediatrician or
intensive care physician in the acute sector. This can lead to a reluctance to initiate, what is perceived by the clinician to be, a futile treatment. The parents with more specific knowledge may disagree with this
view and wish for their child to be treated. Is this reasonable? It has
been shown that 'patients with cancer are much more likely to opt for

radical treatment with minimal chance of benefit than people who do not have cancer, including medical and nursing professionals.'[8] The same logic applies to treatment in ICU. Note also that medical professionals are not systematically better than patients or parents at predicting clinical outcomes or quality of life:

> Data regarding 521 patients including 1,932 daily judgements by nurses and doctors were analyzed. Disagreement on at least one of the daily judgements by nurses and doctors was found in 21% of all patients and in 63% of the dying patients ... Patients only rarely indicated bad quality of life (6%) and severe physical disability (2%) 6 months after intensive care unit admission. Compared with patients' own assessment, neither nurses nor doctors correctly predicted quality of life ... Disagreement between nurses and doctors was frequent with respect to their judgement of futility of medical interventions. Disagreements most often concerned the most severely ill patients. Nurses, being more pessimistic in general, were more often correct than doctors in the judgement of dying patients but proposed treatment withdrawal in some very sick patients who survived. Future quality of life cannot reliably be predicted either by doctors or by nurses.[9]

Of course, there is a strong presumption in favour of life,[10] but there may come a stage when invasive treatment is felt by medical staff to be inappropriate and the focus turns to palliative care. Given the possibility of disagreement and the difficulties often inherent in prognosis, how are decisions of this gravity to be taken, how should judgements about the proper care be made, upon what criteria, and by whom? How does the best interests test apply to babies and children? This chapter considers (a) the evolution of judicial deference to clinical opinion, (b) the assertion of the authority of the court, (c) that there is no right to *demand* medical treatment, (d) resolving irretrievable differences of opinion, and (e) the position of mature children.

Evolution of judicial deference to clinical opinion

In principle, three parties are relevant to a decision as to whether to continue to give a child treatment in intensive care, namely parents, doctors, and the courts. Notice that at each stage, there is potential for the supervision surrounding the decision to increase. In the past, few matters of this nature reached the courts and, in those that did, judges normally deferred to the good sense and judgement of the responsible doctors.

Note first that doctors may never take active steps to hasten the death of a child. However, it may be possible to withhold, or withdraw further treatment if it is no longer in the child's best interests.[11] In *R v Arthur*,[12] for example, a baby was born with Down's syndrome. The parents did not wish the child to survive and the doctor instructed that the baby should be given nursing care only. The child was given sedatives and water, but was not fed and died three days later. The doctor was charged with the attempted murder of the baby,[13] and the trial judge instructed the jury that the child's right to life was not diminished just because a doctor (or his parents) thought his life was not worth living.

> However serious a case may be; however much the disadvantage of a mongol, or indeed, any other handicapped child, no doctor has the right to kill it. There is no special law in this country that places doctors in a separate category and gives them extra protection over the rest of us.[14]

On the other hand, when the judge explained the law to the jury, he emphasized the extent of the doctor's *duties*, rather than the rights of the patient. He said that the crucial issue 'really revolves round the question of what is the duty of the doctor when prescribing treatment for a severely handicapped child suffering from a handicap of an irrevocable nature *where parents do not wish the child to survive.*'[15] Understandably, the jury acquitted the doctor (no charges were brought against the parents for e.g. neglect). Perhaps they took the view that the doctor was reasonably entitled to support the parents in their wish and take steps to withdraw care so that the child would die.[16]

By today's standards, this conclusion seems to ignore the best interests of the child. Is it acceptable for one of the determining factors to be the reasonableness of the doctors' reaction to the parents' decision? Or is it preferable to consider the quality of the life available to the child and respond in a way that promotes best interests? The better response is surely the latter and once we are content to concede that matter, then the courts inevitably have to play a central role in considering best interests. Today, the majority of cases focus attention firmly on the needs and interests of the child, rather than the reasonableness of the actions of others.[17] Equally, although the court regards itself as the ultimate arbiter of 'best interests', in many cases during the 1990s, they accepted uncritically the evidence of doctors in these cases so that, in effect, it was clinicians that governed the outcome. In other words, the outcome was often determined according to a passive application of the *Bolam* test.[18]

Assertion of the authority of the court

More recently, however, a number of cases on the best interests of mentally handicapped patients have emphasized a significant distinction between *Bolam* and the best interests tests. In *Re A (male sterilisation)* Butler-Sloss LJ said: 'I do not consider that the two duties have been conflated into one requirement…In the case of an application for approval of a sterilisation operation, it is the judge, not the doctor, who makes the decision that it is in the best interests of the patient that the operation be performed.'[19] And in *Re SL (Adult sterilisation)*, she said in connection with a proposal by doctors to sterilize a mentally handicapped woman for reasons of contraception:

> There is a question of proportionality and in my judgement the remedy [of hysterectomy] proposed by the judge is out of proportion to the problem to be solved. The patient has the right, if she cannot herself choose, not to have drastic surgery imposed upon her unless or until it has been demonstrated that it is in her best interests… The question…was not was the proposed treatment within the range of acceptable opinion among competent and reasonable practitioners, but was it in the best interests of S. The *Bolam* test, was, in my view, irrelevant to the judicial decision…[20]

These developments refer to sterilization procedures, but they also affect other areas of clinical practice. The change of view with respect to babies and children is illustrated by two cases. First, in *Baby MB*, the patient was diagnosed with Grade 1.1 spinal muscular atrophy at 7 weeks of age; this is the most severe variant that is compatible with survival to birth. There is no known cure, his condition was terminal, and his life expectancy very short. The intensivists believed that suctioning his airways would be painful and distressing and that it was not in the baby's best interests for such treatment to continue. They favoured sedation to ease his suffering which, they fully acknowledged, would quickly be followed by his death. However, the parents disagreed.

They said that they had spent much of their time by his cot, had noticed their baby's ability to communicate, albeit in a limited way, were ever hopeful of improvement, or a scientific breakthrough, and wanted treatment to continue. Who should decide? The Trust sought a declaration from the court that it would not be unlawful to withdraw care from MB. However, the court said that:

> it is positively in his best interests to continue with continuous pressure ventilation and with the nursing and medical care that properly go with it, including suctioning and deep suctioning when required, replacement of the tube as necessary, and chest and lung physiotherapy to clear his secretions. Although that is my opinion, I cannot and do not make an order or declaration to that effect. I merely state it.[21]

Similarly in *Re Wyatt*, the court said: 'There is a strong presumption in favour of a course of action which will prolong life, but that presumption is not irrebuttable. The term "best interests" encompasses medical, emotional, and all other welfare issues. The court must conduct a balancing exercise in which all the relevant factors are weighed and a helpful way of undertaking this exercise is to draw up a balance sheet.'[22] Here too, 'emotional and welfare issues' are not the unique preserve of *Bolam*. In a sense, the 'balance sheet' exercise is crude and simplistic and courts must be astute to the need to distinguish the *quality* of separate components on the lists so as to give them appropriate weight and influence. For example, in a case involving a baby who was 'incapable of even limited intellectual function,' the judge remarked that this was 'a hallmark of our humanity.'[23] Understandably, perhaps, the capacity to relate with others is likely to be especially significant.

Notice, however, that the court's authority is also asserted over parents. For example, shortly after the decision in *Arthur*, the Court of Appeal in *Re B* considered a Down's baby in similar circumstances and whether it was in his best interests that treatment should be withdrawn so he would die. The parents refused their consent to the routine duodenal treatment capable of saving their child's life. However, ordering that treatment should not be withdrawn, the court said 'at the end of the day it devolves on this court...to decide whether the life of this child is demonstrably going to be so awful that in effect the child must be condemned to die, or whether the life of this child is so imponderable that it would be wrong for her to be condemned to die.'[24] Similarly, the refusal of parents to consent to a blood test for their new baby when the mother was HIV+ was rejected because early diagnosis and, if needs be, treatment was so clearly in the baby's best interests. The judge said: '…this is not…about the rights of the parents…[I]f…the father regards the rights of a tiny baby as subsumed within the rights of the parents, he is wrong. This baby has rights of her own.'[25]

Decisions of this nature can be made more difficult by the role of religion and the sincerely held beliefs of parents as to the best spiritual interests of the child. For example, Jehovah's Witnesses may refuse consent to blood transfusion and others may place their faith in prayer alone.[26] Of course, competent adults are entitled to refuse life-saving care for good reason, bad reason, or no reason at all.[27] However, while clinical staff should strive to accommodate so far as practicable the beliefs and preferences of parents in these cases, in the last analysis, the best interest test when applied to children focuses on the best physiological and mental health of the patient, rather than on the sincerity of the parents' beliefs.[28] The reason is not so much the judgement of the doctors, but the view of the court that the right to make a decision of such gravity must be reserved to adults with the mental capacity to do so; it should not be imposed upon children who cannot choose it for themselves.[29] This may lead to a separate, but related question: What are doctors to do in response to parents who refuse to submit their children for routine, but life-saving, treatment? Clearly, doctors have no power to remove children in these circumstances. However, although no case has yet said so, there is surely a duty to notify the relevant statutory authorities of the problem so that child protection facilities can be put in place if needs be.[30]

No right to demand treatment?

This assertion of the judicial role should be tempered, however, by the courts' recognition that doctors must play the dominant role in assessing the *range* of treatments available to the patient. Clarification of the position was given in the case of *Burke*, a competent man suffering spinocerebellar ataxia. He was concerned to die of natural causes. The medical evidence was that he would experience insight and awareness of the pain and discomfort that would arise from dehydration and malnutrition almost until the end. There would be a time when he lost competence (i.e. the capacity to communicate) but would retain awareness of his condition. The issue arose whether he was entitled to *demand* that he be given treatment even after the time at which he lost competence. As the judge put it: 'He does not want ANH (artificial nutrition and hydration) to be withdrawn. He does not want to die of thirst. He does not want a decision to be taken by doctors that his life is no longer worth living'.[31] Although this case concerned a competent adult, its discussion of the clinical duties owed to terminally ill patients must also extend to children. The Court said patients cannot require doctors to administer treatment in these circumstances and endorsed a framework of analysis suggested by the GMC, as follows:

> (1) The doctor, exercising his professional clinical judgement, decides what treatment options are clinically indicated (i.e. will provide overall clinical benefit) for his patient. (2) He then offers those treatment options to the patient in the course of which he explains to him/her the risks, benefits, side effects, etc involved in each of the treatment options. (3) The patient then decides whether he wishes to accept any of those treatment options and, if so, which one. In the vast majority of cases he will, of course, decide which treatment option he considers to be in his best interests and, in doing so, he will or may take into account other, non clinical, factors. However, he can, if he wishes, decide to accept (or refuse) the treatment option on the basis of reasons which are irrational or for no reasons at all. (4) If he chooses one of the treatment options offered to him, the doctor will then proceed to provide it. (5) If, however, he refuses all of the treatment options offered to him and instead informs the doctor that he wants a form of treatment which the doctor has not offered him, the doctor will, no doubt, discuss that form of treatment with him (assuming that it is a form of treatment known to him) but if the doctor concludes that this treatment is not clinically indicated he is not required (i.e. he is under no legal obligation) to provide it to the patient although he should offer to arrange a second opinion.[32]

By analogy, the same approach must also apply to the range of treatments considered proper in neonatal and paediatric care. In theory, then, while it is for judges to assess the best interests of children with respect to treatment, the framework of clinical options within which that decision is made is dominated by medical opinion. However, the theory may be clearer then the practice. As *Re MB* shows above, this framework may be challenged at the margins. Especially when the press appear to support parents, it seems inevitable that cases will continue to be brought to the courts and this brings us to the next question of how to resolve irretrievable differences of opinion.

Resolving irretrievable differences of opinion

What happens when there are insoluble differences of opinion? Whenever there is an irretrievable disagreement between doctors and parents in matters of this sensitive nature, the matter should normally be referred to the courts for advice and guidance. The question arose in the European Court of Human Rights in *Glass v United Kingdom*. Serious dispute arose whether a boy was dying. The doctors believed that the patient was dying, had entered a terminal phase, and required pain relief with diamorphine. However, the family suspected that the patient 'was being covertly euthanased'[33] and a fight broke out at the bed-side. Subsequently, the boy's chest infection recovered sufficiently for him to be discharged home. As the Human Rights Court put it:

> The doctors during this phase all shared a gloomy prognosis of the first appli-cant's capacity to withstand further crises. They were left in no doubt that their proposed treatment would not meet with the agreement of the second applicant. Admittedly, the second applicant could have brought the matter before the High Court. However, in the circumstances it considers that the onus was on the Trust to take the initiative and to defuse the situation in anticipation of a further emer-gency…the Court is not persuaded that an emergency High Court application could not have been made by the Trust when it became clear that that the second applicant was firmly opposed to the administration of a diamorphine to the first applicant…[34]

Therefore, whenever there is unresolved disagreement between doc-tors and parents, the matter should normally be referred to the court for adjudication (if needs be by means of an emergency application).[35] As the GMC says: 'Where there is disagreement between those with parental responsibility and the healthcare team and this cannot be resolved satisfactorily through informal review, you should seek legal advice about obtaining a ruling from the courts.'[36]

This leaves two questions: (a) at what stage in the progression of a fatal illness should the application to the court be made; i.e. what is the balance between an early application, when the prognosis may still be uncertain, and a late one which may prolong a child's suffering and not be in his, or her best interests. And (b) what criteria should be adopted by the court in these cases, i.e. should the court put itself in the position of a responsible parent and make the decision on that basis, or should it look at the merits of the case under its own initiative?

As to (a), the difficulty and sensitivity of the matter was raised in OT,[37] who was aged 10 months and suffered a mitochondrial condition, which caused the breakdown of many areas of his body. He was entirely dependent upon a ventilator, had suffered brain stem damage, a stroke which led to the death of part of his brain, inflammation leading to calcification of his brain; and fits. All the doctors agreed that he would suffer further strokes and would probably die before the age of 3 and certainly before the age of 5. OT was unable to suck, or swallow and secretions had to be cleared from his throat and trachea by suction; a process that caused him discomfort and pain. The parents rejected these pessimistic opinions. There was a hearing lasting 10 days in which the parents were offered access to further medical opinion. However, they applied for an adjournment for further expert opinion to be sought. The judge refused the application and ordered that, should the hospital see fit to do so, it would be lawful as being in OT's best interests, to withdraw and withhold ventilatory support from him and to move to a regime of palliative care in order to lessen his discomfort, and respect his dignity. The parents appealed on the ground that an adjournment should have been granted because alternative views as to diagnosis and prognosis might be available. Relying on Glass, the parents argued that the hospital should have made an application at an earlier date since it knew that they would object to treatment being withdrawn from their son. Where is the balance as to the proper time for an application to be made? The difficulty here was noted by the court in *Portsmouth Hospitals NHS Trust v Wyatt*:

> There was a balance to be struck between: (a) applying in advance of a crisis when the exact medical evidence may be subject to some revision; and (b) waiting for a time which is nearer the crisis but with all the practical problems of a rushed hearing.[38]

In *OT,* the court held that the matter of timing of the application was dependant on the facts of each case. Here, the court supported the judge's decision 'to conduct a full-scale, intensive, efficient yet unhurried determination, calibrated with an urgency commensurate with his generally deteriorating condition, of the most painful and profound issue imaginable, namely in effect whether OT should pass on immediately, or a little later following... profound further pain and misery'.[39] To say that each case is fact-specific may be inevitable, but if there is to be error one way or the other, surely it is better to seek the advice of the court too early, rather than too late.

As to (b), what are the *criteria* to be used when there are differences between the doctors and parents? At present the law appears uncertain. The Court of Appeal has said, for example, that 'the court adopts the same attitude as a responsible parent would do in the case of his or her own child, ... [it] is not expected to adopt any higher or different standard than that which, viewed objectively, a reasonable and responsible parent would do.'[40] But, it has also said: 'the role of the court is to exercise an *independent* and objective judgement. If that judgement is in accord with that of the devoted and responsible parent, well and good. If not, then it is the duty of the court, after giving due weight to the devoted and responsible parent, *to give effect to its own judgement. That is what it there for.*'[41] In the case of paediatric intensive care, for example, the latter view would permit treatment in the ICU to continue, or be withdrawn, at a time determined by the court, rather than responsible parents. Perhaps, however, there is a distinction between (1) cases in which the court finds the parental view clearly contradicts the child's best interests, in which case it must determine the matter on its own initiative (as in *Re OT*); and (2) other cases in which the court would not have reached the same conclusion itself, but it accepts that many others might do so, in which case it may be more hesitant. For example, where parents are desperate for their baby to recover, yet he is terminally ill, has no awareness of his surroundings, and resuscitative care is causing him pain and distress, the court may permit treatment to be withdrawn.[42] On the other hand, as in *Baby MB*, where the doctors feel treatment is unwarranted and even cruel, yet the baby retains a quality of life, albeit that his condition is terminal, the decision may go the other way.[43]

Previously, it was thought that the 'intolerability' test could add certainty to the criteria to be used in these cases. Recall the case of *Re B*, in which the Court of Appeal asked whether the life of the baby was 'demonstrably going to be so awful that in effect the child must be condemned to die.'[44] From this, in Charlotte Wyatt's case, it was argued that, unless her life was going to be *intolerable*, the presumption should be that further life-sustaining care would be provided, perhaps by analogy with the 'unbearable' test considered by the RCPCH (above). The logic is that if treatment is not intolerable, then it should be presumed to be tolerable and should normally be provided. Charlotte suffered severe respiratory damage, brain damage, was blind, deaf and incapable of voluntary response, and the doctors considered that further treatment was not in her best interests. The judge did not consider her life to be intolerable, however, he agreed with the doctors.[45] The case was taken to the Court of Appeal which confirmed the judge's decision that the test remained the 'best interests' test as explained above in the sense that it is not confined to medical opinion and includes emotional and other welfare issues.[46] In a sense, 'intolerability' is more a diagnostic *conclusion* than a legal test[47] and its rejection retains a degree of flexibility that some may welcome. Equally, it preserves the uncertainty of the best interests test and the danger of encouraging more cases into court.[48]

Mature children

In the law of consent to treatment, should 'mature' children be treated as if they are adults? Or should there be an area of overlap in which mature children have some authority over matters within their competence, but allows parents and the courts to consent on their behalf in some circumstances? Take the following example, a boy of 16 has fallen in love with his first 'real' girl-friend. They have being going out for 6 months. She is a Jehovah's Witness and persuades him to join her church and carry a card refusing blood. His parents treat him in this matter as an adult capable of deciding things for himself. However, he is involved in a serious road-traffic accident and urgently requires a blood transfusion to save his life. Had he been over 18, the matter would undoubtedly have been for him alone. What difference should it make that he is a mature child? Should the hospital respond as if he is an adult and not transfuse? Or, as the parents insist, regard his carrying of the card as a symptom of a 16-year-old love affair which has nothing to do with deeply held religious beliefs?

The law in this area is more pragmatic than principled. The *Gillick* case confirms that children have the right to consent to care that their doctors consider appropriate to their needs. As they grow in maturity and understanding, so they acquire greater autonomy to make decisions for themselves. Indeed, Section 8(1) of the Family Law Reform Act 1969 provides that for the purposes of surgical, medical, or dental treatment, the consent of those aged 16 and over 'shall be as effective as it would be if he were of full age; and where a minor has by virtue of this section given an effective consent to any treatment it shall not be necessary to obtain any consent for it from his parents.' This does not present serious difficulty because treatment supported by the child's doctor should never contradict his, or her best interests. But what about the child's *refusal* to consent to treatment? Should the response be the same? *Gillick* is sometimes said to imply that it should? After all, if a child has sufficient competence to *consent* to care, surely it follows that he is equally competent to *refuse* it. However, this 'principled' response is not adopted by English law. Section 8(3) of the Family Law Reform Act continues that:

> Nothing in this section shall be construed as making ineffective any consent which would have been effective if this section had not been enacted.

In other words, there is a period during which mature children may consent for themselves, but if they *refuse* consent to treatment that is in their best interests, the parents, or the court, also retain legal authority to consent on their behalf.

Some say this is wrong;[49] others, that to abandon children at this crucial time of their lives is tantamount to neglect.[50] In the absence of exceptional circumstances, the latter view is surely correct and is supported by the pragmatic response of the law. For example, in *Re E*, a

15-year-old boy and his parents were devout Jehovah's Witnesses. He suffered leukaemia and required chemotherapy supplemented by a blood transfusion to restore his diminished blood count. Both he and his parents were content that he should receive chemotherapy, but they resolutely refused to consent to a blood transfusion. Consistent with all the cases in this area, the court considered that a minor could not reasonably be competent to give serious contemplation to death. The judge said: 'When making a decision ... of life and death, I have to take account of the fact that teenagers often express views with vehemence and conviction ... but I cannot discount at least the possibility that he may in later years suffer some diminution of his convictions.'[51] As the court explained in the case of 16-year-old girl suffering from an eating disorder, it would be wrong to ignore every refusal of consent by a competent minor with which it disagreed.

> I am very far from asserting any general rule that the court should prefer its own view as to what is in the best interests of the child to those of the child itself. [But] if the child's welfare is threatened by a serious and imminent risk that the child will suffer grave and irreversible mental or physical harm, then...the court when called upon has a duty to intervene.[52]

So too in the case of girl suddenly overcome by a fatal cardiac condition requiring an urgent heart transplant, but who refused her consent because she simply could not face living with someone else's heart inside her chest. The court permitted the transplant in her best interests.[53] On the other hand, in matters of less urgency and gravity, it is reasonable and proper to involve mature children in decision-making about their care. Mature children should be given information about the treatment proposed, an opportunity to discuss it with clinicians, and have their views listened to and accommodated wherever possible in the treatment plan. Some may wish to defer to the judgements of others and they should not be burdened with decision-making responsibility they do not wish to shoulder. Clearly, the best course of action will depend on the child's character, their familiarity with their condition, and the treatment regime.

Does this mean, however, that any refusal by a child to life-saving treatment could be overturned? The fictitious story of the 16-year-old

Jehovah's Witness and his girlfriend, raised above, would normally favour a blood transfusion. However, consider another made-up case. Ben is 14 and has been treated for cancer for the past 3 years. None of the treatments have been successful. They have horrible side-effects, which make him feel awful. Those treatments have now been withdrawn and he is expected to die within a month. However, a new drug has become available, which may be suitable. It cannot cure him, but in 50% of patients, it can extend life by up to a further 3 months. His doctors are prepared to offer it to him and his mother wants him to try it because it may be better than expected and, perhaps, something else will be discovered in the meantime. Ben, however, has simply had enough. He would rather enjoy some quality in the last months of his life than face another round of being confined to a hospital drip feeling terrible. Should his wishes be respected? Or is his mother's consent sufficient? Arguably, no one is more competent than Ben to know about the side-effects of treatment, or the frustration of being stuck in bed. The consent of his mother notwithstanding, perhaps he ought to have the final say in these desperate circumstances.

Conclusion

Some time ago, *Re J*, Lord Donaldson emphasized the manner in which the court held a balance between the various interests in these delicate cases. He said in the Court of Appeal,

> No one can dictate the treatment to be given to the child, neither the court, parents, or doctors. There are checks and balances. The doctor can recommend treatment A in preference to treatment B. They can also refuse to adopt treatment C on the grounds that it is medically contra-indicated or for some other reason is a treatment which they could not conscientiously administer. The court or parents for their part can refuse to consent to treatment A or B or both, but cannot insist on treatment C. The inevitable and desirable result is that choice of treatment is in some measure a joint decision of the doctors and the court or parents.[54]

He subsequently said that he could not imagine any circumstances in which a court could order a doctor to treat a patient against the doctor's wish and to do so would be abuse of the court's power.[55] Today, this view may appear optimistic because the role of parents and the courts have become more assertive. Medicine has the capacity to preserve life, sometimes in circumstances many would consider futile. When disagreement is intractable, because of the different perceptions of doctors and parents, or religious conviction, holding a balance may not always be sufficient. Of course, this assertiveness may conceal much uncertainty and unease, perhaps of doctors being required to administer further treatment to a baby in distress, or of parents having treatment withdrawn from a baby for whom they had so much love and hope. In some cases, perhaps, there is no 'right' answer. There will often be profound differences of opinion and decisions may have to be taken in the light of incomplete evidence of what will happen in the future. The role of the court is to listen carefully to both sides and to offer an impartial assessment of the balance of the case on the basis of an imprecise notion of the best interests of the patient. Clearly, the adversarial and distrustful atmosphere of litigation is no place to resolve heart-rending disputes like these.[56] Mediation, candour, and trust are much better solutions. Much better that hospitals have sensitive procedures for arbitration and discussion, which can assist agreement in these difficult cases.[57] Ultimately, however, if all else fails, perhaps the court is the best equipped forum to have the last word.[58]

References

1 Withholding or Withdrawing Life Sustaining Treatment in Children (RCPCH, 2004), 14.

2 Perinatal Mortality (Confidential Enquiry into Maternal and Child Health, 2009), 43.

3 Discussing the difficulties of diagnosing PVS, See for example, Andrews K, Murphy L, Munelay R, and Littlewood C (1996). Misdiagnosis of the vegetative state, *BMJ* **13**: 313 and Practice Note: PVS Withdrawal of Treatment [1996] 4 All ER 766.

4 For a helpful discussion of the evolution of attitudes, see Morris A (2009), Selective treatment of irreversibly impaired infants: decision-making at the threshold, *Medical Law Review* **17**: 347.

5 Withholding and Withdrawing Life-Prolonging Treatment in Children (RCPCH, 2004) 10–11.

6 Considering similar difficulties in connection with premature newborns, see Critical care decisions in fetal and neonatal medicine: ethical issues (Nuffield Council on Bioethics, 2004), where uncertainty arises in connection with babies born at between 22 and 24 weeks gestation and the wishes of parents are accorded more weight.

7 http://www.picanet.org.uk/units.html (accessed 12 November 2009).

8 Slevin ML, Stubbs L, Plant HJ, et al. (1990). Attitudes to chemotherapy: comparing views of patients with cancer with those of doctors, nurses, and general public. *BMJ* **300**: 1458–1460.

9 Frick S, Uehlinger, DE, Zuercher Z, Regula M. (2003). Medical futility: Predicting outcome of intensive care unit patients by nurses and doctors – A prospective comparative study. *Critical Care Medicine.* **31**(2): 456–461.

10 *A NHS Trust v D* [2000] Lloyd's Rep Med 411, 432.

11 In *R v Nigel Cox* (1993) 12 BMLR 38, a jury convicted a doctor of attempted murder for administering potassium chloride to a patient suffering from rheumatoid arthritis who was at the end of her life, was suffering intolerable pain and had expressed a wish to die. Contrast, however, the GMC case of premature babies from whom life-saving treatment had been withdrawn in their best interests. The babies had been injected with morphine and were expected to die quickly, but they started to suffer agonal gasping in the last moments of their lives. The neonatal consultant administered pancoronium to end their suffering and the parents had no complaint about his conduct. He probably hastened the babies' deaths by a very short period of time. However, the charges against him were dropped by the GMC. See O. Dyer (2007), Doctor cleared of act tantamount to murder, *BMJ* **335**: 67.

12 (1981) 12 BMLR 1.

13 The charge was originally murder until it was discovered that the baby had other congenital conditions which might also have been responsible for his death.

14 (1981) 12 BMLR 1, para 5.

15 *Ibid,* para 1 (emphasis added).

16 See Duff R,Campbell A (1973). Moral and ethical dilemmas in the special-care nursery, *N Eng J Med* **17**: 980; Read J, Clements L (2004). Demonstrably awful: the right to life and the selective non-treatment of disabled babies and young children. *Journal of Law and Society* **31**: 482.

17 But note *Re T* [1997] 1 All ER 906, in which it was said: "The welfare of the child is the paramount consideration and I recognize the very strong presumption in favour of a course of action which will prolong life. But to prolong life ... is not the sole objective of the court and to require it at the expense of other considerations may not be in the child's interests ... [T]he court is not concerned with the reasonableness of the mother's refusal to consent *but with the consequences of that refusal and whether it is in the best interests of C for this court in effect to direct the mother to take on this total commitment where she does not agree with the course proposed*" (emphasis added). On this reasoning, parents' wishes that their child should *not* receive a kidney transplantation were respected. (The parents ultimately agreed to the transplant and the boy recovered well.) The case could be used to argue that in judging "best interests," courts may consider how the child's care may be affected by their impact of other people.

18 For example, see *Airedale NHS Trust v Bland* [1993] 1 All ER 821 in which Lord Keith refers to *Bolam* as a legal basis for the decision to withdraw treatment from a patient in PVS.

19 (2000) 53 BMLR 66, para 73.

20 [2000] Lloyd's Rep Med 339, 345–346.

21 *An NHS Trust v MB* [2006] EWHC 507, para 90. This judicial "opinion" really amounted to an order of the court. To fail to provide "best interests" care from which the patient died would expose clinicians to risk to charges of manslaughter.

22 *Wyatt v Portsmouth Hospital NHS Trust,* the court (2005) 86 BMLR 173 (CA), para 87.

23 *Re C (a minor)* [1990] Fam 25, 35.

24 *Re B* [1990] 3 All ER 927, 929 (decided in 1981). The authority of *Re B* is such as to suggest that were circumstances similar to *Arthur* to arise today, the doctor might be susceptible to a charge of manslaughter by neglect.

25 *Re C (HIV test)* (1999) 50 BMLR 283, 294 per Wilson J. The position is summarized by the following: "...whilst the views of the parents must be most carefully considered, those views cannot themselves entirely override the court's view of the ward's best interests. [However,] the court's respect for the sanctity of human life must impose a strong obligation in favour of taking all steps capable of preserving life, save in exceptional circumstances," see: *A National Health Service Trust v DS* [2000] Lloyds Rep Med 411, 417 per Cazelet J.

26 See generally, *Religion and Healthcare in the European Union* (Network of European Foundations, 2009) for a range of special tensions created by religious convictions.

27 *Re T* [1992] 4 All ER 649, 642: "the [competent] patient's right of choice exists whether the reasons for making that choice are rational, irrational, unknown or even non-existent. That his choice is contrary to what is to be expected of the vast majority of adults is only relevant if there are other reasons for doubting his capacity to decide." See also *Re AK* (1991) 58 BMLR 151 and *Re B (adult: refusal of medical treatment)* [2002] 2 All ER 449.

28 See eg *Devon County Council v S* (1993) 11 BMLR 105.

29 In the US case of *Prince v Massachusetts* (1944) 321 US 158, Justice Holmes famously said: "Parents may be free to become martyrs themselves, but it does not follow that that are free in identical circumstances to make martyrs of their children before they have reached the age of full and legal discretion when they can make choices for themselves." The statement was approved in *Re E* (1992) 9 BMLR 1 and *Re R* [1991] 4 All ER 177.

30 In *R v Harris* 23 BMLR 122 (1995), Rastarfarian parents refused to consent to insulin for their nine year daughter who suffered from diabetes. Doctors could not treat her and she died. The parents were convicted of manslaughter by neglect. Although the issue was not argued, should criticism have been directed toward the responsible doctors for failing to notify those with statutory authority to protect the welfare of children?

31 *Burke v General Medical Council* [2005] Lloyds Rep Med 403, para 5.

32 *Ibid,* para 50.

33 (2004) 77 BMLR 120, para 26.

34 (2004) 77 BMLR 120, paras 79–81.

35 The courts can be contacted at any time: 'If you need to make an urgent application to the Court of Protection outside of normal office hours (for example, at the
weekend, or before 9.00 am or after 5.00 pm on a weekday), you should telephone
the Royal Courts of Justice switchboard on 020 7947 6000 and ask for 'Security'.
Security will be able to contact the right urgent business officer or clerk to help
you.' See: http://www.direct.gov.uk/en/Governmentcitizensandrights/
Incapacityandthelaw/DG_176267 (accessed 12 November 2009).

36 *Withholding and Withdrawing Life-prolonging Treatments: Good Practice in
Decision-making* (General Medical Council, London, 2002), 75.

37 *Re OT (A child)* [2009] EWCA Civ 409.

38 [2005] 1 WLR 3995, para 98.

39 *Re OT (A child)* [2009] EWCA Civ 409, para 28.

40 *Re J (a minor)* [1990] 3 All ER 930, 941.

41 *Re Z (freedom of publication)* [1995] 4 All ER 961, 986 emphasis added.

42 See eg *Re J (a minor)* [1990] 3 All ER 930: "J appears to be blind... he is likely to be
deaf... he is unlikely ever to be able to speak, even to the extent of saying Mum or
Dad. It is highly unlikely that he will develop even limited intellectual abilities.
Most unfortunate of all, there is a likelihood that he will be able to feel pain to the
same extent as a normal baby", per Lord Donaldson, 933. See also *Re OT (A child)*
[2009] EWCA Civ 409, above.

43 See *An NHS Trust v MB* [2006] EWHC 507.

44 *Re B* [1990] 3 All ER 927, 929 (decided in 1981). Note that the language of being
"condemned to die" has subsequently been disapproved because it misrepresents
the court's function in these case, which is to determine whether further life-
sustaining treatment is in a patient's best interests.

45 *Re Wyatt (a child)* [2004] EWEHC 2247.

46 *Re Wyatt (a child)* [2005] EWCA Civ 1181. Subsequently, the case was again heard
by the trial judge with evidence of improvements to Charlotte's condition and
further treatment was authorized subject to a fresh application by the court, see
Re Wyatt (a child) [2005] EWHC 2293.

47 See the discussion in *An NHS Trust v MB* [2006] EWHC 507.

48 Although intuitively, *withdrawal* may seem to be different from *withholding* care,
the legal position is not changed merely because treatment has started; See *Airedale
NHS Trust v Bland* (above at note 18). Equally, once treatment has commenced,
the passing of time may help resolve the disagreement between clinician and
parents as the prognosis becomes clearer to all involved.

49 See generally S Elliston, *The Best Interests of the Child in Health Care* (Cavendish,
2007).

50 G. Laurie, "Autonomy of Others: Reflections on the Rise and Rise of Patient Choice in Contemporary Medical Law," in (ed) SAM McLean, *First Do No Harm – Law, Ethics and Healthcare* (Ashgate, 2006).

51 *Re E* [1993] 1 FLR 386, 393. In this case the boy's convictions did not diminish. He refused further transfusions after his 18th birthday and died.

52 Re W *(a minor: medical treatment)* [1992] 4 All ER 627, 648.

53 *Re M (child: refusal of treatment)* (1999) 52 BMLR 124.

54 [1990] 3 All ER 930, 934.

55 *Re J* [1993] Fam 15, 27.

56 On the erosion of trust between doctors and patients, see generally V Harpwood, "The Manipulation of Clinical Practice," in (eds) M Freeman and A Lewis, *Law and Medicine: Current Legal Issues, vol 3* (OUP, 2000).

57 See the helpful discussion in Morris A (2009). Selective treatment of irreversibly impaired infants: decision-making at the threshold, *Medical Law Review* 17: 370–376.

58 The GMC advises in *Treatment and care towards the end of life* (2010): "If disagreements arise about what course of action would be in a child or young person's best interests, it is usually possible to resolve them by, for example, involving an independent advocate; seeking advice from a more experienced colleague; obtaining an independent second opinion; by holding a case conference or ethics consultation; or by using local mediation services. If, after taking such steps, significant disagreement remains, you should seek legal advice on applying to the appropriate court for an independent ruling. Approaching the court should be seen as a constructive way of thoroughly exploring the issues and providing reassurance for the child and parents that the child's interests have been properly considered in the decision" (para 108).

Part B

Issues between doctor and patient

Taking it or leaving it: Demanding and refusing medical treatment in intensive care

Sheila A M McLean and Derek Morgan

Philip Roth's recent novel, *Everyman*, opens with a funeral: what Roth calls 'our species' least favourite activity'.[1] It then moves to the deceased's reflections on his life, as he reflects that time had transformed his body into what—in a memorable phrase—Roth calls 'a storehouse for man-made contraptions designed to fend off collapse.'[2] In modern hospitals, the end of life is now often accompanied by heroic medical interventions, and this situation is more relevant in intensive care units (ICU). While some patients in ICU may consciously confront their own mortality, others may have no awareness of their condition. In each situation, however, decisions will have to be made about whether or not to offer or continue treatment and what kind of therapies should be undertaken. In addition, of course, a patient may be subject to a 'Do Not Attempt Resuscitation' order (DNR order) or come to the ICU with an advance decision or directive already in place. Each of these scenarios poses potential dilemmas, which can become more complex when the patient in question is not an adult. In what follows, we attempt to elucidate and critique some of the most important issues confronting both the patient and the health care team in the ICU, but manifestly it would need an entire book to do full justice to all of them. For this reason, we focus on the adult patient, although we also consider the issues that arise from other cases when relevant, and shed some light on the debate.

The transformation, in little more than a generation, from people made in the image of a deity to people manufactured and maintained by the imagination and capacities of technology, has generated many ethical challenges, which have also tasked the law with negotiating a balance between the various rights and interests at stake. While at a practical level, decisions are often taken at the bedside without reference to the courts, the law will be the ultimate arbiter of whether or not the 'right' decision has been reached. Professional guidance will, of course, assist physicians in reaching a conclusion on testing cases but their behaviour must also accord with what the law requires and the principles underlying such law. In many of these cases, the concern of patients, doctors, and the law will not be about clinical competence, but rather about whether or not life can, or should, be maintained and what role the patient plays in the ultimate decision. It is on these issues that we concentrate since they expose most clearly the kind of dilemmas that can arise.

Patients' rights, doctors' duties

Once patients are accepted into a hospital, medical staff are under a positive duty at common law to care for them. A fundamental consequence of this duty is to take such steps as are reasonable to keep the patient alive. In some cases, a therapeutic plan can be worked out with the patients who, however unwell, will still have an interest in making autonomous decisions about their health care and their future. The best clinical relationship will see the health care team and the patient reviewing the options, sharing information, and concluding on a regime that satisfies the patient's right to self-determination and the clinicians' professional obligations. As we will discuss later, this, of course, is the ideal situation, but not necessarily the only situation in which patients (and sometimes their relatives) and health care professionals may find themselves. Arguably, however, it is legally the most straightforward option and so will be considered first.

The competent patient

A primary issue for consideration is the patient's involvement in health care decisions that affect them. The modern emphasis on patient autonomy, and its legal counterpart the law of consent, supposedly work to ensure that patients are no longer passive recipients of, but active participants in, treatment decisions. The explosion of interest in the concept of patient autonomy in health care has shifted the traditions of medicine away from the Hippocratic or paternalistic model to one that depends on patient authorization of treatment decisions, based on the provision of adequate information. The doctor's obligation is shaped by the legal rules surrounding information disclosure, which are designed to ensure that the patient can be self-governing. While not all information needs to be disclosed, the disclosed information should be sufficient to ensure that the patient is able to reflect on their own values before deciding which option to choose. In the United Kingdom, but not every other jurisdiction,[3] the adequacy of information disclosure is measured against a 'reasonable doctor' test.[4] However, it is now clear that the evidence from a responsible body of medical opinion will no longer be simply accepted by courts, but will be subject to inquiry as to whether or not it rests on a 'logical' basis.[5]

The relationship between patients and health care professionals has supposedly been reshaped by the increased emphasis on autonomy. While for clinicians, this is but one of a range of principles that are important in health care delivery, many patients would prioritize autonomy over other values. Since the law will be the ultimate arbiter of which value dominates when conflicts arise, it is important that we consider how it allocates authority in health care choices and what rules have been developed to delineate doctors' duties. Over 30 years ago, in *The Unmasking of Medicine*, Kennedy argued that doctors 'have a highly developed sense of territoriality' that has been ratified both by government and courts,[6] and elsewhere he criticized the tendency of English courts to defer to medical opinion.[7] He argued that the result of this logic was the twin defects of producing 'idiosyncratic' decision making and sheltering the doctor from 'social responsibility'.[8] In part, his critique was based on the pervasiveness of the test derived from the case of *Bolam v Friern Hospital Management Committee*.[9] This case was one of the earliest to describe what information doctors were legally obliged to disclose to their patients in order that they could make a decision about whether or not to undertake treatment. The so-called *Bolam Test* focused on doctors' duties rather than patients' rights and has been widely criticized, although it survived relatively intact for several decades.[10] Subsequent cases, such as *Sidaway*,[11] *Bolitho*,[12] *Pearce*,[13] and most recently *Chester v Afshar*[14] have seen a gradual move away from complete emphasis on what the 'reasonable doctor' would disclose towards what the 'reasonable patient' would want to know, but unlike other jurisdictions, the shift is still marginal. As in other instances of tort law, the characteristics of the reasonable patient are determined by the public institution of the court. The twin engines now driving review of doctors' professional behaviour are 'logic' (not quite the same as, but close to, 'rationality') and judicial 'review' of the quality of the doctors' disclosure decision. But the singular point that remains to be emphasized is that while the test for adequacy of disclosure has been wrought from the medical profession by, and to, the legal profession, the deference shown by the latter to the former belies the rhetoric of patient choice in reality.

Yet information is vital to the patient's ability to make authentic decisions. Following reflection, patients are said to be free to decide to accept treatment or to choose an alternative, even if it is clinically suboptimal. Doctors cannot force their preferred treatment on an unwilling patient, whose ultimate choice should be respected even if it seems irrational or downright wrong to others.[15] However, the converse of this is that while patients might believe that autonomy is the trumping value, and places them in control of health care decisions, in fact, their rights do not extend to demanding treatment. This was recently clearly established in the case of Mr Leslie Burke. Although the majority of court decisions about end-of-life choices concern the alleged right to have assistance in dying (discussed later in more detail), the importance that people place on the *manner* of their death was highlighted in this case, where the claimant's fear was that he would find his life being brought to an end *against his wishes* by doctors deciding to withhold treatment—in this case withdrawing assisted nutrition and hydration (ANH).[16]

Mr. Burke was 45 years of age. He suffered from a congenital degenerative brain condition known as spino-cerebellar ataxia, which has now confined him to a wheelchair. As a result of his condition, there will come a time when he will be entirely dependent on others for his care and survival. He will lose the ability to swallow and will require ANH to survive. At first instance, Mr Justice Munby observed that medical evidence indicated that Mr Burke was likely to retain full cognitive faculties even during the end stage of the disease and that he would retain, almost until the end, insight and awareness of the pain, discomfort, and distress that result from malnutrition and dehydration. If food and water were to be withheld, he would die of dehydration after some two to three weeks. He was also likely to retain the capacity to experience the fear of choking, which could result from attempts at oral feeding. Medical evidence suggested that Mr. Burke is unlikely to lose his capacity to make decisions for himself and to communicate his wishes, until his death is imminent. Mr Burke's concern was to be fed and provided with appropriate hydration until he dies of natural causes: as Munby J put it, 'he does not want a decision to be taken by doctors that his life is no longer worth living.'[17] He argued that the guidance drawn up by the General Medical Council (GMC) implied that, even if death is not imminent, a doctor may be able to withdraw ANH. Paragraph 81 of the GMC advice states that:

> Where death is not imminent, it usually will be appropriate to provide artificial nutrition or hydration. However, circumstances may arise where you judge that a patient's condition is so severe, the prognosis so poor, that providing artificial nutrition or hydration may cause suffering or to be too burdensome in relation to the possible benefits.[18]

While agreeing with the proposition that merely prolonging life is *not* always in the best interests of the individual, Munby J nonetheless added that 'the starting point ... must be the very strong presumption in favour of taking all steps which will prolong life. Save in exceptional circumstances, or where the patient is dying, the best interests of the patient will normally require such steps to be taken.'[19] As the Court of Appeal was later to put it: '... Mr Burke fears that ANH will be withdrawn before the final stages of his disease, ... he fears that those caring for him may decide that his life is not worth living and withdraw ANH to bring it to an end, notwithstanding that he is able to communicate to them that he wishes them to continue to keep him alive.'[20]

One theme running through Munby J's judgement was that, providing there are no overwhelming resource implications, doctors who have assumed the care of a patient *must* administer such treatment as is in the patient's best interests and that, where a patient has expressed an informed wish for a particular treatment, provision of that treatment will, *by definition*, be in the patient's best interests. In this view, 'best interests' is determined by the wishes of the competent patient rather than by the opinions of health care professionals. For Munby J the 'best interests' test, which is a common decision-making standard in health care law, is broader than best clinical interests; deciding on what they are 'involves a welfare appraisal in the widest sense, taking into account where appropriate, a wide range of ethical, social, moral, emotional and welfare considerations.'[21] The Court of Appeal, in fundamental disagreement with Munby J on both the nature and basis of his approach, also disagreed on this point, saying:

> It seems to us that it is best to confine the use of the phrase 'best interests' to an objective test, which is of most use when considering the duty owed to a patient who is not competent and is easiest to apply when confined to a situation where the relevant interests are medical.[22]

Mr Justice Munby had concluded that Article 3 of the European Convention on Human Rights[23] (the prohibition of inhuman and degrading treatment) would be infringed if doctors failed to offer the treatment against the patient's wishes, because the effect would be to subject Mr Burke to acute mental and physical suffering. Similarly, Article 8 (the right to private and family life) would be engaged because Mr Burke's dignity and autonomy would have been flouted. The Court of Appeal did not deal with the issues raised by this case in anything like the depth or detail that Munby J did, but they clearly disapproved of his decision. Nonetheless, the court agreed that if English law permitted a National Health Service (NHS) doctor deliberately to withdraw life-prolonging treatment from a competent patient *contrary to that patient's wishes*, the state would violate a positive obligation to enforce Article 2 of the Convention (the right to life). This presumption may be displaced *only* where the patient's request that *medical* treatment is withheld, withdrawn, or discontinued, or, if the patient is incompetent, doctors decide that it is not in the patient's best *medical* interests, as objectively judged, for treatment to be initiated or continued. In both cases, the role of medicine is paramount. Only medical treatment may be refused by the patient and only medical interests are to be considered by the doctors. Thus, following *Burke*, English law's position is clear.[24] There is a strong presumption in favour of life and the exceptions to the state's positive duty to safeguard or preserve life are circumscribed narrowly.

In some situations, however, the patients' choices are said to be determinative. The paradigmatic case in point here concerns a lady known as *Ms B*.[25] Briefly, she had become tetraplegic and ventilator-dependent. In 1999 she suffered a haemorrhage of the spinal column in her neck, followed in 2001 by an intramedullary cervical spine cavernoma. Doubts about her legal competence were resolved and she repeatedly asked that the ventilator be removed. The doctors caring for her were unwilling to do accede to her request and suggested instead that she should be weaned off it. Ms B, however, remained adamant and eventually had to resort to law to have her wishes respected. It seems clear that in this case the doctors were prevented by their own moral values from acceding to the refusal of an otherwise competent patient to continue with treatment. Indeed one of them declared that she 'felt she was being asked to kill Ms B.'[26] Whatever the feelings of the doctors, in effect, for as long as she was unwillingly maintained mechanically she was the victim of an assault, which was recognized by Dame Elizabeth Butler-Sloss who said:

> If mental capacity is not in issue and the patient, having been given the relevant information and offered the available options, chooses to refuse the treatment, that decision has to be respected by the doctors. Considerations that the best interests of the patient would indicate that the decision should be to consent to treatment are irrelevant.[27]

On the other hand, some choices are not within the patient's authority in most (but not all) jurisdictions. While medical opinion on whether or not people should legally be allowed an assisted death is by no means unanimous, the law is clear. In England and Wales, the Suicide Act 1961 specifically makes it a criminal offence to assist a suicide,[28] while in Scotland, suicide would be covered by the law of murder or culpable homicide (the Scottish equivalent of manslaughter). Although some jurisdictions have legalized assisted dying,[29] the United Kingdom seems resolutely opposed to doing so. The legality of the United Kingdom's prohibition of assisted dying was recently clarified in the European Court of Human Rights. In the case of *Pretty v United Kingdom*,[30] a woman suffering from motor neurone disease (MND) was denied the relief she sought—assistance by her husband in dying—despite seeking to engage a number of the Articles of the European Convention on Human Rights in her argument. While accepting that other states covered by the Convention had enacted legislation to permit assisted dying, the Court of Human Rights held that Mrs Pretty would have to prove that the United Kingdom was in contravention of the Convention by not doing so. Given the latitude that states have to decide on matters of public morality, the court held that this conclusion would have been untenable. More recently came the case of *R (on the application of Debbie Purdy) v DPP*,[31] which was raised by a woman who now lives with primary progressive multiple sclerosis and who has been a wheelchair user for seven years. Whereas Mrs Pretty had asked the court to review the Director of Public Prosecution's (DPP) refusal to undertake that her husband would not be prosecuted if he provided her assistance in dying that would have fallen foul of the terms of Section 2(1) of the 1961 Act, Mrs Purdy sought judicial review of the failure by the DPP to issue specific guidance on the circumstances in which a prosecution under the section would be brought. As in *Pretty*, the court declined to hold that Mrs Purdy's Convention rights had been engaged, let alone breached, by the DPP's failure to issue specific guidance.[32]

Purportedly, one reason for denying people the right to obtain an assisted death is the principle of the sanctity of life. However, since it has been firmly stated in a number of cases that self-determination trumps the sanctity of life,[33] it is unclear why this principle should suddenly be prioritized when a competent person seeks to act in a self-determining manner but requires assistance to effectuate their decision. It is also the case that many clinicians believe there is a difference between killing and 'letting die', and their views have been highly influential. Indeed, in refusing to recommend law reform in this area, the House of Lords Select Committee on Medical Ethics placed considerable weight on doctors' views—to such an extent that they even speculated that it might appear that too much importance had been attached to them.[34] As its Report says:

> Some people may consider that our conclusions overall give too much weight to the role of accepted medical practice, and that we advocate leaving too much responsibility in the hands of doctors and other members of the health-care team. They may argue that doctors and their colleagues as no better qualified than any other group of people to take ethical decisions about life and death which ultimately have a bearing not only on individual patients but on society as a whole. But no other group of people is better qualified to do so....By virtue of their vocation, training and professional integrity they may be expected to act with rectitude and compassion.[35]

Further arguments against respecting patient choice in this area include fears of the slippery slope—that is, if we once allow people to choose an assisted death, then we will either start permitting it for less serious conditions or people will feel compelled to die; the right will become a duty. Since this chapter is not concerned with the strength of the arguments for or against assisted dying, it is not necessary to go further into either this or any additional arguments. Merely, it is important to note that in this case, patients' wishes are discounted by both courts and legislators, presumably in what are seen as wider societal interests in constraining the choice for death, even although a different approach is taken when that same choice is made by someone like Ms B.

One further issue merits consideration in this issue: that of advance decisions or directives. Although patients may not be competent when the directive is triggered, they are included under this heading because they express choices that were made when the patient *was* competent. For some patients, previous experience or apprehension of deteriorating health may lead to them preparing in advance an account of what they would wish to happen should they become incompetent. These advance decisions have been given the force of law in England and Wales by the terms of the Mental Capacity Act 2005,[36] so long as they are unambiguous and applicable to the circumstances in which the patient now finds himself or herself. This statutory provision puts what had been accepted at common law in a number of earlier cases onto a sure legal footing. At common law, the lawfulness of advance statements had already been considered in cases such as *Re AK*.[37] In this case, a young man who was suffering from motor neurone disease was granted authority to have all life-sustaining treatment withdrawn two weeks after he became unable to communicate. Irrespective, therefore, of his doctors' views he was allowed effectively to choose death; his autonomy or right to self-determination was respected. No similar legislation exists in Scotland, but it is widely assumed that the pre-existing common law position would also be accepted there. Yet again, however, it must be made clear that the law specifically authorizes decisions to *refuse* treatment; patients are not permitted by the 2005 Act, nor by common law, to *insist* on the provision of specific treatment. The decision whether or not to offer treatment (including ANH) remains firmly with the clinician.

The balance between doctors' duties and patients' rights in these examples suggests that when the patient and doctor are in agreement, problems seldom arise. However, when doctors' preferences are at odds with what their patient wishes, the situation becomes more complex. Where the patient wants to refuse even life-sustaining treatment, his or her wishes prevail;[38] should they wish to insist on treatment, the clinical decision is paramount. What we can conclude, then, is that while competent patients can reserve the right to decide which treatments to accept or reject, they cannot compel doctors to behave in ways that breach their best clinical or moral judgements. However, additional concerns arise when the patient is not competent to make decisions and the responsibility become primarily—sometimes solely—that of the health care team.

The incompetent patient

Sadly, some patients without advance directives will lapse into unconsciousness and will obviously be unable to let the health care team know what they would want to be done for them. When this is a temporary situation, all efforts should be made to maintain life until the patient can decide for himself or herself. However, in some cases, for example, where the patient is diagnosed as being in permanent vegetative state (PVS), recovery of consciousness is impossible. First described (as the persistent vegetative state) over 30 years ago by Jennet and Plum,[39] PVS results in the loss of higher brain function. While the patient may survive for some time, he or she will not recover consciousness and will never therefore be able to make self-determining decisions. Historically, management of these patients was problematic, not least because nobody had decision-making authority over another adult. The leading case of *Airedale NHS Trust v Bland*,[40] however, clarified the situation. Patients in PVS will require ANH in order to sustain their continued existence. The dilemma, therefore, is whether or not this should be continued. Albeit by somewhat different routes, all of the judges in the House of Lords in the *Bland* case agreed that removal of ANH was lawful, adding the caveat that all such cases should in future be brought to the attention of the courts for adjudication. A similar case occurred a few years later in Scotland—*Law Hospital NHS Trust v Lord Advocate*[41]— in which the Court of Session (Scotland's highest court) also authorized the withdrawing of ANH from a patient in PVS. Interestingly, however, it did not impose any requirement to bring cases before a court, although the Lord Advocate (Scotland's senior prosecutor) did issue a statement indicating that should doctors obtain court approval, no prosecution would follow. Mason and Laurie argue that this is unsatisfactory since it means that a 'situation has now arisen where the doctor may be required to second guess the criminal law—a position that is hardly desirable.'[42]

Desirable or not, this is how the law stands, and while in some cases family and clinicians will agree as to the proposed course of action, in others there may be dispute between the concerned parties. A few cases are worthy of consideration on this point—even although they concern children—as they demonstrate the tensions that can arise as well as the legal obligations that health care professionals have in the event of dispute. In the case of *Glass v UK*,[43] disagreement arose between the mother of a seriously ill child and the health care professionals who were caring for him. So serious was the disagreement that members of David's family actually became violent towards the doctors. In this situation, it was decided that David's rights under Article 8 of the European Convention on Human Rights had been breached by the failure of the Trust to have sought a court judgement to resolve the matter one way or the other before it spiralled out of control. Mason and Laurie conclude that 'procedurally, then, disputes over care should be referred to the courts in all but the most urgent of circumstances.'[44] The task of the courts then is to weigh the competing opinions and ascribe authority to one or the other of them.

In the case of *Re Wyatt*,[45] the child was profoundly brain damaged; she was blind, deaf, and unable to move. The doctors caring for her sought a declaration from the court that they would not be required to institute ventilation should it become necessary; they described Charlotte's condition as 'terrible' and felt that 'the enduring of further aggressive treatment....[was] intolerable.'[46] The parents on the other hand wanted anything and everything done to keep Charlotte alive for as long as possible, believing that there was quality in her life no matter how disabled she seemed to be. Noting that this is essentially a subjective matter, the court was ultimately persuaded by the clinicians, although the judge did say that nothing in his judgement relieved them of the right or responsibility for advising or giving the treatment that they and the parents think right in the light of the circumstances as they develop. All it does is to authorize them, in the event of disagreement between the parents and themselves, not to send the child for artificial ventilation or similar aggressive treatment.'[47] At a subsequent hearing of this case in 2005, when Charlotte had surprised everyone by continuing to survive, the judge declined to vary his decision although in October of that year he removed his earlier order. Nonetheless, he reiterated that this did not mean that the parents could insist on the provision of assisted ventilation. In February 2006, her condition had worsened and the judge agreed that doctors could choose not to intubate or resuscitate Charlotte should the need arise. In October 2006, Charlotte celebrated her 3rd birthday alive, contrary to the expectations of the doctors caring for her.

In *An NHS Trust v MB*[48] the child was diagnosed as suffering from spinal muscular atrophy (SMA). He was virtually unable to move and also suffered from epilepsy. His parents believed that nonetheless he could experience pleasure and wanted him to be kept alive. The doctors disagreed, believing that keeping him alive could be described as cruel and that his endotracheal tube should be withdrawn. Unlike the *Wyatt* case, the question here was whether or not to withdraw treatment that was already in place, over the objections of the parents. The court, however, was of the view that essentially the same issues arose, a position supported by the Royal College of Paediatrics and Child Health[49] and the Nuffield Council on Bioethics.[50] It concluded that a decision had to be made from the perspective of the child's best interests. After considering a list of the benefits and burdens of treatment, the judge concluded that it was not obvious that immediate withdrawal of ventilation would satisfy that test, but he also agreed that should other interventions that could inflict pain become necessary it would not be unlawful to fail to provide them. It should be noted, however, that the judge made a point of saying that his decision was specific to the particular facts of the case and should not be taken as representing a general policy. It does, however, seem very similar to the judgement of Lord Donaldson in the case of *Re J (a minor) (wardship: medical treatment)*[51] where he said:

> There is without doubt a very strong presumption in favour of a course of action which will prolong life, but ... it is not irrebuttable ... account has to be taken of the pain and suffering and quality of life which the child will experience if life is prolonged. Account has also to be taken of the pain and suffering involved in the proposed treatment itself.[52]

There are other cases on point, but there is no need to consider them in depth here as general conclusions can be drawn from those referred to. What emerges from the majority of them is that courts—while prepared to engage with the debate—have tended to favour the clinical rather than the parental choice. In fact, we are only aware of one case where the converse happened—*Re T (a minor) (wardship: medical treatment)*.[53] This exception to the general rule is peculiar, however, for more than just the fact that it was differently decided; the parents in this case were described as health care professionals themselves and had in any case removed the child from the jurisdiction. These factors may have been important considerations in the court's support for their rejection of a potentially life-saving organ transplant for their child.

Interestingly, the professional guidelines issued to doctors by the Royal College of Paediatrics and Child Health[54] are arguably more nuanced in tone than what has emerged from the courts. In particular, these guidelines explicitly declare that '[a]lthough it is necessary and fundamental to practice within the framework of the law', nonetheless it is also 'important to define best practice in relation to the interests of the family and the child rather than presenting the minimum legal requirement. We must look at what is legally permitted and required, *but also at what is ethically appropriate, which may exceed the minimum standards set by law*'[55] (emphasis added).

Further problematic cases arise where patients are subject to 'do not resuscitate' (DNR) or 'do not attempt resuscitation' (DNAR) orders. These are patients in whose case the health care team has concluded that cardiopulmonary resuscitation (CPR) should not be attempted should the patient suffer a cardiac incident. This may be because CPR is seen as likely to be futile, or because the anticipated quality of life for the patient is thought to be unacceptable. Where DNR orders are made in respect of a patient who is unable to participate in the decision, best medical judgements will apply and are particularly appropriate where the decision is based on clinical futility. However, since quality-of-life decisions are extremely complex and sensitive, it is plausible that they are best made with the agreement of the patient where possible. However, some evidence has suggested that '[a]lthough patients report an interest in discussing DNR issues with their physicians, few report actually having these discussions.'[56] In fact, '[i]n one study, 86% of families but only 22% of patients had participated in discussions about DNR orders.'[57] This same commentary (admittedly rather elderly) pointed out that proxies were more often asked for consent than were the patients themselves. This, of course, may be a result of how ill the patient actually is when decisions are taken, but it disrespects the autonomy of those who could have competently participated in the decision. What does seem clear is that '[a] timely, caring, and open exchange of information involving the appropriate individuals and taking into account the patient's prognosis, quality of life, and value system is vital to humane DNR decision-making.'[58] Of course, patients and doctors may differ as to whether or not a life will have quality, and this may be one situation where patients'—or, as in *Wyatt*, parent's—requests or demands for treatment might be prioritized.

Concern for the rights and sensitivities of patients (and their families) was recently affirmed at a hearing of the General Medical Council's Fitness to Practise Panel.[59] In this case, the respondent doctor decided to withdraw treatment from a Mr S without making the fullest possible inquiry into alternative management of his case. She did not consult with colleagues nor with his family. In finding her guilty of serious professional misconduct, the panel—while recognizing that Mr S might in any event have died—declared that he nonetheless 'had an undeniable right to all reasonable treatments before the decision to withdraw treatment was made. No decision should have been taken until all attempts at diagnosis and treatment had been made.'[60] This case makes it clear that families—and most particularly one would assume, patients—should be involved in decision-making where feasible and reinforces the law's concern for the preservation of life where possible.

Unavailable treatment

One final matter is worthy of consideration before embarking on a more general discussion of modern health care decisions. It is often said that today's patients are better informed than their predecessors. Information is widely available about both disease states and therapies. Anecdotally, most doctors will claim to have had experience of patients who self-diagnose and then demand a particular treatment. However, even if they are correct, not every treatment in the market will be available. It is also a moot point whether doctors have a professional obligation to tell patients about treatments that could be more successful than those made available in the NHS, although it is arguable that permitting co-payments may require some resolution of this question.

In England, Wales, and Northern Ireland, decisions about what drugs will be funded by the NHS are made by the National Institute for Health and Clinical Excellence (NICE).[61] In Scotland, the equivalent body is the Scottish Medicines Consortium.[62] While drugs may receive a licence that allows them to be prescribed, limitations on availability may arise from the fact that a cost–benefit analysis does not come down on the side of benefit. Although NICE has recently backtracked on a number of decisions, for example, in relation to end of life drugs, it remains a powerful gatekeeper of the availability of some products that patients might want to receive.

What has emerged from this section of the chapter is a sense that in the ideal doctor–patient relationship, authority is shared. Trust is supposed to characterize the best medical encounter[63] both the patient and doctor require, and facilitate the sharing of information and the quality of the outcome. However, health care professionals, doctors, and patients (and their families) will not always agree with one another and it is often the law that will have to step in to provide a resolution of their disagreement. While patients can anticipate that their decisions will be given due weightage (in some circumstances), the majority of the examples we have highlighted show the emphasis placed that is placed by courts on clinical decisions. Patients' rights or autonomy, while commonly lionized in bioethical literature, do not seem to carry the weight that commentators attribute to them. In addition, while individual autonomy and choice are often lauded as of supreme importance, further emerging theoretical critiques cast doubt on this model of doctor–patient relationship.

Making markets, constructing consumers, commanding choice

Phillip Bobbitt, in his essay *The Shield of Achilles*,[64] argued that the era of the nation state as the context for the exercise of authority, including legal and moral authority, was coming to an end. Its replacement as the arbiter and enforcer of moral and social values, the new context for legitimacy and the practical reach of power, is the market state. Here, increases in choice and opportunity take precedence over substantive values, leading, as Montgomery has argued,[65] to a promotion of choice *at the expense* of autonomy; what Schwartz has recently identified as 'miswanting' or 'the paradox of choice: more is less.'[66] Bobbitt, and Montgomery, identify health care as an area in which problems can arise, and the limitations of the consumer model are succinctly

articulated by Brazier and Glover, who have cautioned that developments in modern medical care are threatening to circumvent any
'gate-keeping' role for health care professionals. Of course, whether or
not this is a good development depends on the role and function that is
ascribed to the doctor or the nurse. Brazier and Glover argue that a case
can be made that in large part '… the medical role is to protect the
patient …',[67] which means that 'miswanting' generates distinct threats.
According priority to desire or demand alone means that consumer
protection laws could (in theory) '… offer sufficient guarantee of the
quality of the goods supplied and standards of service provision.'[68]
However, whether or not this would result in good patient care or positive outcomes for patients is surely debateable. Where medical law is
subsumed into consumer law, this may be seen as a logical development of regarding it a sub-set of human rights, which can generate an
adversarial relationship and prioritize choice over content. The *potential* harms of the modern obsession with choice were beautifully illustrated by Franz Ingelfinger, the former editor of the *New England
Journal of Medicine* as he lay dying of cancer:

> I do not want to be in the position of the shopper at the Casbah who negotiates
> and haggles with the physician about what is best. I want to believe that my physi-
> cian is acting under a higher moral principle than a used car dealer. I'll go further
> than that. A physician who merely spreads an array of vendibles in front of his
> patient and then says 'Go ahead, you choose, it's your life' is guilty of shirking his
> duty, if not malpractice. [69]

This statement informs a more general thesis that medicine and hence
medical law are not just about treating people *right*, but also about
treating them *gently*. The consumerist model presupposes rational market actors and resources, which, while it may offer 'recreation for the
"worried well"', [70] may also fail to meet the needs of the sick and the
destitute. Individual rights claims have an insidious history of gravitat-
ing towards those who are articulate and affluent,[71] while remaindering
others to the margins of the resource arithmetic. If rights are to serve
their purpose, they must be seen as contextual as well as individual. The
NHS is now 'in the business of customer service'[72] seeking to devolve
the power of making choices about health care and exerting real
influence over those choices to the users of services.[73] While this may

provide the illusion of 'patient power', in addition to the concerns already outlined, Manson and O'Neill suggest that the importance of patient choice is actually over-estimated in health care since '[p]atients are typically asked to choose—or refuse—from a very limited menu (often a menu of one item)....'.[74]

Further, choice—apparently a staple of the consumer model—is no longer free; it is essentially *mandated,* and people have to make not just *a* choice, but the *right choice.* This is clearly illustrated in Ward LJ's judgement in the *Conjoined Twins* case.[75] In this case, the parents refused to authorize the separation surgery that would inevitably result in the death of one of their daughters, knowing well that failure to operate would result in the deaths of both of them. That was their choice, based on their religious convictions. The judge objected to the parents' choice. He did so first by claiming that the courts had jurisdiction over the case, declaring that '[d]eciding disputed matters of life and death is surely and pre-eminently a matter for a court of law to judge. ... If a person having a recognisable interest brings such a dispute to court, the court must decide it.'[76] The person bringing the case was the doctor (or more likely the hospital manager) who disagreed with the parents' decision. Now, the judge could have appealed to the authority that parents generally have in making decisions for their children and declined to hear the case. However, it is obvious that he too disapproved of what the parents wanted, and he proceeded to castigate the parent's decision as being morally reprehensible:

> In my judgement, parents who are placed on the horns of such a terrible dilemma *simply have to* choose the lesser of their inevitable loss. If a family at the gates of a concentration camp were told they might free one of their children but if no choice were made both would die, *compassionate parents* with equal love for their twins *would* elect to save the stronger and see the weak one destined for death pass through the gates.[77] (emphases added)

The evident problem, stemming from Kennedy's analysis of what Harvey Teff later came to call the 'therapeutic alliance', centres on the difference between the rhetoric and the reality of patient choice. Kennedy's argument that an authentic expression of liberty entails that sensitive clinical decisions should not be left to the 'unarticulated judgement of individual medical practitioners' or the 'undefined collectivity of the medical profession'[78] and his call for people's entitlement, 'to expect not only some regularity … in the decisions doctors arrive at, but also some conformity between these decisions and those which the rest of us might make,[79] were and remain aspirational.

As the cases of *Re B*,[80] *Conjoined Twins*,[81] and *Burke*[82] amply demonstrate, the relevant legal tests are delegated back by the courts to the doctor and his or her professional colleagues. Although Ms B was eventually allowed to refuse treatment despite the objections of her doctors, the very fact that they were able to delay respecting her decision forcing her to go to law to have her rights vindicated shows how easy it is to circumvent patient choice. A less articulate or determined patient might have seen her decision disrespected. In *Wyatt*, it was not the parents' choice but the *clinical* assessment of the child's 'best interests' that was respected; in *Burke*, Munby's advocacy of a broad assessment of the 'welfare' interest was recast on appeal as a much narrower revision that focused on medical interests.

Conclusion

The theologian Alastair Campbell, in his Tuohy lectures of 1994, articulated a vision of modern postindustrial society that saw health 'as best understood as an aspect of human freedom' and the essence of good health care as 'a liberation, a setting free.'[83] Although Campbell argued his thesis from an explicitly theological position, he also urged that if the vision of health as liberation is the right one, 'then we shall need to find (or form) some secular "communities of faith" to help us in the quest.'[84] His critique of modern medicine led him to try to draw us away from 'the dazzle of modern medicine's alleged success and try to see things from the perspective of those who suffer and for whom there is no quick technological fix.'[85] His aim, which is not entirely ours, was to 'reorient the debate about justice in health care' by adopting the perspective of liberation theology. This is a perspective, as he explains, that insists that we focus our attention on those most often overlooked in such debates, 'that we listen first and foremost to the voices of those who suffer.'[86] The reason he gives for this is simple, and in our view compelling:

> I do not claim that listening to the voices of the dispossessed is all that needs to be done about health and health care, nor do I claim that I have given a wholly fair and accurate picture of what is currently provided by the health care professions. But I do insist that unless we confront these issues of freedom, oppression and liberation, we will have missed the central problem of modern health care ethics. We will be focusing our attention on secondary issues while refusing to confront or even acknowledge the primary issue – that of the uses and abuses of power in health care delivery and in the very definition of health itself.[87]

Any opportunity for abuse of power could, of course, be limited by focusing on encouraging patients (or their legal representatives where appropriate) to become equal (if not dominant) partners in decisions about their health care and their lives. On the other hand, we will fail patients if we too easily discount what clinical expertise and judgement have to offer. Striking the balance between the authority of the patient and the beneficence of medicine is not easy, and the ambivalence sometimes shown in court judgements makes this entirely clear. What can be concluded is that we are yet to succeed in separating out the patient's interests from his or her 'clinical' interests. Failure to do this results in what sometimes appears to be an over-emphasis on clinical authority at the expense of patient choice. Patients are free to choose, but their decision must be the 'right' one if the law is to support it—very often the 'right' personal choice is taken to be equivalent to the 'right' medical choice. Moreover, the reluctance of the law to impose robust information disclosure requirements or to abandon its emphasis on doctors' duties rather than patients' rights disenfranchizes patients and reduces their autonomy right to a shadow of what we might wish it to be. The decision to 'take it or leave it' is seldom solely that of the patient.

References

1 Roth, P. *Everyman*, London: Jonathan Cape, 2006; 15.

2 ibid, p. 16.

3 See, for example, the Australian cases of *Rogers v Whittaker* [1993] 4 Med LR 79 and *Chappell v Hart* (1998) ALJR 1344; in the United States, see *Canterbury v Spence* 464 F 2d 772 (DC, 1972).

4 *Bolam v Friern Hospital Management Committee* [1957] 2 All ER 118, and to a slightly lesser extent *Sidaway v Board of Governors of the Bethlem Royal Hospital* [1985] 1 All ER 643 (H.L.)

5 See *Bolitho v Hackney Health Authority* (1998) 39 BMLR 1; *Pearce v United Bristol Healthcare NHS Trust* (1999) 48 BMLR 118.

6 Kennedy I (1983). *The Unmasking of Medicine*, London, Granada, at p. 28.

7 For example, see Kennedy, I., *Treat me Right. Essays in Medical Law and Ethics*, Clarendon Press, Oxford, 1988.

8 Kennedy, *The Unmasking of Medicine, supra*, at pp. 119–120.

9 *Supra cit.*

10 For discussion, see McLean SAM, *A Patient's Right to Know: Information Disclosure, the Doctor and the Law*, Aldershot, Dartmouth, 1989.

11 *Supra cit.*

12 *Supra cit.*

13 *Supra cit.*

14 [2005] 1 AC 134 For one of a number of celebrations of *Chester*, see Meyers, D., '*Chester v Afshar: Sayonara, Sub Silentio, Sidaway?*', in McLean, S.A.M. (ed), *First Do No Harm: Law, Ethics and Healthcare*, 255–272. For a more skeptical view, see Veitch, K., *The Jurisdiction of Medical Law*, Aldershot, Ashgate, 2007, pp. 80–81 and more generally at p. 39 *et seq.*

15 '[Whether the patient's] reasons for making the choice are rational, irrational, unknown or even non-existent.' *Re T* [1993] Fam. 95 at 102 (per Lord Donaldson, citing Lord Templeman in *Sidaway v Bethlem Royal Hospital* [1985] A.C. 871, at 904 05 and 116 (Butler-Sloss LJ), a dictum reaffirmed by the Court of Appeal in *Re MB* [1997] 2 F.L.R. 426 at 432, 436–437.

16 *Burke v GMC* [2005] Q.B. 424 (HC); [2006] Q.B. 273.

17 p. 431.

18 *Withholding and Withdrawing Life-Prolonging Treatments: Good Practice in Decision-Making*, London, GMC, 2002.

19 Per Munby J (2005) Q.B. 424, at p. 459. Indeed, he might have gone further and suggested that taking such steps is always in the interest of the patient, absent these unspecified exceptional circumstances.

20 [2006] Q.B. 273, at p. 289 (per Lord Phillips of Worth Matravers, MR).

21 [2005] Q.B. at p. 455.

22 [2006] Q.B. 273 at 289, per Lord Phillips.

23 Which was imported into UK law by the Human Rights Act 1998.

24 This question has yet to reach the Scottish courts, which are under no formal obligation to follow the judgements of their English counterparts.

25 *Re B (adult: refusal of medical treatment)* (2002) 65 BMLR 149.

26 p. 163.

27 p. 174.

28 S. 2 (1).

29 For example, The Netherlands and Belgium. It is not a crime in Switzerland and seems never to have been one in certain circumstances. For further discussion, see McLean, SAM., *Assisted Dying: Reflections on the Need for Law Reform*, London, Routledge-Cavendish, 2007.

30 [2002] 2 FLR 45.

31 [2008] EWHC 2565.

32 This case is currently subject to an appeal.

33 *Re T* (1992) 9 BMLR46.

34 *Report of the Select Committee on Medical Ethics*, HL Paper 21-1, 1994.

35 p.56, para 272.

36 s. 24.

37 *AK (medical treatment: consent)* (2001) 58 BMLR 151.

38 *Re C (adult: refusal of medical treatment)* [1994] 1 All ER 819.

39 Jennet B and Plum F (1972). 'Persistent Vegetative State after Brain damage: A Syndrome in Search of a Name', *The Lancet*, April 1, 734–737.

40 (1993) 12 BMLR 64.

41 1996 SLT 848.

42 *Mason and McCall Smith's Law and Medical Ethics* (7th ed.), Oxford, Oxford University Press, 2006, 590.

43 (2004) 77 BMLR 120.

44 *op cit*, at p. 354, para 10.18.

45 *Re Wyatt (a child) (medical treatment: parents' consent)* (2004) 84 BMLR 206.

46 p. 214.

47 p. 217.

48 [2006] EWHC 507 (Fam) (15 March 2006).

49 *Witholding or Withdrawing Life Sustaining Treatment: A Framework for Practice*, (2nd Ed), London, Royal College of Paediatrics and Child Health, 2004, at p. 13.

50 *Report on Critical Care Decisions in Fetal and Neonatal Medicine: Ethical Issues*, London, Nuffied Council on Bioethics, November 2006, para 2.33.

51 [1990] 3 All ER 930.

52 p. 938.

53 (1996) 35 BMLR 63.

54 *Witholding or Withdrawing Life Sustaining Treatment in Children: A Framework for Practice*, (2nd ed), London, Royal College of Paediatrics and Child Health, May 2004.

55 p. 10.

56 Ebell MH, Doukas DJ, and Smith MA (1991). 'The Do-Not-Resuscitate Order: A Comparison of Physician and Patient Preferences and Decision-Making,' *The American Journal of Medicine* **91**: 255–260, p. 255.

57 pp. 255–256.

58 p. 260.

59 Date of Fitness to Practise Panel Hearing: 3–16 November 2005; Name of respondent doctor: DAVID, Ann Clair

60 Transcript, at p. 6.

61 See http://www.nice.org.uk

62 See http://www.scottishmedicines.org.uk

63 For a discussion of the importance of trust, see O'Neill, O., *Autonomy and Trust in Bioethics*, Cambridge, Cambridge University Press, 2002.

64 Bobbitt, P. *The Shield of Achilles*. London, Penguin, 2002.

65 'Law and the Demoralisation of Medicine' (2006) 2 LS 185 esp at 185–187. In turn, Montgomery's analysis draws from Rowan Williams, The Richard Dimbleby Lecture 2002, at www.archbishopofcanterbury.org and *Lost Icons*, London, T & T Clark, 200, ch. 1.

66 New York, Harper Perennial, 2004.

67 Brazier M and Glover N (2000). 'Does Medical Law Have a Future?' in Birks, P, (ed.) *Laws' Futures*, Oxford, Hart Publishing.

68 *id.*

69 Ingelfinger FG (1980). 'Arrogance'. *New England Journal of Medicine* **304**: 1507–1511.

70 p. 15.

71 *loc cit* at p. 15.

72 Department of Health, *Building on the Best. Choice, Responsiveness and Equity in the NHS*. Cmnd. 6079 (London, The Stationary Office, 2003) at 23.

73 ibid at 12 (ie: Department of Health, *Building on the Best. Choice, Responsiveness and Equality in the NHS*. Cmnd. 6079) (London, The Stationary Office, 2003) at 12.

74 Manson NC and O'Neill O (2007). *Rethinking Informed Consent in Bioethics*, Cambridge University Press, p. 72.

75 *Re A(Children)(Conjoined Twins: Surgical Separation)* [2000] 4 All ER 961.

76 *Re A(Children)(Conjoined Twins: Surgical Separation)* [2000] 4 All ER 961 at 969.

77 pp. 1009–1010. For discussion, see Veitch, K., 'Medical Law and the power of life and death' (2006) 2(2) *International Journal of Law in Context*, 137–157, Munro, V., 'Square Pegs in Round Holes: The Dilemma of Conjoined Twins and Individual Rights' *Social & Legal Studies* 2001, 10, 459–482.

78 Kennedy I (1983). *The Unmasking of Medicine*, London, Granada, at p. 102.

79 *The Unmasking of Medicine* at p. 124.

80 *Supra cit.*

81 *Re A(Children)(Conjoined Twins: Surgical Separation)* [2000] 4 All ER 961.

82 *Supra cit.*

83 Campbell A (1995). *Health as Liberation: Medicine, Theology and the Quest for Justice*, Cleveland, Ohio, The Pilgrim Press, 1.

84 pp. 23–24.

85 p. 17.

86 pp. 1–2.

87 p. 2.

Chapter 5

Dying to know: Legal and ethical issues surrounding death and do not resuscitate orders

Hazel Biggs[*]

Introduction

If you were a hospital patient, would you want to know that no attempt would be made to revive you if your heart stopped beating or you stopped breathing? And, how would you feel if you did know? There are no definitive answers to these questions, and this forms the central theme of this article. The answers are imponderable, not only because every individual has their own opinion about such matters, but also because they depend upon a great many variables. For example, is your heart expected to stop in the near future? What are your chances of surviving such an event? How great is your life expectancy with or without resuscitation? And, will resuscitation cause pain and distress to yourself or your loved ones? These questions appear to turn on issues of life and death: if you are resuscitated, you will survive; if not you will die. The reality, however, is far more complex and far less certain.

Contemporary medical law and ethics revere individual autonomy and the patient's ability to choose as key aspects of medical care. In general, the ability to exercise autonomy is thought to require the provision of sufficient information to enable the patient to decide which interventions to accept or reject. Yet in some circumstances, including the scenario described above, perhaps it would be better not to know.

* The author wishes to thank Richard Austen-Baker and Stuart Brittle for their very helpful comments on an early draft of this chapter.

This chapter explores the legal and ethical responsibilities of health care professionals involved in do not resuscitate (DNR) decisions for adults with decision-making capacity, to determine whether, in practice, they can be/are easily reconciled with the needs and wishes of patients. The primary focus will be on issues of medical decision-making, consent, information provision, and communication, alongside an examination of the relationship between withholding and withdrawing treatment. Particular emphasis will be placed on the relationship of trust between doctors and those they care for in the context of medical futility and end of life decisions. Further to this, some of the ethical and legal distinctions between intention and foresight, as illustrated by the case of *Dr Ann David v The General Medical Council* will be discussed to assess their impact upon the potential legal liability of clinicians making these difficult decisions.

To resuscitate or not to resuscitate?

Resuscitation can involve a number of different procedures and treatments but it is most widely associated with the technique known as cardio-pulmonary resuscitation (CPR) and, since DNR or DNAR (do not attempt resuscitation) orders apply only to CPR, this chapter will focus solely on resuscitation involving CPR. CPR first began to be used successfully in the 1960s[1] after it was described in a seminal article by Kouwebhoven et al.[2] as closed chest cardiac massage. In the early days, it was mostly used on young and relatively fit patients who had suffered sudden and often unexpected cardiac failure, but has now become a common-place procedure that has 'saved the lives of countless cardiac arrest patients'.[3] As such it may be realistically described as an emergency medical procedure and is one of a very few medical interventions that is regularly and legitimately administered without explicit consent. Similarly, because of the nature of the technique, in a genuine emergency it may also be performed without prior discussion amongst the members of the clinical team, although that is relatively unlikely to occur in the intensive therapy unit.

CPR involves forceful manual compressions of the chest to stimulate cardiac function and encourage the circulation of oxygenated blood to the brain and heart. Traditionally, especially in non-hospital settings, this procedure would be accompanied by ventilation of the lungs via mouth-to-mouth aeration. However, some recent research concerning resuscitation by non-health professionals suggests that chest compression alone is equally valuable when resuscitation takes place in the community.[4] An international review of all data relevant to this proposition is currently underway and due to be reported in 2010 and in the meantime the evidence for resuscitation in the community using chest compression alone is regarded as inconclusive.[5]

In the hospital setting, it is the clinical circumstances, such as the patient's underlying medical condition, their age, and whether or not the cardiac event was anticipated, that dictate the precise approach to be taken for resuscitation. In this context, CPR typically involves chest compressions and ventilation of the lungs using a range of equipment depending on the location of the cardiac arrest patient and local policy. For example, a pocket mask and oral airway may be all that is available in some settings, while laryngeal mask airways and self-inflating bags, tracheal intubation, and defibrillation are commonplace in other situations. Drugs may also be administered to help stimulate cardiac output and circulation. It is, however, chest compressions, regarded by some as 'a desperate measure that involves somewhat brutal force to revive a non-pulsating heart',[6] that have become one of the more contentious aspects of CPR. Indeed, in the frail elderly CPR has been described as a 'violent and undignified' technique.[7] In critical, or intensive care, where the patient's prospects of survival may already be severely compromised, the possibility of causing injury through strenuous CPR will be a significant factor in deciding whether or not to attempt resuscitation.

Survival rates following CPR are always low, and it is claimed that only 15–20% of those resuscitated in hospital survive to be discharged, while out of hospital at best only 5–10% of cardiac arrest victims survive after attempted resuscitation.[8] Of course, everybody who dies suffers a cardiac arrest; it is the ultimate clinical sign of death. Sometimes therefore, cardiac arrest simply represents the natural end to life, particularly when associated with the end stages of terminal illness. Arguably, to subject a patient to an invasive and potentially harmful medical intervention such as CPR once that stage is reached would be contrary to their best interests. Quality of life after the procedure would almost inevitably be diminished and as such its imposition would offend the ethical principle of non-malfeasance, meaning that it would no longer be ethical, and probably not legal. But knowing this does not necessarily make the decision clear cut.

According to Mason and McCall-Smith, 'It is appropriate to consider making a DNR order when attempted CPR will almost certainly not restart the patient's heart, when there is no benefit in so doing or when the expected benefits are outweighed by the burdens.'[9] However, despite the apparent clarity of their statement, there remains a distinct imprecision in what they say. Certainly a patient faced with a choice of whether or not to accept CPR might, at a minimum be expected to question the meaning of 'almost certainly' before opting in or out. They might also be interested in how accurately the prospective benefits and burdens can be assessed in order to determine which was the most significant. For instance, is CPR expected to be of no benefit because it is unlikely to succeed in any event, or because the prognosis is very poor and successful resuscitation would simply prolong the dying process? Or, would it be that, because the patient is already frail, the burdens of painful and distressing potential side effects of CPR, such as severe bruising and fractured ribs or sternum, clearly outweigh any possible benefits. The difficulty in making a decision is not limited to the patient. The clinician also needs to be able to identify those individual patients in whom the benefits of CPR might be expected to outweigh the burdens and lead to a successful outcome that extends life without compromising its quality.

Clinically the potential burdens of providing CPR relate both to the nature of the intervention and the quality of life the patient will enjoy afterwards. A number of factors, including age, terminal illness, cancer, sepsis, pneumonia, and renal failure, among others, are known to have a detrimental influence on the outcome of CPR. As a consequence, CPR is usually regarded as inappropriate in patients with these conditions except in rare cases where the cardiac crisis results from a temporary and readily reversible cause such as choking or blocked tracheostomy tube.[10] Further, if the coronary failure is directly related to the disease process, then successful resuscitation will often achieve nothing more than simply prolonging the dying process. In these cases, where it is unlikely that performing CPR will enhance, or even maintain the patient's quality of life, it will not be regarded as in the patient's best interests and a DNR order will usually be appropriate. In other patients, the prognosis following CPR may be more optimistic and here the decision about whether and when it will be appropriate to resuscitate turns on a number of factors. Both medical ethics and law dictate that calculating a patient's best interests involves social and welfare concerns as well as the purely medical,[11] implying that quality of life measures are as important as quantity of life. Best interests is also central to the decision-making process because the doctor has a duty to treat the patient according to her best interests. Hence in end-of-life decision-making, a best interests analysis is pivotal to the determination of what treatment options to offer, including CPR.[12]

Related to this, it has long been the legal position, based on sound moral and ethical principles such as beneficence and non-malfeasance that there is no requirement to 'strive officiously' to keep a patient alive when to do so would be futile.[13] Furthermore, even the major religions have accepted that CPR represents extraordinary treatment that will not benefit every patient, thereby recognizing that quality of life may override sanctity of life in some cases.[14] Despite this, deciding not to treat based on an assessment of an individual's quality of life has always been controversial, especially where the patient is unable to decide for themselves:

> We do not believe that it would be appropriate for a court to designate a person with authority to determine that someone else's life is not worth living simply because, to that person, the patient's 'quality of life' or value to society seems negligible.[15]

Regardless of the contentious nature of these treatment withholding decisions however, the courts have confirmed that it is lawful to withhold CPR from a patient who lacks decision-making capacity where it would be contrary to their best interests.[16,17]

Ordinarily, unless there is a dispute between the patient or, if she is incapacitated, her representatives, and the doctor, a DNR decision is not one that needs to be taken by a court. Ideally it is a decision that should be taken as part of advance care planning for any patient to whom it may be relevant, which will include many of those receiving critical care. Because DNR it is not solely a clinical decision, involving as it does best interests and quality-of-life measures, patient autonomy requires that where possible the patient should be involved in the decision-making process.[18] It is here that extra-clinical factors, including the patient's own personal and subjective understanding of quality of life will undoubtedly influence her decision whether or not to agree to CPR. For instance, even if there appears to be a good chance that CPR will revive the patient, other factors, perhaps the perceived indignity of the process, or the effects on those close to her, may dictate that she regards resuscitation as undesirable and cause her to reject it. In this regard, as David Price explains, 'the threshold of burdensomeness will differ from one person to another'.[19] The nature of the treatment and the decision-making process also lends itself to the inevitability that some patients will lose their resolve and change their minds when faced with their mortality.[20,21]

Accepting that patients' views will vary according to their own preferences and experiences, those with the mental capacity to make a decision should be provided with sufficient information to enable them to exercise their autonomy. Where CPR is being proffered as a clinical option, this will satisfy ethical imperatives and allow the patient to give an informed and legally valid consent or refusal. Similarly, where a DNR order is proposed current guidance[22] insists that ordinarily the patient should be appraised of the decision and the reasons behind it. For various reasons, some patients may not be content to accept a DNR decision having 'specific reasons for wanting to try to delay death',[23] and this wish may persist even after full and frank discussion of the potential risks and benefits of CPR and the prospects of success. If in these circumstances no agreement can be reached, the clinician faces a real ethical dilemma: whether to disregard a potentially dying patient's wish or to provide a potentially harmful treatment against clinical judgement.

There is little English case law applying specifically to CPR decisions, but the courts have occasionally been called upon to adjudicate where doctors and patients, or their representatives, disagree about a clinical decision to withhold treatment. These cases draw heavily upon jurisprudence relating to medical decisions about patients who lack capacity to decide for themselves and therefore tend to turn on issues related to the assessment of the individual patient's best interests.[24] Perhaps most influential amongst these is *Burke*,[25] where the Court of Appeal determined conclusively that 'autonomy and the right to self determination do not entitle the patient to insist on receiving a particular medical treatment regardless of the nature of that treatment'.[26] Put simply, a doctor cannot be required to provide treatment, even resuscitation, against her clinical judgement[27] and, the patient has an absolute right to refuse any treatment offered, but not to demand treatment that the doctors believes is not clinically indicated.

Since the factors to be considered for each decision about CPR are complex, and may be specific to each patient, it is logical that they should be made on an individual basis. In the past however, great controversy has been generated by blanket policies applied to specific classes of patients, for example the elderly or those with dementia. Blanket policies clearly have discriminatory tendencies. It would therefore be unethical and almost certainly unlawful under the Human Rights Act 1998 for health care institutions to implement such a policy. In the case of older people, they would also contravene the National Service Framework for Older People.[28]

Discussion and communication therefore seem central to the decision-making process, and there is a great deal of evidence to suggest[29] that most patients welcome discussion, or at least some consultation, about CPR and its relevance to them[30,31] indicates that failure to discuss CPR with competent patients can in some cases lead others to make decisions that would actively be contrary to their wishes. Certainly, given that CPR is regarded as a treatment like any other, performing it without consent based on an elective decision taken when the patient would have been competent to consent or refuse could constitute a battery. Accordingly, there is a strong argument in favour of discussing the matter with the patient as part of their advance care planning, and prior to CPR becoming necessary. Arguments suggested by Manisty et al. among others, run counter to this however, suggesting that it may be detrimental, even psychologically harmful, to engage some patients in the decision-making process.[32] The debate about inviting patients to consider whether they would wish, and indeed are suitable, for CPR has spanned many years and disciplines. Several scholars have identified pitfalls associated with the practice[33,34] but on balance, although it requires excellent communication skills, the conclusion reached by Schade and Muslin that doctors have a duty 'to ascertain whether the patient wishes to enter into such a discussion'[35] and then to have the discussion, seems compelling.

DNR discussions are undoubtedly difficult to broach and the 2007 guidance published by the BMA and the Royal College of Nursing states that when it has been decided clinically that CPR should not be attempted 'it is not necessary or appropriate to initiate discussion with the patient' who has not expressed a wish to discuss the matter.[36] Failing to have the discussion with patients and their representatives may however raise concerns about communication and trust, and the recent past has witnessed accusatory headlines as a consequence.[37] Where an undisclosed DNR order is discovered while the patient's treatment is ongoing it would not be surprising if the resultant distress and mistrust led to disagreements between medical staff and patients and to possible legal action.

It is widely accepted that the public, and often members of the medical professions, 'have unrealistic expectations about the likely success and benefits of CPR.'[38] On the whole, these are represented by idealistic optimism fuelled by dramatizations and media depictions of successful outcomes as the expected norm, with miraculous recoveries being by no means atypical. This glamorization of CPR is largely responsible for instilling false perceptions about the potential benefits of CPR and its likelihood of success, together with real ignorance about what the physical process of resuscitation involves.[39] Consequently, a decision not to attempt resuscitation is often perceived as a harbinger of imminent death, particularly in the environment of the intensive care unit, and that reality may be difficult for patients and their loved ones to accept. As a result, these decisions are frequently contentious and can result in misunderstandings and loss of trust between doctor and patient. The ensuing confusion, anger, and grief can often give rise to challenges to the decision-making process, and sometimes to legal action. This has important implications for both medical ethics and law, and the remainder of this chapter will now focus on the potential legal liability that may flow from disagreements or misunderstandings about DNR decisions.

Potential liability for failure to administer CPR?

The imposition of a DNR order combined with subsequent failure to provide CPR resulting in death is perhaps the most obvious, or at least the most foreseeable, reason for a legal challenge to decision-making of this type, particularly if the existence of a DNR order was not known to patients and relatives. Whether or not such a challenge would succeed depends on a number of factors but is most likely to turn on whether, in the circumstances that arose, the clinician concerned was in breach of a legal obligation to provide such treatment to the specific patient. As has been explained above, the overriding legal duty of any doctor is to treat each patient according to their best interests. The determination of what constitutes the best interests of a specific patient depends upon their medical condition, the treatment proposed, and the views and wishes of the patient, if known. In the case of the non-competent patient, the medical, social, and welfare implications of providing, or not providing the treatment[40] and similar issues are likely to influence decisions made by a competent patient. Where a clinical assessment indicates that a particular intervention, such as CPR, would be contrary to the patient's best interests the doctor is not obliged to offer that treatment, even if the patient requests it. Specifically, where a treatment is regarded as futile or where any potential benefit is outweighed by the concomitant harms the principle of non-malfeasance dictates that it would be unethical to provide it and a clinician is under no obligation to do so.[41,42] That is settled law and ethically justifiable, but in relation to CPR, where the decision might seem to the lay person to turn on a choice between certain death and the promise of survival, discord is perhaps predictable.

Death resulting from a failure to resuscitate would be characterized as death by omission, that is to say, withholding treatment in this way represents a failure to act. In criminal law liability does not ordinarily attach to omissions, except where the defendant has a duty to act. Establishing that a clinician owes a duty of care to her patient is not difficult,[43] but since best interests is a central aspect of the duty to provide care, it may be less straightforward to demonstrate that the duty extended to administering resuscitation. The very poor success rates associated with CPR, combined with evidence about the harmful effects of the procedure, would seem to make it relatively easy to demonstrate that CPR would not be in a patient's best interests and therefore no duty to treat with CPR would be established. However, the anxiety associated with medical care at the end of life, coupled with the difficulty of communicating bad news, may mean that the information may just be too hard for the patient and their relatives to hear. People may simply not want to know that the prognosis is so poor that CPR would futile, or at least too burdensome, and that makes for an environment where misunderstandings and disputes are probably inevitable.

On casual inspection, the case of consultant anaesthetist Dr Ann David,[44,45] who was struck off the medical register in 2005 appears to epitomize many of these issues. The case revolved around concerns about decisions to both withhold and withdraw treatments from patients in the intensive care unit (ICU). Although it was not the main factor in the complaint made against her, it is Dr David's decision to withhold treatment, including CPR, that resonates with this discussion.

The police investigated the circumstances of the deaths of 40 patients in her care, but no criminal charges were brought. The family of one patient then complained to the General Medical Council (GMC) arguing that she had withdrawn and withheld care despite their objections. In finding her guilty of serious professional misconduct, the Professional Conduct Committee of the GMC held that she had removed the patient from the ventilator at a time when it was 'clinically unjustified' and would have accelerated his death. Dr David's conduct straddles the boundary between act and omission. Not only did she withhold care, (an omission), after initially withdrawing it (an action), she also gave the patient a large dose of sedatives, which would have hastened his death. This aspect of the case clearly distinguishes it from instances involving DNR decisions alone.

When clinical discretion dictates that CPR would not be in a patient's best interests and a DNR decision is taken, the treatment is subsequently withheld with the intention of minimizing the patient's suffering. In Dr David's case, not only did the administration of the sedative constitute a positive act, it appeared to have been performed with the intention of accelerating his death. This would be a crucial element in demonstrating criminal responsibility, and one that would be absent in bone fide DNR decisions. It would not in itself be sufficient to secure a conviction however, as it would also be necessary to show that the act of giving the sedative was a causal factor in the death. Presumably in this regard, the evidence was insufficient to clearly establish culpability, hence no charges were brought.

Providing that a DNR order is made on the basis of a sound clinical judgement that CPR would be contrary to the best interests of the patient, no liability will be incurred if the patient dies without resuscitation being attempted. That in itself does not avoid the upset and mistrust felt by patients and relatives who have not been permitted to participate in the decision-making process. Good communication is therefore essential to ensure that the pros and cons of CPR and the environment within which decisions are made are clearly understood. Where that happens, it is possible that the patient will agree with a DNR decision, or even request that CPR is not attempted, which should prevent misunderstandings, leading to action over failure to intervene. Communication is a two-way street however, and it is not inconceivable that the law may be called upon because a patient's rejection of CPR is not respected or even overridden.

Potential liability for administering CPR without consent(?) or against refusal

It would seem counterintuitive to argue that clinicians, whose primary professional imperative is to save life, should be held accountable for preserving the life of a patient. Likewise, one might expect that morally most of society would regard life as preferable to death. Further, conventional legal wisdom would suggest that the law would not construe continued life, or existence, resulting from cardiopulmonary resuscitation as a harm. Rather, being alive would usually be perceived as a beneficial outcome that would be unlikely to permit a patient to successfully sue for damages.[46] However, 'some people have a profound abhorrence of being kept alive in a state of total dependency or permanent lack of awareness, or of undignified death,'[47] which leads them to decide not to accept CPR if it is offered. Others may simply feel that when their 'time has come' they would prefer to experience death without the intrusion of invasive medical procedures. In these circumstances, the imposition of CPR could represent a grave violation of personal autonomy, and continued life, an outrage.

The competent patient who deliberately refuses life-saving treatment has an absolute right to do so[48] and may exercise this right for her own personal reasons, or indeed for no reason at all.[49] Contrary to prevailing morality therefore, she may well regard continued existence as detrimental to her well-being and suffer emotional and psychological harm as a consequence. Of course, such a patient would be at liberty to bring an action for battery in relation to the resuscitation or any other physical life-saving treatment administered against her wishes. This was indeed the route followed by Ms B[50] in what seems to be the only UK case to date to address this kind of issue. Ms B's life was being maintained by mechanical respiration following complications resulting from a cavernoma in her neck. Once it became clear that she was irreversibly paraplegic and could not survive without artificial ventilation, she withdrew her consent to the treatment and requested that the life support system be removed. The hospital declined to do so, arguing inter alia that she was not competent to make the decision. She challenged the hospital's failure to comply with her wishes and, having ascertained that she was competent to decide for herself, the court found in her favour. In the absence of consequential harm, she was awarded nominal damages of £100 for battery in respect of the violation of her physical integrity. The hospital was also required to respect her autonomous refusal of consent and withdraw the treatment.

There is then ample precedent that can be drawn upon to support a claim that harm has resulted from CPR performed unlawfully; that is, without the patient's consent. Various heads of claim could be brought to obtain compensation not just for any pain and suffering relative to the physical aspects of the treatment, but also for the affront to the patient's autonomy and the denial of their wishes.[51] But, what remedy might be available to the patient who argues that they have been wrongfully kept alive? Here the argument would not be simply that physical and emotional pain and suffering had resulted from the treatment, but also that the continued existence which the patient had sought to avoid amounted to a harm.

Damages in tort are designed to put the claimant in the position they would occupy had the tort not occurred, as far as money can do so. Clearly had the patient not been resuscitated they would be dead, and no amount of money can 'restore' them to that position. The alternative is to claim special damages, the quantum of which would be calculated according to the costs associated with their continued existence. In our publicly funded National Health Service system, the direct costs of medical care would probably not be available, but the patient might seek additional costs, such as ordinary living expenses and perhaps the costs of social care, which would have been avoided by death. In *Re T*[52] Butler-Sloss doubted that compensation of this type would be available, even though substantial damages were awarded in the Canadian case of *Malette v Shulman.* [53] Her position seems to be supported by authorities from the United States[54,55] where the courts appealed to social morality as the foundation of their refusal to recognize a prolonged life as harm capable of compensation. Consequently, the cases adjudicated to date suggest that any redress will be for the harm caused by the denial of autonomy in relation to the actual resuscitation, rather than any injury brought about by the fact that the patient is alive against their express wishes.[56] But for some patients, this denies the reality of the situation.

There seems little doubt that some individuals reach a point in their lives when they would genuinely rather not be alive any longer. This is evidenced by the numbers who access assisted dying in states where it is permissible, and those who are prepared to travel from the UK to the

Dignitas clinic in Switzerland for an assisted death.[57] These people represent a small but significant minority, and public opinion polls suggest that a large proportion of the population supports assisted dying in certain circumstances, at least in theory.[58,59] Assuming that they are properly informed and counselled therefore, it seems highly probable to suppose that people who refuse CPR do so out of strongly held convictions that they do not wish their life to be prolonged if they suffer a cardiac arrest. Having argued that ethics and law require that patients should be informed of the brutal truths about CPR and its chances of success before reaching a decision, surely that decision ought to be respected and the law should make amends if it is not. It is one thing to treat a patient in the absence of consent, but quite another to do so over their express refusal, especially in a life and death situation.

Public policy considerations probably dictate that compensation is not available for such claims[60] at least not under battery. Arguably however, the claim arises *prima facie* out of a disregard for the autonomy of the patient who has agreed a DNR order and effectively declined this treatment. It is, as Strasser argues, a claim born of the derogation of the right to physical integrity.[61] As such, it is difficult to see why the ordinary principles of tort law should not be applied to allow people whose valid refusal of life-saving treatment has been disregarded to succeed.[62] Failing to compensate in these situations leaves the patient with no remedy in circumstances where the clinician was in clear breach of a professional duty and 'a claimant ought not to be without a remedy, even if it involves some extension of existing principle' because otherwise that duty would 'in many cases be drained of its content'.[63]

Conclusions

It is a truism that death, like taxes, is inevitable. That said, it should come as no surprise that eventually a time will arise when no amount of medical intervention can save or prolong a person's life. Regardless of this, most of us do not seek death and are relieved that modern medicine holds out the promise of cure and recovery against all the odds. As a consequence, the public perception of intensive therapy often includes expectations of miraculous outcomes. Frequent optimistic fictional depictions in television and film fuel these expectations[64] so it is perhaps predictable that the issue of do not resuscitate orders sometimes causes controversy.

The concerns provoked by DNR orders are not only born of unrealistic expectations however. Fear of death is a deep-seated aspect of human life, such that in his seminal work of 1974. Ramsey[65] described the experience of dying as the 'ultimate indignity'. Imagine then the situation of a patient for whom initial resuscitation had proven successful but who must confront the realization that death would come again. Saunders describes this prospect as part of his vivid depiction of the physical insult of bodily invasion by tubes and monitors that frequently accompanies the post-resuscitation state,[66] exemplifying the moral and human dilemmas associated with CPR and DNR orders. Those faced with the immediacy of their own mortality, or that of a loved one, are then rightly fearful.

Law and medical ethics ordinarily require that legitimate consent is obtained prior to the imposition of medical treatment. And, although intuitively different, especially in the public consciousness, CPR is the same as any other therapy. In the case of a DNR order however, where the clinician has designated CPR as not clinically indicated, no treatment is to be provided and so technically there is no therapy for which consent or refusal can be obtained. It is arguable therefore that the patient need not be involved in the decision-making process if a DNR order is to be made. But in this respect CPR is not a treatment like any other. It is regarded as making the difference between living and dying and accordingly 'failure to discuss end-of-life decisions with competent patients is under most ... circumstances, a form of crass paternalism'[67] and such a position cannot be regarded as ethical.

Given this, it would seem crucial that CPR is only performed in appropriate circumstances and when the patient has a proper appreciation of the procedure and the implications associated with success or failure. But the forgoing discussion suggests that this is not the case. The recent guidance published by the BMA/RCN (2007)[68] locates communication and the provision of information about CPR as one of its main messages, except where there is no expectation that the patient will suffer a cardiac arrest.[69] It insists that CPR decisions should form part of advance care planning and that the patient should be involved in the decision-making process. Yet this is difficult to reconcile with the statement that 'where the patient has not expressed a wish to discuss CPR, it is not necessary to initiate discussion with the patient or explore their wishes'.[70] Combined with the general presumption promoted by the guidance that CPR will be attempted where no decision has been made or there is no DNR in place, this seems to take no account of the desires of those who would opt not to be resuscitated had they been asked. It also perhaps even encourages avoidance of discussion. The central premise here seems to be that a decision about CPR only needs to be discussed with the patient if there is some hope of success, and only then if the patient expresses a desire to discuss it. Given the evidence that patients generally welcome participation in the decision-making process, such a stance can surely only lead to mistrust and anger.

References

1 Resuscitation Council UK (2004). *Advanced Life Support Course: Provider Manual*, 4th ed. Resuscitation Council UK & European Resuscitation Council, London.

2 Kouwenhoven WB, Jude JR, Knickerbocker GG (1960). Closed chest cardiac massage. *J Am Med Soc*, **173:** 1064–1067

3 Weisfeldt LM, Ornato JP (2008). Closed-chest cardiac massage: progress measured by the exceptions. *JAMA*, **300**(13): 1582–1584 at 1582

4 KftS-Ksg Nagao (2007). Cardiopulmonary resuscitation by bystanders with chest compression only (SOS-KANTO): an observational study. *The Lancet*, **369**: 920–926.

5 Koster RW, Bossaert LL, Nolan JP, Zideman D on behalf of European Resuscitation Council (31 March 2008). Advisory statement of the European Resuscitation Council on basic life support. European Resuscitation Council. Available at: www.erc.edu (accessed 4 January 2009)

6 Gelbman BD, Gelbman JM (2008). Deconstructing DNR. *J Med Ethics*, **34:** 640–641 at 641.

7 Wilson J (2008). To what extent should older patients be included in decisions regarding their resuscitation status? *J Med Ethics*, **34:** 353–356 at 354.

8 British Medical Association, Royal College of Nursing & Resuscitation Council (UK) (2007). *Decisions relating to cardiopulmonary resuscitation*. BMA, London

9 Mason JK, Laurie G (2006). *Mason & McCall-Smith's Law and Medical Ethics*, 7th ed. Oxford University Press, Oxford, p. 636.

10 British Medical Association, Royal College of Nursing & Resuscitation Council (UK) (2007). *Decisions Relating To Cardiopulmonary Resuscitation*. BMA, London, p. 8.

11 *Re A (Male Sterilisation)* [2000] 1 FLR 549, at 556.

12 See for example the Mental Capacity Act 2005, s. 4.

13 Bayliss R (1982). Thou shalt not strive officiously. *BMJ* **285**: 1373–1375.

14 Pius XII, the prolongation of life, *The Pope Speaks* 4 1958, as cited by Saunders J (1996). Medical Futility: CPR in Lee R, Morgan D (1996). *Death Rites: Law and Ethics at the End of Life*. Routledge, London, p. 76.

15 *Re Clare Conroy* 486 A 2d 1209 (NJ. 1985).

16 British Medical Association, Royal College of Nursing & Resuscitation Council (UK) (2007). *Decisions Relating to Cardiopulmonary Resuscitation*. BMA, London, p. 10.

17 *Re R (Adult: Medical Treatment)* [1996] 2 FLR 99.

18 British Medical Association, Royal College of Nursing & Resuscitation Council (UK) (2007). *Decisions Relating to Cardiopulmonary Resuscitation*. BMA, London at 10.

19 Price D (2009). What shape euthanasia after Bland? Historical, contemporary and futuristic paradigms. *Law Quarterly Review* 142–174 at 152.

20 Wilson J (2008). To what extent should older patients be included in decisions regarding their resuscitation status?. *Journal of Medical Ethics* **34**: 353–356.

21 Morgan D (1994). Odysseus and the binding directive: only a cautionary tale. *Legal Studies* **14** (3): 411–442.

22 British Medical Association, Royal College of Nursing & Resuscitation Council (UK) (2007). *Decisions Relating to Cardiopulmonary Resuscitation*. BMA, London.

23 British Medical Association, Royal College of Nursing & Resuscitation Council (UK) (2007). *Decisions Relating to Cardiopulmonary Resuscitation*. BMA, London at 10.

24 *Re R (Adult: Medical Treatment)* [1996] 2 FLR 99.

25 *Burke v General Medical Council* [2005] EWCA Civ 1003.

26 *Burke v General Medical Council* [2005] EWCA Civ 1003 at para 31.

27 *Re J (A Minor) (Wardship: Medical Treatment)* [1993] 3 All ER 930

28 Department of Health (2001). *National Service Framework for Older People*. DoH, London.

29 Mason JK, Laurie G (2006). *Mason & McCall-Smith's Law and Medical Ethics*, 7th ed. Oxford University Press, Oxford, p. 637.

30 Hill ME, MacQuillan G, Forsyth M, Heath DA (1994). Cardiopulmonary resuscitation: Who makes the decision? *BMJ* **308**: 1677.

31 Morgan R, King D, Prajapati C, Rowe J (1994). Views of elderly patients and their relatives on cardiopulmonary resuscitation. *BMJ* **308**: 1677–1678.

32 Manisty C, Waxman J (2003). Doctors should not discuss resuscitation with terminally ill patients. *BMJ* **327**: 614–615.

33 Schade SG, Muslin H (1989). Do not resuscitate decisions: discussions with patients. *J Med Ethics* 15: 186–189; Gillon R (1989). *J Med Ethics* 15: 171–172.

34 Loewy EH (1991). Involving patients in do not resuscitate (DNR) decisions: an old issue raising its ugly head. *J Med Ethics* 17: 156–160.

35 Schade SG, Muslin H (1989). Do not resuscitate decisions: discussions with patients. *J Med Ethics* 15: 186–189 at 188.

36 British Medical Association, Royal College of Nursing & Resuscitation Council (UK) (2007). *Decisions Relating to Cardiopulmonary Resuscitation*. BMA, London, p. 9.

37 Hull L (25th March 2008). Family's fury as they discover 'do not resuscitate' order in mother's file after she dies. *The Daily Mail* Available at: http://www.dailymail. co.uk/news/article-543374/Family's-fury-discover-resuscitate-order-mothers-file-dies.html (accessed 25 January 2009)

38 British Medical Association, Royal College of Nursing & Resuscitation Council (UK) (2007). *Decisions Relating to Cardiopulmonary Resuscitation*. BMA, London, p. 10, s.7.

39 Diem S, Lantos JD, Tulsky JA (1996). Cardiopulmonary resuscitation on television: miracles and misinformation. *N Engl J Med* 334(24): 1578–1582.

40 *Re SL (Adult Patient) (Medical Treatment)* [2002] 2 FCR 452, and Mental Capacity Act 2004.

41 *R (Burke) v General Medical Council* [2005] EWCA Civ 1003.

42 *Re J (A Minor) (Wardship: Medical Treatment)* [1990] 3 All 930

43 *R v Cheshire* [1991] 3 All ER 670

44 The facts are rehearsed in *Dr Ann David v The General Medical Council* [2004] EWHC 2977 (Admin).

45 BBC News (16 November 2005). Hospital doctor struck off by GMC. Available at: http://news.bbc.co.uk/1/hi/England/essex/4443354.stm (accessed 25 January 2009).

46 *McFarlane v Tayside Health Board* [2000] 2 AC 59 HL.

47 British Medical Association, Royal College of Nursing & Resuscitation Council (UK) (2007). *Decisions Relating to Cardiopulmonary Resuscitation*. BMA, London, p. 10.

48 *Re T (Adult) (Refusal of Medical Treatment)* [1992] 4 All ER 649.

49 *Re MB* [1997] 2 FLR 426.

50 *Ms B v An NHS Trust* [2002] EWHC 429.

51 Michalowski S (2007). Trial and error at the end of life: no harm done? *Oxford Journal of Legal Studies* 27(2): 257–280.

52 *Re T (Adult: Refusal of Treatment)* [1993] Fam 95 CA at 117.

53 (1990) 67 DLR (4th) 321.

54 *Anderson v St Francis-St George Hospital, inc.,* 671NE 2d 225 (Ohio 1996).

55 *Allore v Flower Hospital* 699 NE 2d 560 (Ohio App6th Dist. 1997).

56 Michalowski S (2007). Trial and error at the end of life: no harm done? *Oxford Journal of Legal Studies* **27**(2): 257–280 at 268.

57 Gibb F (2 October 2008). Swiss clinic Dignitas has helped 100 Britons to die: Dignitas reveals total as test case begins. *The Times* Available at: http://business. timesonline.co.uk/tol/business/law/article4863771.ece (accessed 19 January 2009).

58 BBC News (9 September 2004). Half would help loved ones die. Available at: http://ves.c.topica.com/maacDiZaa9QNpb23Jjvb/ (accessed 30 January 2009).

59 Telegraph.co.uk (9 September 2004). Many Britons would assist suicide. *The Telegraph*. Available at: http://www.telegraph.co.uk/news/1471357/Many-Britons-would-assist-suicide.html (accessed 30 January 2009).

60 *McFarlane v Tayside Health Board* [1999] 4 All ER 961 HL.

61 Strasser M (1999). A jurisprudence in disarray: on battery, wrongful living and the right to bodily integrity. *San Diego Law Review* 997–1041.

62 Knapp W, Hamilton F (1992). 'Wrongful living': resuscitation as tortuous interference with a patient's right to give informed refusal' *Northern Kentucky Law Review*. 253–227

63 *Chester v Afshar* [2004] UKHL 41.

64 Birtwistle J, Nielsen A (1998). Do not resuscitate: an ethical dilemma for the decision-maker *British Journal of Nursing*. **7**(9): 543–549, at 543 plus refs used previously.

65 Ramsey P (1974). The indignity of "death with dignity". *Hastings Centre Studies* **2**: 47–62.

66 Saunders J (1996). Medical Futility: CPR in Lee R, Morgan D (1996). *Death Rites: Law and Ethics at the End of Life*. Routledge, London at 77.

67 Loewy EH (1991). Involving patients in do not resuscitate (DNR) decisions: an old issue raising its ugly head. *Journal Medical Ethics* **17**: 156–160.

68 British Medical Association, Royal College of Nursing & Resuscitation Council (UK) (2007). *Decisions Relating to Cardiopulmonary Resuscitation*. BMA, London, p. 3.

69 British Medical Association, Royal College of Nursing & Resuscitation Council (UK) (2007). *Decisions Relating to Cardiopulmonary Resuscitation*. BMA, London, p. 3.

70 British Medical Association, Royal College of Nursing & Resuscitation Council (UK) (2007). *Decisions Relating to Cardiopulmonary Resuscitation*. BMA, London, p. 9, para 6.1.

Chapter 6

Diagnosing death

Andrew Lawson

Death is nothing to us, since when we are, death has not come, and when death has come, we are not.[1]

Poor Smith! One can't help feeling sorrow for him. First he loses his job; then his wife leaves him and now, to top it all off, he's dead.[2]

Introduction

If the diagnosis of death was without dissent, a chapter on diagnosing death would be superfluous. The problem of the significance of death has troubled the ancients and more recent philosophers as exemplified by the quotations above. Notwithstanding the vexed question as to whether the dead person suffers by being dead, it is clear that relatives and others may be deeply affected by the death of a loved one. What is perhaps of greater contemporary significance is the modern nature of death. In the era of organ transplantation, death has attained a new cultural and ethical significance, as a diagnosis of death may facilitate the removal of organs. Until mechanical ventilation was introduced in the 1950s, there was little to separate the concepts of neurological and cardiovascular death. Cessation of brain function was swiftly followed by cardiac failure or if the heart failed, the consequent circulatory failure led to anoxic brain death. As technology has become available to maintain respiratory and cardiovascular function, social policy and ethical considerations have become as central as biology in determining when death occurs.

Death

There are many definitions of death. To expire is to literally breathe out the last breath (in Latin, *exspirare*). In Yiddish, we find the term

Oyshoykhn di neshome, the breathing out of the soul, and for hundreds of years mirrors have been used to determine the lack of breathing and so determine death. In more primitive cultures such as in the Pidgin English of the Solomon Islanders, we find a way of characterizing the varying states of consciousness leading up to death.

Himi die lilbit (Fainting)
Himi die toomas (Unconscious)
Himi die finis (Dead)

The Solomon Islanders neatly encapsulate an intuitive approach to death; he is finished when he is dead, and on the way to dying there is a change in consciousness. Implicit in this is the idea that the loss of consciousness is part of what we call death. However, the simple act of not being conscious cannot of itself be sufficient to determine death, otherwise sleep or being anaesthetized would involve dying. Aside from religious concerns, which will be alluded to in this chapter, it seems that there must be something about consciousness or lack of it that is relevant to death.

There is no specific legal definition of death in the United Kingdom; in law, the opinion of a registered medical practitioner with suitable experience is sufficient. Recent guidelines from the Academy of Medical Royal Colleges have stated that in the absence of obvious signs (rigor mortis, hypostasis, decapitation, etc.) death occurs when there has been simultaneous and irreversible onset of apnoea and unconsciousness in the absence of circulation.[3] In most states in the United States, the Uniform Determination of Death Act has been adopted. According to this law, an individual who has sustained either irreversible cessation of circulatory and respiratory functions or the irreversible cessation of all functions of the entire brain, including the brain stem, is dead. That determination must also take place in accordance with accepted medical standards. The declaration that a patient is brain dead has become equated legally to the actual death of the patient by U.S. state legislatures and has been upheld by the courts.

Cardiovascular death or death following on from irreversible cessation of circulation seems unproblematic. Without circulation one dies and apnoea follows swiftly from cardiovascular cessation. However, the problems of diagnosing death in the Intensive Care Unit stem from the usage of brain death criteria in apparently 'living patients' and also from the consequences of the diagnosis of brain death—organ retrieval and withdrawal of 'treatment'. In the latter, there are issues of linguistic dissonance, as one cannot 'treat' a dead person.

This confusion over what it means to be dead was exemplified in a legal ruling over 30 years ago in Florida when a judge ruled on 3 December 1976 that 'this lady is dead and has been dead since November 21st 1976 and is being kept alive artificially …' The case produced much interest and produced an article in the *Journal of Legal Medicine* entitled '"Dead" woman allowed to die.'[4]

Defining death

Lamb described three criteria for a definition of death.[5] It must be irreversible, selective, and universal. In the absence of any kind of divine intervention there must be an irreversible physical change in the status of the patient. It must be selective in that as death is a process leading to the destruction of every cell of the body, there is a point at which there is a loss of the integrated function of the whole body before universal cell death when death can be said to have occurred. The definition of death must also be universal, that is, the criteria for death must be unambiguous and repeatable. The Academy of the Medical Royal Colleges code of practice for the diagnosis and confirmation of death states that death 'entails the irreversible loss of those essential characteristics which are necessary to the existence of a living human person and, thus, the definition of death should be regarded as the irreversible loss of the capacity for consciousness combined with the irreversible loss of the capacity to breathe'.

Broadly speaking, the essential characteristics that determine the existence of a living person are firstly the functioning of the higher centres of the brain, the loss of which has been described as the death of the person. This death of the 'person' or loss of personhood occurs when damage from any cause produces the loss of mental function in the higher centres. There is no ability to speak, think, interact, or observe. On its own, it cannot suffice to describe death as individuals with a persistent vegetative state (PVS) or anencephalic babies would be diagnosed as 'dead'. The loss of 'personhood' has, however, been described as a relevant criterion for whether an individual should be allowed to die. Higher function may be assessed clinically and also by EEG and functional brain imaging.

Secondly, we need the integrative function of brain stem both to allow us to breathe spontaneously but also to be conscious. The ascending reticular activating system (ARAS) in the upper brain stem is a prerequisite for consciousness. Brain stem tests can be used to determine the loss of function. The loss of brain stem function leads to cessation of circulatory activity in a variable period of time in the absence of any cardiovascular support. This validity of brain stem tests has been confirmed in published series.

Brain death in intensive care

Why is it important for us to be able to adequately diagnose death in the intensive care unit and to have a morally cogent terminology? If we diagnose a patient as being dead we may then, subject to sociological mores, consent and pre-mortem requests treat that person as being dead. Artificial ventilation and other supportive measures may be withdrawn without the patient being illegally killed, and we may remove organs for transplantation.

It is not ethically or legally problematic for the intensive care physician, nor conceptually difficult for most relatives, to diagnose or understand the concept of the cessation of cardiovascular function. If cardiovascular function ceases, then by definition, brain death and brain stem death follows as a result of hypoxia. The patient is dead and looks dead to all concerned. Where there seem to be conceptual and ethical difficulties, and potential for conflict with relatives, is where the patient has been diagnosed as 'brain dead', as the sociologist Professor Kellehear put it in 2007:

> Corpses are not warm, they are not pink, they do not move, they are not pregnant—but a person who is brain dead can be all of these things.[6]

Traug and Robinson[7] considered the issue of brain death by comparing the features of being alive, being brain dead, and being cardiovascularly dead using a number of criteria. What distinguishes brain death from being alive is the 'capacity for consciousness'. Patients who are brain dead share more features with 'living patients' than they do with those who are cardiovascularly dead, a feature captured by Professor Kellehear above. While brain dead patients are ventilated and have no capacity for self-ventilation, this distinction does not make them any less alive as relying on artificial ventilation does not equate to death. There are many quadriplegics who are ventilator-dependant.

On its own this loss of capacity for consciousness cannot be a definition of death, even though there has never been a case of a brain dead patient recovering consciousness. Currently it is accepted (notwithstanding any religious concepts of the soul) that this consciousness is based in the higher centres of the brain as mentioned previously. While a functioning ARAS is a prerequisite for consciousness, there are beings with no or extensively destroyed neocortex such as anencephalic babies and people in a PVS who do have a functioning brain stem. A usage of a definition of pure loss of capacity for consciousness would then make anencepahalics and people in a PVS 'dead', and we might then morally be obliged to treat them as dead, for example, by burying or cremating them. Veatch[8] has sought a way out of this problem by proposing that a solution lies in making a moral decision about whether a person may be treated 'as if they are dead' rather than trying to decide if they are 'really dead'. However, this solution does not remove the problem of there being two classes of dead people, those who are clearly biologically dead and those who are 'brain dead'; or the problematic prospect of organs being removed from spontaneously breathing patients being fed by a NG tube because they are 'morally' dead!

As mentioned, the criteria for diagnosing death have been recently published by the Academy of the Medical Royal Colleges. Tables 6.1 and 6.2 summarize the criteria and brain stem tests, respectively.

Table 6.1 Criteria for diagnosis of death

Basic criteria under which death may be diagnosed and confirmed
• Condition due to known aetiology of irreversible brain damage
• Reversible causes of coma must be excluded
• No evidence of depressant drugs
• Primary hypothermia must be excluded: temperature > 34°C
• Exclusion of reversible circulatory, metabolic and endocrine disturbances
• Exclusion of reversible causes of apnoea
• Absence of brain stem reflexes

Table 6.2 Brain stem death tests

Brain stem reflex testing
No pupillary response to light
No corneal reflex
No vestibulo-ocular reflex (caloric test)
Doll's eye reflex
No motor response to pain in Vth nerve distribution
No gag reflex in response to suction through endotracheal tube (ETT) or tracheostomy
Apnoea despite $PaCO_2$ > 50 mmHg (6.6 kPa) with normal PaO_2

Religion and ITU death

Judaism

There is no agreement within the Jewish community, or even among orthodox Jews, about the appropriate medical definition of death. The Jewish concept of death varies depending upon an orthodox or a reform perspective. Lord Jakobovits, former chief rabbi of the United Kingdom and expert on Jewish medical ethics, has stated that '[S]o long as the heart still functions and the blood circulates, death has not yet set in'. This is the majority view in the orthodox tradition: that death has occurred only when there is neither breathing nor beating of the heart. A ventilated patient with a diagnosis of brain death may well have good cardiac function to an orthodox Jew, therefore, such a patient would not be 'dead'.

In the Mishnah (the first part of the Jewish Talmud; a collection of early oral interpretations of the scriptures that was compiled about

AD 200) physical decapitation of an animal is said to be a conclusive indicator of death. Subsequent movements, provided that they are *pirchus be'alma*, or like the 'severed tail of a lizard that twitches spasmodically', do not signify life. Some Jews, who accept brain stem death as a valid determinant of death within the Jewish tradition, argue that it is physiologically equivalent to decapitation; that destruction of the brain stem means inability to breathe and that any movement of the heart as it beats falls into the category of 'pirchus'.

Islam

Traditionally, Muslim jurists regarded the complete cessation of heartbeat as signifying death. Along with other faiths, modern medical technology has thrown up challenges to this traditional view. In 1986, the Council of Islamic Jurisprudence (majma` al-fiqh al-islami) looked at the problem of the patient in intensive care, and the issue of brain death. Its deliberations concluded that the person is considered legally dead, and all the guidelines provided by the Shari`a to determine death are applicable when following signs are confirmed:

1 When complete cessation of the heart or respiration occurs, and the expert physicians ascertain that the cessation is irreversible.

2 When complete cessation of all functions of the brain occurs, and the expert physicians ascertain that the cessation is irreversible and the brain is in the state of degeneration. In this condition it is permissible to discontinue the life supportive system from the patient even when some of the patient's organs are kept functional by artificial means.

Christianity

To a Christian, death has always been the separation of the soul from the body. The Catholic Church looks to the medical community to determine the biological signs that indicate with moral certainty that death has occurred. It is accepted in the Western medical tradition that irreversible loss of brain function provides a firm indicator of death, thus the use of neurological criteria for the determination of death is legitimate according to the Catholic Church. Pope John Paul II approved this approach in an address he gave to the 18th International Conference of Organ Transplant Specialists in August 2000. Pope Pius XII and Pope John Paul II both said the Church has no competency in determining death; this properly belongs to medical science.

Buddhism

Buddhist religious law, such as exists, imposes no special requirements or limitations on medical practice. Death is thought to occur when the body is bereft of three things: vitality, heat, and sentience. A difficulty for Buddhists comes because of the putative existence of yogic trances when no vital signs can be discerned, a state into which the Buddha himself is believed to have entered when he died. There is disagreement amongst Buddhists as to when death may be diagnosed; some may accept brain death as being approximate to the state of death of the Buddha.

Hinduism

In 1993, a bill was passed by the Indian legislature allowing brain death criteria for the determination of death. It has been estimated that brain death occurs in up to 60,000 patients per year in India.[9] The importance of the brain in Hinduism can be seen in the narratives of the Hindu physician of the gods, Dhanwantari: 'During the great war of the gods, Rudra severed the head of Yadnya. The gods then approached the famous celestial twin surgeons, Aswinikumaras. They successfully united Yadnya's head to his trunk restoring him to life'.[10] The restoration of life coming from the reconnection of the head to the body.

Summary

The diagnosis of death may be straightforward or subject to multiple complicating factors from social mores, religious imperatives, and neurophysiologic variability. The major conflict in the diagnosis of death in ITU seems to have emanated from the problems of consequent organ retrieval and withdrawal of supportive, but not life-saving or -sustaining, therapy. It is always going to be problematical to describe a warm, pink 'person' with a beating heart as dead. Hopefully advances in genetic technology will lead to the development of organs for transplantation in vitro, leading to the consignment of many of the ethical problems of transplantation to history.

References

1 Letter to Menoceus (1977). *Epicurus in Classics in Western Philosophy*, Hackett Pub Co, Indianapolis, pp. 215–217.

2 Mothersill, M (1971). Death (Chapter 10), in Rachels J (Ed.), *Moral Problems*. Harper Collins College, New York.

3 A code of practice for the diagnosis and confirmation of death. Academy of Medical Royal Colleges (October 2008).

4 Fatteh A (1977). Dead woman allowed to die: a unique case in Florida. *J Leg Med (NY)* 5(1): 24.

5 Lamb D (1994). What is death? in Gillon R (Ed.). *Principles of Health Care Ethics*, John Wiley & Sons, Chichester, UK.

6 BBC News: http://news.bbc.co.uk/1/hi/6987079.stm. Accessed 12 September 2007.

7 Truog R, Robinson M (2003). Role of brain death and the dead donor rule in the ethics of organ transplantation. *Critical Care Medicine* 31: 2391–2396.

8 Veatch RM (2003). The dead donor rule: true by definition. *Am J Bioethics* 3: 10–11.

9 *The Hindu*, Thursday, July 25, 2002.

10 Sushrut Samhita, Sl/17.

Chapter 7

Ethics and law in critical care: Research in intensive care

Thomas E Woodcock

History

Commitment to the advancement of medical knowledge by research can be found in the seventeenth century; An 'Invisible College' was meeting at Gresham College, London, as early as 1645, and an 'Experimental Philosophy Club' at Wadham College, Oxford in 1649. Under the patronage of King Charles II, 12 men decided to found a 'College for the Promoting of Physico-Mathematicall Experimental Learning', in London in 1660 and among the topics of interest to this group were William Harvey's observations on the circulation of blood and Robert Boyle's description of respiration.[1] This group went on to become the Royal Society. Research on humans had been substantially restricted to post-mortem examination of convicted felons, as demonstrated by the remarkable story of Anne Green. Hanged by the neck at Oxford's Cattle Yard in 1650, her cadaver was taken to the rooms of William Petty for dissection. On discovering signs of life, Petty and Thomas Willis directed and meticulously recorded her resuscitation by the physicians gathered there[2]; described in a pamphlet of the time by an anonymous 'Scholler in Oxford' entitled *Newes from the Dead or A True and Exact Narration of the miraculous dekiverance of Anne Green*, this is one of the earliest critical care case reports of the scientific age. Philosophers of the Enlightenment did not specifically address the ethical challenges of research on humans, but in 1797 Immanuel Kant gave us a glimpse into the reason why convicts were preferred subjects. He reasoned that every human being 'at least has the dignity of a citizen. The exception is someone who has lost it by his own crime, because of which, though he is kept alive, he is made a mere tool of another's choice.' (AK 6:330). In justifying the importance of capital punishment in a civilized society, he goes on to argue 'What, therefore, should one think of the proposal to preserve the life of a criminal sentenced to death if he agrees to let dangerous experiments be made upon him and is lucky enough to survive them, so that in this way physicians learn something new of benefit to the commonwealth?' (AK 6:332). In 1724 Emmanual Timoni described the Turkish practice of vaccination against smallpox in a communication to the Royal Society. In 1796 Edward Jenner set about a systematic investigation into the theories and reports of vaccination, and was praised by the King of England and the President of the United States for his work, which involved exposing subjects to the risk of contracting disease.[3] Unfortunately, the outcome from research is not always positive. Following a national scandal over a trial of vaccination against syphilis, which went horribly wrong, a Prussian minister issued a directive in 1900 on the conduct of medical research, which includes many of the standards of practice now expected.[4] In Germany, there were active concerns for the rights of subjects in medical research in the early part of the twentieth century,[5,6] but the Kantian distinction between citizens and prisoners was applied by medical researchers of the Third Reich. The Nuremberg doctors trial established the need for guidelines on ethical research in 1946,[7] but there were some notable apologists for these war crimes in Britain even after the war.[8] The World Medical Association adopted The Declaration of Helsinki in Finland in 1964. Physicians were to obtain consent from research subjects (or proxy consent) 'if at all possible'. In the light of the declaration, contemporary examples of unconsented research were sought and soon found. In the United Kingdom, Maurice Pappworth exposed some practices in a 1966 magazine article and his book *Human Guinea Pigs: Experimentation on Man* in 1967.[6] He called for formal regulation of research with lay representation and clear accountability. In response, the Royal College of Physicians issued a report and the Minister of Health requested health authorities to establish Research Ethics

Committees in 1968. Sheila Sherlock at the Royal Free Hospital was one of the researchers named and shamed by Pappworth and it was said that 'she never forgave Maurice'.[9]

In the United States, Harvard anaesthesiologist Henry Beecher studied the research methods of the Nazis and was initially opposed to the application of the Nuremberg Code.[10] He himself carried out unconsented studies on the effects of LSD (Lysergic acid diethylamide) and advised the CIA on interrogation techniques,[11] yet in the 1960s he campaigned tirelessly against research without consent, eventually bringing the issue to national attention with his 1966 landmark paper on 'Ethics and Clinical Research'.[12] The Center for Disease Control nevertheless continued with the Tuskegee Study of Untreated Syphilis in the Negro Male until a national newspaper expose in 1972. Senator Ted Kennedy led Congressional hearings and the National Commission for the Protection of Subjects of Biomedical and Behavioural Research was formed as Title II of the National Research Act. The Belmont Report on the ethical principles to be applied in research was published in 1979, and can even now be accessed from the current home page of the Office for Human Research Protections at the U.S. Department of Health and Human Services. Federal regulations were made and Institutional Review Boards were mandated. At a White House ceremony in 1997, President Bill Clinton on behalf of the American people formally apologized to Tuskegee Study participants.[13-15]

In the United Kingdom, the Department of Health issued its first national guidance on Research Ethics Committees in 1991. Following David Southall's publication in 1998 of a randomized controlled trial of ventilation techniques for newborns with respiratory distress, an action group of parents alleged research misconduct and the government commissioned an Inquiry led by Rod Griffiths.[16] Published in 2000, the report was critical of Southall and his colleagues and prompted the Department of Health to publish its first Research Governance Framework document in 2001 (revised 2005).[17] The Griffiths Report in turn was heavily criticized. It is now claimed that Professor Southall has been exonerated of the allegations against him concerning that study.[18]

European legislation (Directive 2001/20/EC) obliged the Government to put in place the Medicines for Human Use (Clinical Trials) Regulations 2004.[19] At first neither of these instruments allowed for unconsented research even for emergency treatment.[20] An amendment in 2006 addressed this problem for England and Wales.[21] Directive 2005/28/EC provides detailed guidelines on Good Clinical Practice and will be integrated into UK law.[22] Good Clinical Practice is the standard provided by the tripartite (United States, EU, and Japan) International Conference on Harmonisation. The European Union only recognizes the fourth revision of the Declaration of Helsinki (1996), ignoring the controversial fifth revision of 2000.[23] The EC Directives and UK Statutory Instruments only apply in law to 'clinical trials of investigational medicinal products' (CTIMPs), but they form the basis of all research policies and are therefore enforceable by the requirements of the researcher's employer or professional body. They include regulations about the process of independent ethical review of any research proposal and the monitoring of adverse events. The General Medical Council issue specific guidance on Research[24] and their Indicative Sanctions Guidance April 2005 states

> Research misconduct…undermines the trust that both the public and the profession have in medicine as a science, regardless of whether this leads to direct harm to patients. Because it has the potential to have far reaching consequences, this type of dishonesty is particularly serious.

The Bristol Royal Infirmary Inquiry (Professor Sir Ian Kennedy) and the Royal Liverpool Children's Inquiry (Michael Redfern QC) published critical Reports in 2000 and 2001 and inspired Parliament to deliver the Human Tissue Act 2004.[25] Most recently, the disastrous experiments at Northwick Park Hospital with a monoclonal antibody called TGN1412, which caused cytokine release syndrome and critical illness in six volunteers, have led to new advice on the management of Phase 1 trials.[26]

Classification

Medical research comes in many shapes and sizes, with differing legal and ethical issues attached. Authorities have sought to classify research activities in various ways. The Medical Research Council uses the Declaration of Helsinki's distinction between 'clinical' and 'non-clinical' research. The former is defined as medical research combined with professional care, in which the research is directed at the disease afflicting the subject patient, who must be assured of receiving the best proven diagnostic and therapeutic methods, which can include placebo where no proven better method exists. The latter is defined as non-therapeutic biomedical research conducted on volunteers who are healthy persons, or patients for whom the experimental design is unrelated to the patient's illness.[27] Dr Robert Levine's evidence to the President's Commission on Bioethics explains the illogicality of this distinction.[28]

The European Medicines Agency defines clinical trial or study as follows:

> Any investigation in human subjects intended to discover or verify the clinical, pharmacological and/or other pharmacodynamic effects of an investigational product(s), and/or to identify any adverse reactions to an investigational product(s), and/or to study absorption, distribution, metabolism, and excretion of an investigational product(s) with the object of ascertaining its safety and/or efficacy. The terms clinical trial and clinical study are synonymous. (CPMP/ICH/135/95 2002 1.12)[29]

It then subclassifies clinical research into therapeutic or non-therapeutic on the criterion of 'anticipated direct clinical benefit to the subject' (CPMP/ICH/135/95 2002 4.8.13).[29] It is the European Medicines Agency's Note for guidance on good clinical practice which underpins UK legislation, and also the Australian National Statement.[30] The most recent European Directive 2005/28/EC on the ethical principles of research makes no therapeutic/non-therapeutic distinction.

Case Study: *Halushka v. University of Saskatchewan* (1965) 52 WWR 608 (Sask CA)

Drs Wyant and Merriman were experienced researchers at the University of Saskatchewan. In 1961 they were recruiting volunteers for $50 each to undergo general anaesthesia with direct pulmonary artery pressure monitoring, and their subject one day was Walter Halushka, a 21-year-old student who had been referred by the university's employment office. Walter signed a brief consent form, which included the clause 'I do release the chief investigators... from all responsibility and claims whatsoever, for any untoward effect or accidents due to or arising out of said tests, either directly or indirectly.' The anaesthetic used on Walter was trifluoroethylvinyl ether, and a catheter was passed from Walter's antecubital fossa to his pulmonary artery without apparent difficulty. However, Walter suffered a sudden cardiac arrest under anaesthesia, and the doctors took immediate steps to open the left side of his chest for internal cardiac massage. They gave adrenaline to restart his heart, and urea to combat swelling of the brain. Walter remained unconscious for four days, and was a patient in the hospital for two weeks. On the day before discharge, Dr Wyant visited Walter and gave him the promised $50. Walter thought he deserved more, and decided to seek redress through the law. His claim for damages was in part based on trespass to his person because of inadequate disclosure of risks, which rendered his consent ineffective.

The common law makes no exceptions for the conduct of research, and it is always open to patients to seek damages from those whose negligence causes harm. The judge in this case emphasized that the duty to disclose 'all the facts, possibilities and opinions which a reasonable man might be expected to consider' was particularly important in research from which the subject would not benefit, and there could be no therapeutic privilege to limit disclosure for the protection of the subject as there might be in obtaining consent for treatment the patient clearly needs. Modern legal and ethical thought even throws doubt on therapeutic privilege as a defence against incomplete disclosure of risks of treatment. In the light of *Chester v Afshar* a patient could conceivably claim damages for any foreseeable injury, about which warnings should have been, but were not, given.[31,32] It is in the nature of research than unforeseeable harms might occur, and so modern good practice[32a] demands that arrangements are in place to compensate subjects harmed by trial participation without the need to establish negligence. We consider compensation arrangements below.

The duty to obtain consent in clinical trials

The law on consent in health care is mostly derived from cases involving surgical practice, and so the process of consent to surgery has become extensive and formalized. A similarly meticulous and well-documented approach to consent to trial participation is necessary. While in surgical practice there is an underlying presumption that the procedure is anticipated to bring direct benefit to the patient, in a clinical trial, it must be made very clear to the participant whether or not personal therapeutic benefit is intended.[30] A particular difficulty in randomized trials is that the researcher must explain, and the patient must comprehend, each of the possible treatments before randomization determines which will be provided. Patient information sheets are now required, and need to be drafted in such a way that the majority of the intended subjects will understand. In practice, this means the material should be written to a reading age of 12 years. The patient information sheet must support, and not replace, verbal explanations with opportunities for the consent-giver to ask questions. Understanding can be enhanced by follow-up opportunities to explain the study.

Possible scenario

Sedated ICU patients give rise to particular problems in research. Providing the ratio of benefit to risk is clear, it is permissible enroll patients who lack capacity into a clinical trial with the assent of a legal representative.[30a] For example, in a trial of early versus late tracheostomy, patient P (who was sedated for her treatment) was recruited into a trial with the agreement of her husband Mr P. Randomization was performed and P was allocated to late tracheostomy at day 10. On day 6, Mr P contacted the investigator to say that he believed his wife would be more comfortable and under less sedation once the tracheostomy was performed, and asked for it to be done earlier. The investigator explained to Mr P the scientific importance of compliance with the trial protocol, but Mr P was insistent. He then chose to withdraw P from the trial so she could have the tracheostomy earlier than day 10.

In non-blinded trials, a subject or legal representative disappointed with the outcome of randomization might choose to withdraw, to the detriment of the power of the trial. The investigator has conflicting interests in preserving the scientific integrity of his study and protecting the interests of his subject. There is no doubt that a subject's decision to withdraw must be respected, but a legal representative has a duty to act in the subject's best interests, and so a question arises as to where those interests lie. The investigator would be wise to consult carefully in a situation like this and will usually accept the legal representative's withdrawal.

The nature and purpose of blinding is not easily understood by the layman. Even a legal textbook states: 'There are doctors and researchers who believe the randomized controlled trial is most effective if conducted "blind", that is the patient is told nothing at all' and then procedes to discourse on the vulnerability in law of such research.[33] To be clear, in a blinded trial, the consent giver must be informed of all the possible randomizations and must understand that he will not be informed which treatment he was randomized to until the trial is completed. He can be reassured, however, that blinding can be broken and treatment allocation disclosed if circumstances arise that make it necessary for the treatment of a possible adverse event.

Estimating the risks that subjects are exposed to, and communicating those risks for the purpose of informed consent, are further challenges for the researcher. First, the consent giver needs to understand that interventions may put the subject at risk of an undesired outcome without being the immediate cause of the outcome. Minimal risk is a widely used phrase and has been defined as 'the probability and magnitude of harm or discomfort anticipated in the research are not greater in and of themselves than those ordinarily encountered in daily life or during the performance of routine physical or psychological examinations or tests'.[33a] Risks can be explained as absolute risk (of a specific complication over a specified period of time) or relative risk (for the subject relative to someone not exposed to the research intervention). Merely giving numeric descriptions of risk is of little help to many people, and some statement of common experience comparison may be helpful.

As we saw in Halushka's case, it has long been argued that the research subject's altruism deserves an even more detailed presentation of relevant information, and the argument is especially strong where the subject is to receive treatment he might not otherwise be offered. The outcome of the TGN1412 trial reminded us of the need for subjects to understand that any medical intervention can rarely cause death or serious morbidity. The potential subject must be given as much information as is necessary in order to make a choice about participation.

The consent process will involve both verbal and written information provision, with sufficient time allowed for consideration and deliberation. The research concepts of standard, control or placebo treatments for comparison with the experimental candidate, and the principle of equipoise, which morally justifies randomization and blinding are often difficult to explain. People with serious or life-threatening diseases, or their representatives, may hold unrealistic hopes of benefit from participating in trials of 'new' drugs or procedures and they will need careful and compassionate counseling. It would obviously be of dubious morality to allow a desperate patient to consent to a trial in false hope of a cure.

Case Study

Ellen Roche was a technician at the Johns Hopkins Asthma and Allergy Center. On 4 May 2001, she was the third healthy volunteer to receive inhaled hexamethonium in an Institutional Review Board (IRB) approved study at her institution. Next day, she developed a dry cough, and her condition slowly deteriorated so that she was admitted to the Medical Center on day 5 with acute respiratory distress syndrome. Admitted to intensive care on May 12, she died on June 2 of progressive hypotension and multiorgan failure. On October 11, a financial settlement with the Roche family was announced.[34]

Healthy volunteers are often coerced by financial considerations. The boundaries between reasonable expenses and financial incentives are obviously grey, but the typical basic remuneration offered to healthy volunteers is £150–200 per day, and the volunteer's involvement may last for many days. It remains a fact of life that people can earn a significant income from 'volunteering' to research projects, and advertisements for 'volunteers' are regularly placed on the world wide web and in the street magazine *Big Issue*.

Another concerning form of coercion is colleague pressure. It could be reasoned that any researcher ought to be prepared to be a subject in any study he designs, but whether it is incumbent on any member of the research team to show similar confidence is less sure. In legal principle, compulsion or coercion can render consent invalid, but would be difficult to establish.

There is some concern about the knowledge doctors actually pocess about consent and capacity.[35] In an observational study of 302 consecutive acute medical admissions to a UK hospital, at least 40% were determined to lack mental capacity.[36] Capacity can be difficult to determine in critically ill patients, and it seems to be widely accepted that the acute administration of narcotics renders a patient incapable of consent. It is perhaps too easy to presume all patients in a critical care facility lack capacity and to use this approach to gaining consent to research. On the other hand, perhaps more could be done to establish guidelines on capacity to consent to research during acute illness or under the influence of narcotics and to train critical care physicians to undertake detailed assessments so that more patients could be empowered to make decisions for themselves. A systematic approach is necessary.[37] The assessing physician needs to be familiar with the patient's background, medical records, and reports, and if appropriate must make enquiries of others who know the patient about their normal behaviour, values, and aspirations. If the person suffers from a mental disorder, the diagnosis must be recorded. The mental state examination may then procede under the following headings.

Appearance and behaviour, making allowances for the effects of the illness and the fact that in-patients don't get to choose their dress! Speech, where it is physically possible, whether minimal and monosyllabic or garrulous, whether focused or going off on flights of fancy. Mood, which may be labile after cerebral ischaemia, or unreasonably pessimistic after prolonged illness. Thought abnormalities may include delusions or pre-occupations. Perception can be impaired by hallucinations, which we know affect survivors of prolonged critical illness. Cognition is given much weight, and most psychiatrists would apply the Mini-Mental State Examination. Orientation problems will suggest defects of long- or short-term memory impairment, and will not preclude all decision-making, but arguably would preclude consent to research. Intelligence needs to be taken into consideration, especially whether the person's current abilities to reason, calculate, or function match those that are normal for this person. Finally, insight (or lack of it) does not readily preclude capacity to consent to research, and should only be claimed with recording of clear examples.

The Adults with Incapacity (Scotland) Act 2000, Part 2, gives power to guardians, attorneys, or close family members to provide proxy or surrogate consent to research,[38] but there is no legal basis for proxy consent to research on behalf of an adult who lacks capacity to make the decision in England and Wales. This inconvenient fact did not prevent research being approved and conducted on the incapax, sometimes with a 'waiver of consent' and sometimes with proxy consent, which some referred to as assent in recognition of the fact that the law did not embrace proxy consent. Such practices were justified by being compatible with International Guidelines on Good Clinical Practice, and approved by a Research Ethics Committee. The Mental Capacity Act 2005, section 33, requires the researcher to identify somebody close to the patient who knows the potential subject well and is prepared to accept the duties and responsibilities of a 'Personal Consultee'. Where there is a patient-nominated attorney or court-appointed deputy, this person may undertake the role of a consultee. In cases where no such person can be identified, the researcher may instead invite someone to accept the duties of a 'nominated consultee'. The consultee is given all the relevant information about the proposal to enlist the incapax, and his duty is to advise the researcher whether the incapax would have consented or refused. Guidance emphasizes that the consultee should put to one side any personal views on the proposal and should understand that he is not giving or withholding consent. Nonetheless, his advice will be determinative of whether or not the incapax participates and is self-evidently equivalent to the proxy consent required by international standards. It is recommended that the consultee be given access to 'independent' advice about their duties and responsibilities in law.[39] There are regulations addressing the rare instance of unanticipated loss of capacity during a research project, which reflect the principles applied to the care of the incapax.[40]

Where the investigation is into emergency interventions which preclude prior involvement of a consultee, the Act requires the researcher to identify one or more doctors who are knowledgable about but not connected with the trial, and who are willing to accept the responsibility to decide whether or not to agree to the inclusion of each patient into the trial. Recruitment will only be lawful with an agreement. In trials where there is no opportunity for agreement by an independent doctor, the Research Ethics Committee may grant a waiver of the requirement for advice by a consultee or agreement by a doctor, though consent of the patient or the advice of a consultee must be sought at the earliest possible opportunity after the emergency. The guidance is silent on what to do in the case of fatal outcome, though common sense dictates that 'next of kin' and the coroner should be appraised of what happened.

European legislation's Directive 2001/20/EC included a number of safeguards for vulnerable subjects beyond arrangements for proxy consent by 'natural or legal persons, an authority and/or body provided for by national law'. It dictates that 'consent must represent the subject's presumed will', which is a commonly quoted aspiration in many fields, including arguments for 'presumed consent' to organ donation. However, this is a very subjective test and the reality is that proxies are often ignorant of a person's previously expressed preferences.[41,42] and there can be no grounds for presuming the will of someone who has never had capacity. Moreover, there must be reservations about the ability of a distressed personal proxy to take responsibility.[43] The English Common Law concept of decision-making according to the subject's best interests (an objective test) is surely to be preferred.

Recognizing that some patient subjects may have diminished but not absent capacity, the directive requires that the subject 'has received information according to his/her capacity of understanding regarding the trial, the risks and the benefits'. It also gives advice that any indication of dissent by the incapacitated subject must be respected. This will be a particular challenge within the critical care setting, where the capacity of a temporarily impaired patient subject will be expected to fluctuate rapidly, and communication is heavily impeded by oral tubes or tracheostomies.

Case Study

Polyheme is a solution of human polymerized haemoglobin. Researchers were granted an emergency research waiver of informed consent for the study in which randomization occurred in the pre-hospital phase of care and continued for the first 12 hours of in-hospital care. The decision by the IRB to grant the waiver was controversial, and when recruitment commenced in July 2006 ABC News ran a television and Internet story about the cities in which the study was operating, and advising people how to obtain a blue bracelet stating 'I decline the Northfield Polyheme Study'.

Sensationalist reporting of this trial, and extensive debate in the *American Journal of Bioethics*, led to barely concealed allegations of misconduct circulating on the Internet, but they should have been muted by publication of the results in a peer-reviewed journal.[44] The Department of Health and Human Services and the Federal Drugs Agency in the United States enacted complementary regulations on emergency research without consent in 1996.[45] An Institutional Review Board may approve an Emergency Research Waiver (ERW) if it is satisfied on the following criteria:

1 The subject must be suffering from a life-threatening condition for which immediate treatment is necessary.

2 It is impractical to obtain consent within the time available to start treatment.

3 Clinical evidence suggests substantial therapeutic benefit for the subject.

4 Efforts must be made to contact a legal representative or proxy.

5 An independent committee must review the progress of the study.

6 The available treatments must be 'unproven and unsatisfactory'.

7 Investigators must engage with the communities from which subjects will be drawn and publicly disclose pertinent aspects of the study including risks as well as potential benefits.[45a]

Similar conditions are expected before waiving of consent in UK statutes. A full description of the community consultations in the

Polyheme trial was published.[46] Practical aspects of emergency research without informed consent in the United States and steps taken to satisfy the requirements for community consultation and public disclosure could be used in the UK.[47,48] Legitimate concerns about the potential for abuse of waiver rules remain and will continue to be debated.

The matched cohort is an alternative to the randomized controlled trial, which is exploited in emergency research. Researchers at the National Taiwan University Hospital carried out a three-year prospective observational study of in-hospital cardiac arrest and developed a propensity score to equalize the potential prognostic factors so that patients who received the experimental treatment could be optimally matched with a similar patient who received standard treatment.[49]

Professional recommendations on the principles of ethical conduct of critical care research in North America have been published by the American Thoracic Society.[50]

Compensation for injury

The Clinical Trials Directive[50a] requires that insurance or indemnity is in place for the compensation of subjects harmed by trial participation. The Association of British Pharmaceutical Industries operates a scheme to provide compensation for an injury arising from a trial involving one of its member companies.[50b] In the United Kingdom, indemnity will typically be provided by the National Health Service where it employs the researcher, or by an insurance arrangement made by a university or pharmaceutical company. Payment will either be ex gratia, as in Ellen Roche's case above, or after proving negligence, as in Walter Halushka's case.[51] The situation for clinical research is more complex. When the experimental treatment group achieves better outcomes than the control group, it is reasoned and generally accepted that the control group patients were not unfairly denied a chance of cure or survival, and it presumed that future patients will benefit from their sacrifice. But what happens when the experimental treatment group fare worse?

Case Study

A study was desiqned to determine whether the application of continuous negative expiratory pressure (CNEP) to pre-term neonates could reduce the need for oxygen therapy or intubation and ventilation. Published in a major Journal in 1996, the results were la small benefit for early respiratory outcomes, but a smaller (though statistically non-significant) harm for survival to discharge. A family who lost not one, but two children after treatment with CNEP at one of the trial Units, lodged a formal complaint about the trial.[52a] Other families of the subjects became alarmed and a national newspaper ran the headline 'Guinea pig trial killed our babies'.[52b]

It is part of the grieving process to want to know why a loved one died, and it can be very difficu lt for them to understand statistical nuances and probabilities. Anger is another part of the grieving process, and can be directed at doctors or investigators.

Case Study

522 recovering but ventilator-dependent critically-ill patients were randomized to receive recombinant growth hormone (rGH) or placebo. In the Finnish part of the study, the placebo group of 123 patients experienced 25% mortality rate, and so the expected number of deaths amongst the 119 allocated to rGH treatment was 30. In fact, 47 died, an excess of 17 deaths. In the multinational study, 23% of the 115 subjects receiving placebo died, so that the expected number of deaths among 139 patients treated with rGH was 32, against the observed number of 61, or 29 excess deaths. In the whole of this study, therefore, 46 people died as a result of experimental treatment with rGH.

In practice, no compensation will be paid in a situation like this. We cannot identify among the 108 patients who died after receiving rGH the 46 who would otherwise have survived. Yet all the treatment group patients were harmed to a greater or lesser extent, in terms of prolonged hospitalisation and additional treatments needed. Should there not be acknowledgment of this, and at least nominal compensation paid? When we consider the fallout following the TGN1412 study, in which 6 men were seriously but not fatally injured, that it generated so much national and international concern about subject safety and compensation arrangements, we must wonder why there was no such debate about the rGH study which killed 40 to 50 people and harmed some 250.

Patient information and retained tissue

Case Study

In an international observational study of end-of-life practices in European intensive care units, the trial organizers realized that some practices are lawful in some countries, while unlawful in others. Specifically, there was concern about palliative drug use and the reasons doctors claimed for using them. In the United Kingdom, it is unlawful to administer a drug with the intention of ending life, and yet in the Netherlands that could be quite acceptable if performed appropriately. It was therefore agreed to use a terminology, which had less connotation of killing, and 'actively shortening the dying process' was agreed upon. This practice was claimed to occur in seven countries, in as many as 19% of deaths in one of these, and in no deaths from other countries. It is likely that fear of prosecution affected reporting of palliative drug use.[53,54]

Law normally requires consent from the individuals concerned before 'sensitive' data concerning their health is acquired and processed, or before the removal, storage, and use of their tissues. Users of any health care system have, however, an interest in, and ethical responsibility to contribute to, quality assurance procedures. In return for this small infringement upon their autonomy, patients should presume that use of their data will be ethically sound and likely to be of benefit to the service.[55] The relevant Statutes are the Data Protection Act (1998),[56] the Human Tissue Act (2004)[25] and the Human Fertilization and Embryology Act (1990)[57] concerning live gametes and embryos. In the United Kingdom, the law does permit ethically approved research access to anonymized medical data and to 'residual' tissue. For England and Wales, Section 60 of the Health and Social Care Act 2001 confirmed that patient information can be shared for medical purposes, which include research and the establishment of disease registers, in the interests of improving patient care.[58] The Patient Information Advisory Group (PIAG) was established as a statutory committee to be consulted about the regulations under Section 60. The Health and Social Care Act 2008 establishes the National Information Governance Board to replace the PIAG.[59] The Ethics and Confidentiality Committee of the NIGB is now empowered under Section 251 of the NHS Act 2006 to set aside the common law duty of confidentiality. Applications are made through the Integrated Research Application System at https:www. myresearchproject.org.uk. Privacy Advisory Committees in Scotland and Northern Ireland fulfill a similar function in those countries. Anonymized data can be linked to the appropriate tissue, but there must be nothing in the information supplied to the researcher that would allow an individual 'donor' to be identified. Coding (that is, substituting the individual's name for a number linked to the name) is not an adequate anonymization.

Proposal and publication ethics

The World Health Organization advocates clinical trial registration, and an increasing number of journal editors (including the prestigious Vancouver Group, now known as the International Committee of Medical Journal Editors) will require registration of a trial before they consider publication.[59a] The purpose of registration is to make the research process more effective and efficient. It is expected that publication bias of the evidence base (towards positive outcome trials rather than 'no difference' outcome) will be reduced and selective reporting will be easier to detect. Unnecessary duplication of experiments will be less likely to occur, and those designing future trials will be better informed about existing knowledge and ongoing research directions. Effective collaborations will be more frequent, and recruitment could be facilitated. A number of registries exist, including www.clinicaltrials.gov in the United States and www.actr.org.au in Australia. For an up-to-date list, visit the International Clinical Trials Registry Platform at www.who.int/ictrp/about/details/en/index.html.

Editors, reviewers, or readers may notice in submitted or published articles unethical research conduct, which has escaped the initial ethical review process. They may feel they have a duty to report this to an appropriate authority. There are also a number of areas of misconduct specific to the publication process.

Redundant or duplicate publication

Researchers must take care to identify in their manuscript any data or analyses that have been previously published in any format.

Plagiarism

It is in the nature of research that we build on the attainments of others, and there is something to be said for quoting directly their opinions and conclusions, lest by Chinese whispers we come to misrepresent their original message. Copying becomes unacceptable when the perpetrator is perceived to be passing the work of others off as his own, whether short unattributed phrases or substantial paragraphs of text lifted from any source. In 2008 the General Medical Council found Rajendra Persaud guilty of dishonesty and of bringing the profession into disrepute for inadequately acknowledging the work of others in his books, articles, and other media. Dr Persaud is a well-known broadcaster and author of books on psychiatric topics for the public.[60] The non-professional nature of these media does not reduce the obligation to give clear acknowledgement of the work of others.

Fabricated data

Examples go from total fabrication of data to selective use of data whose aggregation results in unwarranted statistical results. Dr Julio Cruz published three remarkable papers on the treatment of unsurvivable severe head injury with high-dose mannitol between 2001 and 2004. He died in 2005. Doubts were raised about the veracity of his reports in 2006, and enquiries found no evidence that he had conducted such research in any of the hospitals he claimed to have worked at.[61] In retrospect, it is easy to say that the results he claimed were so remarkable and so inconsistent with the experience of clinicians that doubts should have been expressed much earlier, including by those who reviewed the manuscripts prior to publication. Even simple checks could have revealed doubts about their veracity. However, we are in general trusting of our professional colleagues' probity. A British cancer researcher was removed from the Medical Register in 2007 for plagiarism and misrepresentation.[62]

Unwarranted authorship

A number of reputable doctors who claimed co-authorship of the papers describing Dr Cruz's experiments had, when questioned, no good evidence that the work was 'real'. With authorship comes responsibility.

Undisclosed conflict of interest

Researchers will benefit from the publication of their work, but it is to be expected that they will present their results objectively and that their conclusions will uninfluenced by financial or commercial considerations. The extent to which a sponsor's generosity towards researchers can influence their objectivity is debatable. Any affiliation, which could be seen to be a conflict of interest, must be declared to the journal editor.

Publication ethics is increasingly formalized with guidance from bodies such as the World Association of Medical Editors[63] and the Committee on Publication Ethics.[64]

The joy of critical care research

After reading this chapter, it would not be surprising if a young critical care physician were to feel that this particular domain of our specialty now has too many bureaucratic and regulatory hurdles to clear, and poses too many threats to a career, to be worth pursuing. I want to end on a positive note, to give personal encouragement to those who are brave enough, bright enough, and determined enough to push the limits of knowledge and make their own contribution to ever-improving outcomes for patients. Research is still portrayed as involving a small minority of patients who are asked to allow themselves to be exposed to dangerous experiments for the benefit of the majority. If it could become the norm that every patient be enrolled in a trial of some sort, medical progress would accelerate, and the public would be less fearful of the approach of the investigator. National collaborations and international multicentre trials are increasingly providing the high-quality evidence we need to assure our patients they are receiving the best possible care, and much more can be achieved. The researcher gets to experience the excitement of being involved in discovery, and always has the possibility of immortality as the name associated with a major advance. I do not forget, and never will, the courage of those patients who volunteer to let us perform dangerous experiments upon them, and I reflect on the memories of those who have died. I also recall with admiration one patient who resolutely refused my best exhortations to let me enrol him, and put an end to my efforts by rolling up his sleeve to show me a number tattooed on his arm by Nazi prison authorities. 'I have done my bit for medical research', he said.

It can be tempting to attempt to answer a research question by 'audit' of existing practices in order to bypass many of the hurdles, and there can be no doubt that young intensivists are conducting audits where they would have carried out research in times gone by. The distinctions between clinical audit and clinical research can be very unclear[67] A defining characteristic of research is that its results can be trusted to inform evidence-based practices, and so there is an imperative for all of us to help researchers through the jungle of regulations and facilitate good practice in research.

For those seeking up to date practical guidance, a number of organizations provide useful websites.

References

1 Proctor DF (1995). A history of breathing physiology. *Informa Health Care* 87.
2 Hughes JT (1982). Miraculous deliverance of Anne Green: an Oxford case of resuscitation in the seventeenth century. *Br Med J (Clin Res Ed)* **285**: 1792–1793.
3 Davies H (2007). Ethical reflections on Edward Jenner's experimental treatment. *J Med Ethics* **33**: 174–176.
4 Vollmann J, Winau R (1996). The Prussian regulation of 1900: early ethical standards for human experimentation in Germany. *IRB* **18**: 9–11.
5 Sauerteig L (2000). [Ethical guidelines, patient rights and physician behavior in clinical drug trials (1892–1931)]. *Medizinhist J.* **35**: 303–334.
6 Lock S (1995). Research ethics – a brief historical review to 1965. *J Intern Med.* **238**: 513–520.
7 Katz J (1996). The Nuremberg Code and the Nuremberg Trial. A reappraisal. *JAMA* **276**: 1662–1666.
8 Weindling P (1996). Human guinea pigs and the ethics of experimentation: the BMJ's correspondent at the Nuremberg medical trial. *BMJ* **313**: 1467–1470.
9 Richmond C (2002). Dame Sheila Sherlock: World authority on the liver and Professor of Medicine, Royal Free Hospital, London. *BMJ* **324**: 174.
10 Kopp VJ (1999). Henry Knowles Beecher and the development of informed consent in anesthesia research. *Anesthesiology* **90**: 1756–1765.

11 Mashour GA (2005). Altered states: LSD and the Anesthesia Laboratory of Henry Knowles Beecher. *Bull Anesth Hist.* **23**: 11–14.

12 Beecher HK (1966). Ethics and clinical research. *N Engl J Med.* **274**: 1354–1360.

13 Rockwell DH, Yobs AR, Moore MBJ (1964). The Tuskegee Study of untreated syphilis; the 30th year of observation. *Arch Intern Med.* **114**: 792–798.

14 White RM (2006). The Tuskegee study of untreated syphilis revisited. *Lancet Infect Dis* **6**: 62–63.

15 Carmack HJ, Bates BR, Harter LM (2008). Narrative constructions of health care issues and policies: the case of President Clinton's apology-by-proxy for the Tuskegee syphilis experiment. *J Med Humanit.* **29**: 89–109.

16 Hey E (2006). The 1996 Continuous Negative Extrathoracic Pressure (CNEP) trial: were parents' allegations of research fraud fraudulent? *Pediatrics* **117**: 2244–2246.

17 Health Do. Research Governance Framework for Health and Social Care. 2005.

18 Gornall J (2008). Three doctors and a GMC prosecution. *BMJ* **337**: a907.

19 The Medicines for Human Use (Clinical Trials) Regulations 2004.

20 Silverman HJ, Druml C, Lemaire F, et al. (2004). The European Union Directive and the protection of incapacitated subjects in research: an ethical analysis. *Intensive Care Med* **30**: 1723–1729.

21 The Medicines for Human Use (Clinical Trials) Amendment (No.2) Regulations 2006.

22 Verheugen G. Commission directive 2005/28/ec laying down principles and guidelines for good clinical practice as. Official Journal of the European Union. 2005.

23 Goodyear MD, Krleza-Jeric K, Lemmens T (2007). The Declaration of Helsinki. *BMJ* **335**: 624–625.

24 Research: The Role and Responsibilities of Doctors. 2002.

25 Human Tissue Act 2004.

26 Goodyear MDE (2006). Further lessons from the TGN1412 tragedy. *BMJ.* **333**: 270–271.

27 Medical Research Council. MRC Guidelines for Good Clinical Practice in Clinical Trials. 1998.

28 Levine R. President's Council on Bioethics. Chairman E Pellegrino. Session 3: Children and Clinical Research. 2006.

29 Note for guidance on Good Clinical Practice. European Medicines Agency; 2002.

30 National Health and Medical Research Council, Australian Research Council, Committee AV-C. National Statement on Ethical Conduct in Human Research. 2007: 3.3.14.

30a EMEA CPMP/ICH/135/95: ICH Topic E 6 (R1) Guideline for Good Clinical Practice, Section 4.8 and Statutory Instrument 2004 No. 1031 and The Medicines for Human Use (Clinical Trials) Regulations 2004, Schedule 1, Part 5.

31 Hassan M (2008). Informed consent and the law – an English legal perspective. *Dig Dis.* **26**: 23–27.

32 Garfield J (2005). *Chester v. Afshar*: a surgeon's view. *Br J Neurosurg.* **19**: 120–121.

32a Statutory Instrument 2004 No. 1031, The Medicines for Human Use (Clinical Trials) Regulations 2004, para 15(5).

33 Brazier M, Cave E (2007). *Medicine, Patients and the Law.* Penguin, London, p. 429.

33a Code of Federal Regulations Title 45 Public Welfare Department of Health and Human Services Part 46 Protection Of Human Subjects, para102(i) (US).

34 Steinbrook R (2002). Protecting research subjects – the crisis at Johns Hopkins. *N Engl J Med.* **346**: 716–720.

35 Jackson E, Warner J (2002). How much do doctors know about consent and capacity? *JRSM* **95**: 601.

36 Raymont V, Bingley W, Buchanan A, et al. (2004). Prevalence of mental incapacity in medical inpatients and associated risk factors: cross-sectional study. *The Lancet* **364**: 1421–1427.

37 Society BMAaTL (2004). *Assessment of Mental Capacity.* BMJ Books, London.

38 Adults with Incapacity (Scotland) Act 2000.

39 Mental Capacity Act 2005, Section 33

40 The Mental Capacity Act 2005 (Loss of Capacity during Research Project) (England) Regulations 2007.

41 Sulmasy DP, Terry PB, Weisman CS, et al (1998). The accuracy of substituted judgements in patients with terminal diagnoses. *Ann Intern Med* **128**: 621–629.

42 Coppolino M, Ackerson L (2001). Do surrogate decision makers provide accurate consent for intensive care research? *Chest* **119**: 603–612.

43 Jones C, Skirrow P, Griffiths RD, et al. (2004). Post-traumatic stress disorder-related symptoms in relatives of patients following intensive care. *Intensive Care Med.* **30**: 456–460.

44 Moore EE, Moore FA, Fabian TC, et al. (2009). Human polymerized hemoglobin for the treatment of hemorrhagic shock when blood is unavailable: the USA multicenter trial. *J Am Coll Surg.* **208**: 1–13.

45 Ellis GB, Lin MH. (45CFR Part 46) OPRR Reports: Informed Consent Requirements in Emergency Research. 1996.

45a Federal Regulation 21CFR 50.24 allowing Exemption of Informed Consent. Title 21 – Food and Drugs, Chapter I – Food And Drug Administration, Department of Health And Human Services, Part 50.

46 Longfield JN, Morris MJ, Moran KA, Kragh JFJ, Wolf R, Baskin TW (2008). Community meetings for emergency research community consultation. *Crit Care Med.* **36**: 731–736.

47 Salzman JG, Frascone RJ, Godding BK, et al. (2007). Implementing emergency research requiring exception from informed consent, community consultation, and public disclosure. *Ann Emerg Med.* **50**: 448–455. 455.e1–4.

48 Halperin H, Paradis N, Mosesso VJ, et al. (2007). Recommendations for implementation of community consultation and public disclosure under the

Food and Drug Administration's "Exception from informed consent requirements for emergency research": a special report from the American Heart Association Emergency Cardiovascular Care Committee and Council on Cardiopulmonary, Perioperative and Critical Care: endorsed by the American College of Emergency Physicians and the Society for Academic Emergency Medicine. *Circulation* **116**: 1855–1863.

49 Chen YS, Lin JW, Yu HY, et al. (2008). Cardiopulmonary resuscitation with assisted extracorporeal life-support versus conventional cardiopulmonary resuscitation in adults with in-hospital cardiac arrest: an observational study and propensity analysis. *Lancet* **372**: 554–561.

50 Luce JM, Cook DJ, Martin TR, et al. (2004). The ethical conduct of clinical research involving critically ill patients in the United States and Canada: principles and recommendations. *Am J Respir Crit Care Med*. **170**: 1375–1384.

50a Statutory Instrument 2004 No. 1031, The Medicines for Human Use (Clinical Trials) Regulations 2004, para 15(5).

50b http://www.abpi.org.uk/publications/pdfs/Clinical-Trial-Compensation-GLs.pdf, accessed December 17 2009

51 Steinbrook R (2006). Compensation for injured research subjects. *N Engl J Med*. **354**: 1871–1873.

52a Laurance J. Chance remark alerted parents. The Independent 2000 May 9.

52b Hey E (2006). The 1999 Continuous Negative Extrathoracic Pressure (CNEP) Trail: Were Parents' Allegations of Research Fraud Fraudulent? *Pediatrics* **117**: 2244–2246.

53 Sprung CL, Cohen SL, Sjokvist P, et al (2003). End-of-life practices in European intensive care units: the Ethicus Study. *JAMA* **290**: 790–797.

54 Sprung CL, Woodcock T, Sjokvist P, et al. (2008). Reasons, considerations, difficulties and documentation of end-of-life decisions in European intensive care units: the ETHICUS Study. *Intensive Care Med*. **34**: 271–277.

55 Wade D (2007). Ethics of collecting and using healthcare data. *BMJ*. **334**: 1330–1331.

56 1998 DPA.

57 Human Fertilisation and Embryology Act 1990 – an illustrative text.

58 Health and Social Care Act 2001.

59 Health and Social Care Act 2008.

59a http://www.icmje.org/publishing_10register.html, accessed 17 December 2009.

60 Jenkins R (2008). TV psychiatrist Raj Persaud suspended for plagiarism.

61 Roberts I, Smith R, Evans S (2007). Doubts over head injury studies. **334**: 392–394.

62 Fitness to Practice Panel, General Medical Council: Dr Subhajit Dutta-Roy.

63 World Association of Medical Editors.

64 Ethics CoP.

65 Wilmshurst PT (2007). Research misconduct: can Australia learn from the UK's stuttering system? *Med J Aust.* **186**: 662–663.

66 Kennedy I (2008). UK Panel for Research Integrity: more than a smokescreen. *Lancet* **372**: 1877.

67 Wade DT (2005). Ethics, audit, and research: all shades of grey. *BMJ* **330**: 468–471.

Part C

Management-focused issues

Chapter 8

NHS governance of critical care

David Pittaway QC and Nicholas A Peacock

In this chapter, we explore governance in the National Health Service (NHS), with particular emphasis on critical care. In particular, we seek to answer and explore the following issues:

1 What is governance?

2 How has clinical governance been rolled out in the NHS?

3 How does clinical governance affect the delivery of critical care?

4 Governance, critical care, and the law.

What is governance?—A definition

Clinical governance is, according to the Department of Health: '...the system through which NHS organisations are accountable for continuously improving the quality of their services and safeguarding high standards of care, by creating an environment in which clinical excellence will flourish.'[1]

Fine words, but they do not permit an immediate understanding of what is a difficult concept. An in-depth review of governance in the NHS would not only take far longer than many readers of this text might wish to spend; it would also become rapidly out of date, for (notwithstanding voluminous documents generated at regular intervals) the essence of governance in practice is that it is dynamic. We hope therefore to draw attention to key concepts and landmark publications which the reader needs to know about.

Governance is a notion that was borrowed from, and has many parallels with, the corporate world. In health care, it is intended to embody three key attributes: recognizably high standards of care, transparent responsibility (accountability for those standards), and a constant dynamic of improvement. Properly understood, it is fundamental to patient safety.

How has clinical governance been rolled out in the NHS?

Modernization is a word or concept that might well set teeth grating, but it lies at the heart of the NHS reform and the introduction of clini cal governance since the late 1990s. Drivers for change were legion but there seemed to be a real concern that the NHS, and health care practitioners within it, were unable or unwilling to meet the challenges that had arisen since the NHS was created. Patients, as all clinical negligence lawyers know, had become increasingly likely to question health care service providers, and to complain or even litigate in the event of an adverse outcome. Changes were required at all levels: national and local; organizational and personal.

In the late 1990s, the then recently elected Labour government was particularly concerned about variation in performance and practice between different areas following the introduction of the so-called internal market. It wished to introduce a new NHS model. Embarking on a ten-year modernization programme, it published: 'A first class service—quality in the NHS'.[2] Key aspects in delivering this new service would be as follows:

+ National Service Frameworks (NSFs), together with the National Institute of Clinical Excellence (NICE).

+ Clinical governance, coupled with professional self-regulation and lifelong learning.

+ The Commission for Health Improvement to monitor standards, which would be set out in the National Performance Framework and assessed by a National Patient and User Survey.

Those aims reflect the need not just to set high standards, but to implement and monitor them (as well as, in terms of self-regulation, adjudicate on infringements). Those notions may have developed beyond all recognition today, organization and name changes included, but they still lie at the heart of NHS governance.

In 'Clinical Governance: Quality in the new NHS'[3] the Department of Health set about putting the key elements of its vision into practice. In particular, NHS trusts, health authorities and primary care groups were tasked by April 1999 with identifying lead clinicians for clinical governance and setting up appropriate structures (including, for NHS trusts, board sub-committees) for overseeing clinical governance within their organization.

Picking up the notion of learning from adverse outcome, the next major landmark in the series of clinical governance reforms was the publication of 'An organisation with a memory',[4] which sought expressly to formulate the ways in which NHS organizations could learn from past errors and prevent their recurrence. The problem was starkly identified:

3. Currently, NHS reporting and information systems provide us with a patchy and incomplete picture of the scale and nature of the problem of serious failures in health care. We know, for example, that every year:

- 400 people die or are seriously injured in adverse events involving medical devices;

- nearly 10,000 people are reported to have experienced serious adverse reactions to drugs;

- around 1,150 people who have been in recent contact with mental health services commit suicide;

- nearly 28,000 written complaints are made about aspects of clinical treatment in hospitals;

- the NHS pays out around £400 million a year settlement of clinical negligence claims, and has a potential liability of around £2.4 billion for existing and expected claims;

- hospital acquired infections—around 15% of which may be avoidable—are estimated to cost the NHS nearly £1 billion.

4. Just as none of these statistics can be attributed wholly to service failures, research in this country and abroad suggests that they give no indication of the potential true scale of the problem. This issue has been the subject of major pieces of academic research in Australia and the USA, but work in the UK is in its infancy. Yet the best research-based estimates we have reveal enough to suggest that in NHS hospitals alone adverse events in which harm is caused to patients:

- occur in around 10% of admissions—or at a rate in excess of 850,000 a year;

♦ cost the service an estimated £2 billion a year in additional hospital stays alone, without taking any account of human or wider economic costs.

5. In addition, there is evidence that some specific types of relatively infrequent but very serious adverse events happen time and again over a period of years. Inquiries and incident investigations determine that 'the lessons must be learned', but the evidence suggests that the NHS as a whole is not good at doing so. Still less is known about the situation in primary care, despite the fact that it accounts for the great majority of NHS patient contacts and can still experience service failures, which have serious consequences for individual patients.

It is unlikely that any better or more pithy summary of the underlying reason for clinical governance could be found. Ten recommendations were made; each of them remains important to our current understanding of patient safety:

♦ Introduce a mandatory reporting scheme for adverse health care events and specified near misses.

♦ Introduce a scheme for confidential reporting by staff of adverse events and near misses.

♦ Encourage a reporting and questioning culture in the NHS.

♦ Introduce a single overall system for analysing and disseminating lessons from adverse health care events and near misses.

♦ Make better use of existing sources of information on adverse events.

♦ Improve the quality and relevance of NHS adverse event investigations and inquiries.

♦ Undertake a programme of basic research into adverse health care events in the NHS.

♦ Make full use of new NHS information systems to help staff access learning from adverse health care events and near misses.

♦ Act to ensure that important lessons are implemented quickly and consistently.

♦ Identify and address specific categories of serious recurring adverse health care events.

Interspersed with these landmark publications came a series of equally landmark news events about health care practices and practitioners, which reflected and/or generated huge public concern, among them the

Bristol paediatric heart unit, the Royal Liverpool Children's Hospital (Alder Hey), and Dr Harold Shipman. All in their own way fed into and increased the need for change in the NHS, an organization which must have been reeling under constant shocks to its system. Small wonder that clinical governance became the tool for promoting and improving patient safety.

The Department of Health set about implementing the above recommendations in 'Building a safer NHS for patients',[5] setting a series of dates over the next 18 months or so by which various targets should be met. Today the above notions seem to be in almost everyday usage, but the importance of these policy-framing documents cannot be underestimated. It is time to see how the specific elements and recommendations have come to effect the modern NHS, and critical care in particular.

Clinical governance in practice

Various agencies and specific concepts were mentioned in 'A first class service—quality in the NHS'. Each will be considered, though briefly, in turn below.

National service frameworks (NSFs)

National service frameworks (NSFs) are long-term strategies for improving specific areas of care. They set national standards, identify key interventions, and put in place agreed time scales for implementation.

To date, the following NSFs have been published: blood pressure, cancer, children, COPD, coronary heart disease, diabetes, long-term (neurological) conditions, mental health, renal, stroke, and vascular.

National Institute of Health and Clinical Excellence

The National Institute of Clinical Excellence was set up in 1999, and on 1 April 2005 joined with the Health Development Agency to become the new National Institute for Health and Clinical Excellence (still abbreviated as NICE).

NICE produces guidance in three areas of health: (i) public health—guidance on the promotion of good health and the prevention of ill health for those working in the NHS, local authorities, and the wider public and voluntary sector; (ii) health technologies—guidance on the use of new and existing medicines, treatments and procedures within the NHS, and (iii) clinical practice—guidance on the appropriate treatment and care of people with specific diseases and conditions within the NHS.

Professional self or shared regulation

Key to the NHS reforms was the notion that the professions would continue to self-regulate. The principal regulators remain:

- the General Medical Council[6] (for doctors).
- the General Dental Council[7] (for dentists, dental nurses, dental technicians, dental hygienists, dental therapists, clinical dental technicians and orthodontic therapists).
- the Nursing and Midwifery Council[8] (for nurses and midwives).
- the Royal Pharmaceutical Society of Great Britain[9] (for pharmacists and pharmacy technicians).
- the Health Professions Council[10] (for arts therapists, biomedical scientists, chiropodists/podiatrists, clinical scientists, dietitians, occupational therapists, operating department practitioners, orthoptists, paramedics, physiotherapists, prosthetists/orthotists, radiographers, speech and language therapists).
- the Council for Healthcare Regulatory Excellence,[11] which monitors the above regulators and promotes good regulatory practice.

In 'Good doctors, safer patients'[12] the Chief Medical Officer published his response to consideration by Dame Janet Smith in the Shipman Inquiry of the GMC's regulatory proceedings. He recommended that the adjudicatory function of the GMC should be hived off to a new organization. In the consequent white paper 'Trust, assurance and safety'[13] and the simultaneously published 'Safeguarding patients',[14] the government proposed a new Office of the Health Professions Adjudicator, which was then introduced in the Health and Social Care Act 2008.

The regulation of professionals, and the interaction between NHS organizations and the regulatory bodies, is a complex and fast-moving area, beyond the scope of this chapter.

Lifelong learning

The Department of Health set out its visions for lifelong learning and continuing education in 'Working together, learning together—a framework for lifelong learning in the NHS'. Lifelong learning should not be seen solely as a personal responsibility—note how its importance is framed in the Introduction:

> Lifelong Learning and development are key to delivering the Government's vision of patient centred care in the NHS. Our main aim is to ensure that the NHS, working with its partners and related sectors, develops and equips staff with the skills they need to:
>
> ♦ support changes and improvements in patient care;
>
> ♦ take advantage of wider career opportunities; and
>
> ♦ realise their potential.
>
> This is not simply a good thing in itself. There is increasing evidence that lifelong learning, as part of good employment practice, lies at the heart of effective organisational performance.

The commitment to lifelong learning included setting up the so-called NHS 'university' (NHSU). However, in September 2004, it was announced that the NHSU would be merged with the NHS Modernisation Agency to form the new NHS Institute for Learning, Skills and Innovation, now the NHS Institute for Innovation and Improvement.

The Healthcare Commission

The Healthcare Commission took over the role of the Commission for Health Improvement (CHI) on 1 April 2004 and also assumed some of the responsibilities of the National Care Standards Commission (NCSC) and the Audit Commission, as well as a number of additional functions.

It seeks to promote continual improvement in England's health care services, focusing on what matters to the public. It does this by assessing

NHS and independent health care services, identifying where improvement is needed and investigating any serious problems. It publishes its findings, making the information as accessible as possible, to help everyone make informed decisions about their health care.

National Patient Safety Agency

The National Patient Safety Agency incorporates three agencies whose aim is to improve patient safety in different respects:

- The National Reporting and Learning Service, which deals with rapid responses to incidents, analysis of incidents that come to it via the National Reporting and Learning System and the collaborative development of actions that can be implemented locally.

- The National Clinical Assessment Service (NCAS), which helps local health care managers to understand, manage and prevent performance concerns. To resolve performance concerns NCAS offers: advice from experts with backgrounds in clinical practice, health care and human resources management, signposting to other resources to help you manage the concern; specialist interventions, including facilitation, mediation, performance assessment, action planning and back to work support and; shared learning, providing workshops and conferences to build local skills.

- The National Research Ethics Service (NRES), which was launched on 1 April 2007. NRES comprises the former Central Office for Research Ethics Committees (COREC) and Research Ethics Committees (RECs) in England. In particular, it provides ethical guidance and management support to Research Ethics Committees in England and will deliver a quality assurance framework for the Research Ethics Service.

Clinical audit

Clinical audit is a key aspect of governance and patient safety. The National Clinical Audit Advisory Group (NCAAG) was established to drive the reinvigoration programme following the CMO's report 'Good doctors, safer patients' and to provide a national focus for discussion and advice on matters relating to clinical audit.

The NCAAG is also the steering group for the expanded National Clinical Audit and Patient Outcomes Programme (NCAPOP), which is now hosted by the Healthcare Quality Improvement Partnership (HQIP), established in April 2008 to promote quality in health care, and in particular to increase the impact that clinical audit has on health care quality in England and Wales. It is led by a consortium of the Academy of Medical Royal Colleges, the Royal College of Nursing and National Voices (formerly the Long-term Conditions Alliance).

How does clinical governance affect the delivery of critical care?

The story of clinical governance in the NHS is one of governmental policy initiatives (often but not exclusively driven by catastrophic adverse outcomes), which then drive national framework initiatives, which are in turn rolled out to local level (organizational and personal).

Our starting point in the light of the governance programme we have set out above is the Department of Health's 'Comprehensive critical care—a review of adult critical care services'[15]. Reflecting many of the key concepts above, the Executive Summary states:

> Comprehensive critical care is not simply a new name for intensive care, but is a new approach based on severity of illness. Services delivered in accordance with this report will be comprehensive, inclusive and take responsibility for the critical care needs of their population. This is essential to the modernisation of the service, and to ensuring that patients, their families and friends receive first class critical care wherever they live. The report recommends that the existing division into high dependency and intensive care beds be replaced by a classification that focuses on the level of care that individual patients need. Staff numbers, skills and expertise should depend on the workload and complexity generated by the condition of individual patients.
>
> Comprehensive critical care must be planned and delivered systematically across the whole health system. The characteristics of such a service should ensure:
>
> *Integration*—A hospital wide approach with services which extend beyond the physical boundaries of intensive care and high dependency units, making optimum use of available resources including beds
>
> *Networks*—A service that is provided across NHS Trusts, working to common standards and protocols, taking responsibility for all the critically ill in all specialties within a geographical area

Workforce development—A planned approach to workforce development including the recruitment, training and retention of medical and nursing staff, and balancing the skill mix so that professional staff are able to delegate less skilled and non-clinical tasks.

A data collecting culture promoting an evidence base—A service underpinned by reliable information which will ensure the delivery of effective clinical care, demonstrated through comparative audit.

So we see that the drive for modernization includes uniformity of service by means of, among other initiatives, networking between different service providers and data collection.

In 'Quality Critical Care: Beyond 'Comprehensive Critical Care'[16] the Critical Care Stakeholder Forum set out the ways in which critical care providers from Strategic Health Authorities (SHAs) downwards could set and maintain proper standards in critical care.

Filtering down from the policy and framework level, some of the national organizations above have produced reports on critical care.

In July 2007, NICE published clinical guidelines on 'Acutely ill patients in hospital'[17]. It has also issued, for example, 'Technical patient safety solutions for ventilator-associated pneumonia in adults'.[18]

- In March 2009 NICE published 'Critical illness: rehabilitation after a period of critical illness'[19]. The clinical need for such guidelines is stated to based on, among other issues:

  More than 100,000 people are admitted into critical care units in the UK each year. Many of these people experience significant and persistent problems with physical, non-physical (such as psychological or cognitive) and social functioning after discharge from critical care. This morbidity is frequently unrecognized and, if identified, may not be appropriately assessed or managed.

- In July 2008, the Healthcare Commission published its report on 'Acute inpatient mental health',[20] which assessed the quality and safety of care in NHS acute inpatient mental health wards and psychiatric intensive care units in England. Its findings showed marked differences in standards between Trusts, and sometimes between wards within the same Trust. In particular, no Trust was scored 'excellent' on all four of the criteria; 39% were scored 'weak' on involving service users and carers; around one in nine Trusts was scored 'weak' on providing individualized care; no Trust was scored 'excellent' for the effectiveness of its care pathway from admission to discharge. Based on these findings the Healthcare Commission identified the following key areas for improvement:

- A greater focus on the individual service user and personalized care.
- Making sure that service uses, staff and visitors are safe.
- Providing appropriate and safe interventions.
- Increasing the effectiveness of the acute care pathway.

Closer to individual practitioner level, there is plenty of further guidance available. Possible sources include:

- The first port of call is probably the Intensive Care Society[21], which publishes 'Critical Insight—An Intensive Care Society (ICS) introduction to UK adult critical care services'. Beyond that there are guidelines in many different areas, divided into: Administration and Organisation (including in particular guidelines on Levels of Critical Care for Adult Patients (revised) 2008, which was written to help apply the levels of care described in 'Comprehensive Critical Care'); Clinical Practice, Guidance and Patient Safety (including critical incident reporting). The set of guidance is comprehensive and seeks to take up the governance framework initiatives listed above. For the critical care healthcare practitioner, as well as lawyers, it is invaluable.

- The Royal College of Anaesthetists[22] publishes clinical guidelines for anaesthetists (though none specifically yet which deal exclusively with critical care).

- The Royal College of Anaesthetists' 4th National Audit Project, in conjunction with the Difficult Airway Society, will deal with 'Major Complications of Airway Management in the UK', noting that:

  During every operation and admission to intensive care, it is vital to ensure that the patient can breathe through a 'clear airway'. Multiple options for achieving this are available. While these procedures are routinely performed and are usually very safe, we know that important complications occasionally occur. NHS litigation authority (NHSLA) data indicates that such events certainly do occur, but their frequency and consequences are unclear. It is likely that several patients die or suffer serious brain damage each year. The Royal College of Anaesthetists has undertaken to try to enumerate this problem as its 4th National Audit Project. This sets out to determine the number of major complications arising from airway management during anaesthesia and the number of these procedures performed per year. As similar events also occur during care in the emergency department and intensive care the project will capture these events too.

Reports of such events are often incomplete and the subject remains controversial even within the profession. This makes learning from such events difficult. Gaining a more accurate idea of the incidence of these complications will allow anaesthetists (and those involved in emergency airway management) to make better risk:benefit assessments in patient care and allow more robust disclosure of risk to patients. As well as learning how often such events occur, by studying the cohort of complications that we detect we hope to gain insight into the causes of the problems, clarify best practice and improve patient safety in England, Scotland, Northern Ireland and Wales.

- Local critical care networks and NHS Trusts will have published strategy and guidance documents.

- Regulators (e.g. the GMC) set rather less specific professional standards.

Governance, critical care, and the law

There seem to us to be a vast number of ways in which clinical governance and its constituent elements can and should be considered by lawyers in practice.

Dreaming up areas for possible legal intervention and advice is difficult, but there seem to us to be two main areas where clinical governance issues might be raised in particular: (i) poor professional standards which may lead to challenges to decisions by health care organizations or their employees or to cases brought against medical practitioners by the regulatory authorities; and (ii) applications to the Court of Protection or, exceptionally, the Family Division of the High Court, seeking declarations in respect of the treatment of patients who lack the capacity to make decision for themselves.

This chapter assumes a certain level of knowledge about the principles that apply to the judicial review of administrative actions, in particular the requirement that the decision which is impugned will be subject to review if it was unlawful, procedurally improper, or irrational in the *Wednesbury* sense.

Poor professional standards

At the most mundane level, a medical or nursing director should under his or her local clinical governance arrangements consider whether or not to refer to the GMC (or NMC) a doctor (or nurse) whose poor performance or conduct has led to adverse patient outcomes. To date, we are not aware of any reported decision which has sought to challenge such a decision at local level by way of a private claim pursuant to a contract of employment of engagement.[23] However, there have been cases where doctors have sought to challenge the issuing of an 'alert letter' issued under HSC 2002/011.

In *R (Dr D) v Secretary of State for Health*[24] the Court of Appeal considered a case in which a doctor had been accused but acquitted of five counts of indecent assault on patients. Having relinquished his registration, he was granted limited registration by the GMC. Two further allegations of indecent assault were made against him and an alert letter was issued by the Regional Director of Public Health. The doctor was informed that he would not be prosecuted in respect of the new allegations, and the alert letter was cancelled. However, the doctor's Medical Director was concerned that prospective employers might only know that allegations had been made if an alert letter remained in force; a second alert letter was issued, which the doctor sought to challenge. The Court of Appeal held that there was nothing unlawful in the issuing of the second alert letter:

> The test for disclosure is 'pressing need'…It must I think be obvious that the ascertainment of such a pressing need will require a balance to be struck between the interests of the person who is the subject of the allegations and the interests of the party to whom disclosure is proposed to be made (or those for whom that party is responsible, such as a health provider's patients); and a clear conclusion that in the circumstances the latter must prevail over the former. The nature and strength of the allegations and the vulnerability of the class of persons to be protected are likely to be at the centre of the decision-maker's consideration.[25]

In *R v Regional Director of Public Health (Trent), ex parte Dr X*[26] a paediatric registrar had been suspended for failure to follow clinical guidelines for treatment, non-cooperation with consultant colleagues, and a failure to perform duties. It was accepted that an alert letter was lawfully issued. However, the matter having been referred to the GMC, the GMC's Preliminary Proceedings Committee determined that the allegation should not proceed further. The regional director refused to withdraw the alert letter, pending completion of a performance review. The doctor challenged that refusal. The High Court held that there remained reasonable grounds within the spirit of the applicable guidelines for questioning the doctor's performance and that it was reasonable not to withdraw the alert letter. As to alert letters generally the Judge (Moses J) noted that:

> ...the alert letter was only neutral in the context of a reference to the General Medical Council. It did not imply guilt; but it is not neutral in any other sense. It is clearly a matter that could be gravely prejudicial to a practitioner seeking employment.[27]

We thought that the clinical governance issues that were considered to be relevant to the issuing of alert letters in these two cases are of general application. Not all decisions of this nature will raise questions of public law.

Health care regulators can in general take action on a practitioner's registration in cases where there are concerns about a professional's conduct, performance or health (and other scenarios which need not unduly concern the reader of this chapter). Most regulators have in recent years adopted procedures that allow them to take action against a professional's registration where his or her fitness to practise is impaired. The whole notion is fraught with controversy, and was considered at length in respect of the GMC in the Fifth Report of the Shipman Inquiry.

Nonetheless it seems to us that, where a critical care practitioner does not follow relevant guidelines, a regulator can in principle allege that a practitioner's fitness to practise is impaired by reason (in grave cases) of misconduct and (in repeated or persistent cases) of deficient performance because he or she failed to have due regard to guidelines, which were applicable at the time.[28] Such cases would involve many of the strands of clinical governance we have considered above, including the requirement for a health care practitioner to keep up to date and the requirement for regulators and employers to set standards.

Patients who lack capacity

Many, if not most, patients in critical care will at law lack the capacity to make decisions for themselves because they are not conscious. The practitioner must have regard to the Mental Capacity Act 2005 and act in the patient's best interests. The Act provides a comprehensive statutory framework based on established common law principles of best interests and the presumption of capacity.

Section 1(5) of the Mental Capacity Act 2005 states: 'An act done, or a decision made, under this Act for or on behalf of a person who lacks capacity must be done, or made, in his best interests'. Best interests are not defined in the Act. The Code of Practice provides that a person's best interests must be the basis for all decisions made and actions carried out on their behalf in situations where they lack capacity to make those particular decisions themselves.[29] Section 4 set outs a checklist, which must be considered before a decision is made, or an act is carried out. The checklist sets out a number of matters which are required to be taken into account, namely to encourage participation, identify all the relevant circumstances, find out the person's views, avoid discrimination, in decisions relating to life-sustaining treatment not to be motivated by a desire to bring about a person's death and to consult others.

Section 4(7) states that: 'He must take into account, if it is practicable and appropriate to consult them, the views of—(a) anyone named by the person as someone to be consulted on the matter in question or on matters of that kind, (b) anyone engaged in caring for the person or interested in his welfare, (c) any donee of a lasting power of attorney granted by the person, and (d) any deputy appointed for the person by the court.'

Section 4(9) provides that 'In the case of an act done, or a decision made, by a person other than the court, there is sufficient compliance with this section if (having complied with the requirements of subsections (1) to (7) he reasonably believes that what he does or decides is in the best interests of the person concerned.' The Code of Practice advises that the checklist is only the starting point: in many cases, extra factors will need to be considered.[30]

Section 5 provides protection from liability for acts done in connection with care and treatment, where reasonable steps are taken to establish whether the person lacked capacity, and when the act is done there is a reasonable belief that the person lacks capacity and that it is in the person's best interests for the Act to be done.

The Code of Practice advises that cases referred to the court include those involving ethical dilemmas in untested areas or where there are otherwise irresolvable conflicts between professionals or between professionals and family members.[31] Where the dispute relates to medical treatment the NHS Trust should in most cases make the application to the court.[32]

Where difficult decisions have arisen as to whether an a decision made or act done is in the best interests of the person lacking capacity, the courts, in particular circumstances, have found a way through to find that the act to be carried out was in the best interests of that person. In the case of *In Re Y (Mental Patient: Bone Marrow Donation)* [1997] 2 WLR 556, the court granted declarations that blood tests and a bone marrow harvesting operation could be lawfully performed on the person lacking capacity for the benefit of her sister where it would prolong the life of the mother and sister and she would receive an emotional, psychological, and social benefit from the operation and suffer minimal detriment. However, Connell J made it clear at page 560A that the best interests have to be those of the person who lacks capacity and not any other person.

We consider that Section 1(5) of the Act is engaged where the health body transfers a person from an ICU to another ICU or, indeed, out of an ICU. We also consider that a similar situation would have existed before the Act came into force. Commentaries to the Act make it clear that those parts of the Act relevant to this case are based upon an established line of authority, for example, *F v West Berkshire HA* [1989] 2 All ER 545 [HL].

However, we do not believe that as a matter of principle a person who lacks capacity should be in a better position than a person with capacity.

In the latter case, the decision to transfer a person from an ICU to another ICU or out of an ICU is likely to fall squarely within the dicta of Sir Thomas Bingham MR, in the case of *R v Cambridgeshire Health Authority Ex parte B* [1995] 1 WLR 898 at paragraph 905. If that is correct, then, the courts would only be willing to overturn decisions made by the bodies charged with allocating NHS resources where the decision was in some way irrational, illogical, or flawed though it is debatable the extent to which this principle has been consistently applied in practice.

While the Act does impose an obligation on health bodies providing care and treatment in the circumstances of a person who lacks capacity to make decisions or carry out actions in his best interests, we consider that there should be a notional parity of outcome between a person with and a person who lacks capacity.

There is likely to be a policy document in place, accompanied by a flow chart, regulating the procedure to be adopted for the admission, transfer, and discharge of patients from critical care. It will play a vital role in determining the health body's actions. The key feature of the patient's care and treatment is the practitioner's decision on clinical grounds whether that person requires critical care. If the person does not, then, he can be discharged. The health body will then be exercising its clinical judgement that admission for critical care is no longer in the person's best interests. If the person does require critical care, then it is the care itself which is in that person's best interests. Similar principles will apply to transfer to another critical care unit. The safeguards are likely to be found in the procedure to be adopted for a transfer, particularly the decisions by the practitioner as to whether a patient can be safely transferred. Unless the practitioner decides that a patient can be safely transferred, then that person will not be transferred.

Where the health body has addressed the issue of best interests within the statutory framework of the Act and reasonably believes that the person who requires critical care can be safely discharged or transferred to another unit, then, the issue arises whether the health body itself should make an application to the court in cases where the patient's family object to discharge or transfer to another unit.

The Code of Practice advises that one of the circumstances where such an application should be made is where there is an irresolvable conflict between the professionals and the family. The practicalities and expense of making such an application on notice to the family before transfer may present significant obstacles. However, if it does not make the application, then, it will not exercise control of the litigation process, and on balance, until such time as the matter has been considered by the courts we consider that the guidance in the Code of Practice that the health body should make the application should be followed.

Conclusion

It can be seen that although clinical governance has become firmly embedded in the culture of the NHS, we should be aware that it is, in the final analysis, only a system to promote the continuous monitoring, regulation, and sustained improvements in the standards of clinical care. It is dependent on the commitment of managers and health care professionals to participate, not only in the procedures, but also to adopt the ethos and philosophy of clinical governance into their practise, and not merely to practice defensively and become slaves to protocols and form-filling.

The NHS is a large publicly funded government institution and requires responsible operational management. Where the principles of clinical governance come into conflict with those of corporate responsibility, it appears that the overreaching priority is the maintenance of reasonable standards of clinical care, and even resource issues will not be allowed to interfere with safe practice and the avoidance of unacceptable risk to patients.

However, even with increased monitoring and regulation of the quality of care, there is a danger that, in the event of further deficits in clinical care coming to light, it will still be the individual hospitals and doctors that remain in the firing line, rather than the institutional shortcomings of the NHS.

The standard of care, which the law sets, is simply stated: a health care provider must treat his or her patient with reasonable skill and care; however, such a professional is not guilty of negligence if he or she acts in accordance with a standard accepted as proper by a responsible body of opinion, skilled in that particular area, provided that opinion stands up to logical analysis.[33]

As in regulatory cases, in these cases, it would be argued that a health-care professional's failure to have due regard to applicable professional standards would be a breach of duty on his or her part. For such an argument to succeed, it would have to be demonstrated that (i) the guideline in question had been sufficiently well promulgated and/or that the practitioner should have been aware of it. Standards set by the Intensive Care Society will normally fit into this category; (ii) there was no good or sufficient reason to depart from the guideline. Failure to follow a guideline in these circumstances would in our view be powerful evidence of negligence. Increasingly our experience is that clinical guidelines are referred to by expert witnesses as supporting their view, and recent High Court judgements are scattered with references to applicable clinical guidelines.

References

1 http://www.dh.gov.uk/en/publichealth/patientsafety/Clinicalgovernance/index. htm.

2 Department of Health; HSC 1998/113; 1 July 1998.

3 Department of Health; HSC 199/065; 16 March 1999.

4 Department of Health; 13 June 2000.

5 Department of Health; 17 April 2001.

6 www.gmc-uk.org

7 www.gdc-uk.org

8 www.nmc-uk.org

9 www.rpsgb.org.uk

10 www.hpc-uk.org

11 www.chre.org.uk

12 Department of Health; 14 July 2006.

13 Department of Health; 21 February 2007.

14 Department of Health; 21 February 2007.

15 Department of Health; HSC 200/017; 25 May 2000; HSC 2000/017.

16 Critical Care Stakeholder Forum; 12 October 2005.

17 NICE; July 2007; ref CG50.

18 NICE; August 2008; ref PSG002.

19 NICE Clinical Guideline 83 (issue date March 2009).

20 Healthcare Commission; July 2008.

21 www.ics.ac.uk

22 www.rcoa.ac.uk

23 Though we are aware of cases where doctors have sought damages for breach of
    contract, their employer having suspended them or referred them to the GMC,
    which have settled out of court.

24 [2006] Lloyd's Rep Med 457, CA.

25 Per Laws LJ, para 29.

26 [2001] Lloyd's Rep Med 338.

27 Para 43.

28 For a useful summary of the current law on the meaning of misconduct and
    deficient performance, see R (Calhaem) v GMC [2007] EWHC 2606 (Jackson J),
    in particular part IV of the judgement.

29 Principle 4 Code.

30 Code 5.6.

31 Code 8.23.

32 Code 8.8.

33 The Bolam test, from Bolam v Friern Hospital Management Committee [1957] 2 All
    ER 118, last restated and explained by the House of Lords in Bolitho v City &
    Hackney HA [1998] AC 232.

Chapter 9

Reverse triage? Managing scarce resources in intensive care

Christopher Newdick and
Christopher Danbury

Introduction: Current practice and predicted demand

Intensive care medicine (ICM) is a young specialty that has developed
over the last 50 years. It epitomizes the statement of a former Secretary
of State for Health: 'Every advance in medical science creates new
needs that did not exist until the means of getting them came into
existence.'[1] Prior to the development of ICM, the vast majority of
patients who became critically ill died. Recent studies demonstrate
the mortality of critically ill patients who are not admitted to intensive care is approximately 48% compared with a 30% mortality in
those receiving ICM.[2] Therefore, from a purely medical viewpoint,
there is a clear need for critical care to be provided. However, it has
been argued that there is no country able to provide state-of-the-art
treatment to all of its citizens.[3] As Syrett puts it, 'resources for the
delivery of healthcare (supply) are finite—both funds used to finance
it and the physical resources needed (hospitals, medical staff, equipment etc) are limited—but demand for access to care is, at the least,
highly elastic and potentially infinite.'[4]

In February 2009, the spread of critical care provision across the
country varied between 83 general critical care beds in Guy's and St
Thomas' NHS Trust to 2 in the Liverpool Women's Hospital NHS
Trust.[5] This equates to a variation in critical care provision of between
11 critical care beds per 100,000 in Central London to 1.5 per 100,000
in West Berkshire.[6] Demand for ICU beds is not static. The data in

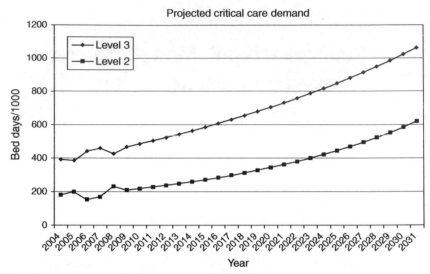

⁷Fig. 9.1 Projected Future Need for Critical Care Resources Modelled by the Intensive Care National Audit Centre (ICNARC).

Fig. 9.1 has been derived by the Intensive Care National Audit Rearch Centre (ICNARC) and predicts the increase in number of level 3 and level 2 bed days on ICU for the next two decades.[7]

This data shows a clear rise in ICU bed days over the last few years and demonstrates the projected increased need to come. The estimate is that the number of ICU bed days will double over the next 15 years. Bearing in mind the ageing population and increase in complexity of medical procedures, this is not an unexpected result. It is likely therefore that the increase in provision of ICM beds will not keep pace with demand. In the late 1990s, the relative lack of critical care beds became acute with the consequence that the emergency bed service handled up to 1200 requests per month to transfer critically ill patients between hospitals.[8]

It has been shown by a number of studies that transferring critically ill patients between hospitals has a detrimental effect on clinical outcome.[9] Since the implementation of the report Comprehensive Critical Care in 2000 discussed below, it is clear that the number transfers has fallen dramatically. However, there continues to be a need to transfer critically ill patients, especially during the annual pressure of winter

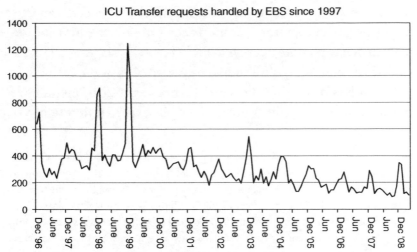

8Fig. 9.2 ICU transfer requests handled by the emergency bed service since 1997. (Supplied by the Emergency Bed Service under a Freedom of Information request).

(Fig. 9.2). Due to the expected increased demand, it is distinctly possible that further crises of the sort witnessed in 1998 and 1999 will take place again and that transferring critically ill patients between hospitals for non-medical reasons will again become commonplace. Rationing in intensive care, it seems, will become more common and more controversial.

The process of ICM rationing has been subject to relatively limited research. The Values, Ethics and Rationing in Critical Care (VERICC) Task Force[10] examined the process and came to the unsurprising conclusion that a number of factors were associated with refusal of admission to intensive care; they include advanced age, high illness severity, medical diagnosis, poor performance status, and bed shortages. As the review concludes:

> In practice, intensivists make the majority of triaging and rationing decisions a priori, acting as gatekeepers ... Although these decisions have important ramifications, they are not always objective. It remains unclear how clinicians reason and ration ethically. Moreover, as the health of our aging population deteriorates, and as critical care becomes more expensive, the need to optimize triage and rationing decisions will intensify ... Additionally, the synthesis of these studies into this systematic review does not provide clear recommendations or guidance for rationing critical care resources. The medical community would ideally work toward consistent definitions for rationing and triage.[11]

How can such practice be defended? A purely Hippocratic approach might insist that doctors should focus only on the best interests of the patients they are treating in the present. As Harris argues: 'Each person's desire to stay alive should be regarded as of the same importance and as deserving the same respect as that of anyone else, irrespective of the quality of their life or its expected duration.'[12] He continues:

> The principle that each individual is entitled to an equal opportunity to benefit from any public health care system, and that this entitlement is proportionate neither to the size of their chance of benefiting, nor to the quality of the benefit, nor to the length of lifetime remaining in which that benefit may be enjoyed ... It is my contention that any system of prioritisation of the resources available for healthcare or for rationing such resources must be governed by this principle.[13]

Although Harris argues that the adoption of utilitarian approaches may lead to 'de facto discrimination against groups of people needing health care,'[14] he also concedes that 'the crucial issue is that of distributive justice, of how public resources may be allocated to do justice to the equal claims of individual citizens.'[15] Perhaps this brings us to the crucial question in intensive care—that of respecting the equal rights of all to *equal access* to intensive care, rather than a crude application of the 'first come first served' rule to the exclusion of all others irrespective of their need. There is a story (which neither of us can now trace) of a field doctor operating on patients damaged in the trenches during the First World War. Prior to the development of triage, his consistent practice was to devote all his time to the patient in front of him before moving to consider the needs of the next. In one sense, this is laudably 'Hippocratic', but is it reasonable? Is it ethically acceptable to ignore the needs of patients bleeding to death in order to complete the tying of a bandage or fastening a sling? One suspects that many soldiers in desperate need of treatment for their wounds might have been helped, but under such a regime, were left in a queue and may have died awaiting the treatment of others with superficial injuries.

The logic of this clinical dilemma suggests that triage has an ethical basis. In circumstances where hard choices have to be made in the allocation of scarce resources, one often has to take a broader, more community-centred approach to medical ethics. It is not solely the patient's interests that have to be considered.[16] Logic notwithstanding, this approach could also confuse the doctor-patient relationship. Would it incline doctors to embark on a crude quality adjusted life year (QALY)-at-the-bedside calculation of the patient's capacity to benefit from care?[17] Would it encourage institutional ageism by discriminating against older patients?[18] Given the dangers, we should be clear how such a system would work. The following considers how this imprecise and general rule about triage, which we may accept in principle, can be clarified and applied in practice. We examine (B) priority setting in intensive care, (C) withdrawing care and the risks of *transferring* patients, and (D) institutional negligence.

Priority setting in intensive care?

Tony Bland's case demonstrates that it is proper to ask whether a continuation of *futile* treatment is in the patient's 'best interests', and this is heavily, although not exclusively, influenced by the *Bolam* test.[19] But what happens when resource constraints force upon doctors the need to decide between patients in none of whom the treatment is futile? The literature shows that transferring patients between acute units is detrimental to their outcome.[20] If demand for intensive care exceeds the facilities available, and the entire group would benefit from intensive care, it is never in their best interests to be removed from the unit, or denied access to the care it offers. In these circumstances, it seems, *micro*-issues of an individual's best interests cannot be considered in isolation. The question also has to address *macro*-issues to do with fairness in access to finite resources and distributive justice. How should the matter be considered?

As a starting point, human rights law permits resource allocation in health care, even to the extent of policies that do not fund (or adequately fund) life-saving, or life-prolonging treatment. In *Pentiacova v Moldova*, a group of patients suffered chronic renal failure and required haemodialysis. They alleged that they were victims of a breach of the right to life protection of Article 2 of the European Convention on Human Rights because public health services for the illness had declined and were inadequate compared to the haemodialysis services available in other countries. However, the Court declared the complaint inadmissible. Accepting the truth of the complaint, it said

> the applicants' claim amounts to a call on public funds which, in view of the scarce resources, would have to be diverted from other worthy needs funded by the taxpayer... While it is clearly desirable that everyone should have access to a full range of medical treatment, including life-saving medical procedures and drugs, the lack of resources means that there are, unfortunately, in the Contracting States many individuals who do not enjoy them, especially in cases of permanent and expensive treatment... the Court is of the opinion that in the circumstances of the present case it cannot be said that the respondent State failed to strike a fair balance between the competing interests of the applicants and the community as a whole.[21]

This demonstrates a distinct reluctance on the part of an international court to involve itself in difficult issues of national priority setting, 'opportunity costs', and the conflict that may arise between competing demands. As we shall see, our own courts have a similar reticence. Should this approach also apply to decisions made within an intensive care unit intended to optimize the best interests of *a group* of patients, without abandoning any of them? The view of the GMC is that

> Decisions about what treatment options can be offered may be complicated by resource constraints – for example, funding restrictions on certain treatments in the NHS, or lack of availability of intensive care beds. In such circumstances, you must balance sometimes competing duties towards the individual patient, the wider population, funding bodies and employers. There will often be no simple solution and, ideally, decisions about access to treatments should be made on the basis of an agreed local or national policy, which takes account of the human rights implications. Decisions made on a case-by-case basis, without reference to agreed policy, risk introducing elements of unfair discrimination or failure to properly consider the patient's human rights.
>
> You must ...
>
> j   Provide the best service possible within the resources available.
>
> k   Be familiar with any local and national policies which set out agreed criteria for access to the particular treatment (such as national service frameworks and NICE/SIGN guidelines).
>
> l   Give priority to patients on the basis of need, where you are able to do so, considering the overall benefit that treatment offers to the patient.
>
> m   Be fair and non-discriminatory in decisions about prioritising patients.
>
> n   Be open and honest about the decision-making process and the criteria for prioritising patients in individual cases.[22]

This professional and ethical guidance supports the need for resource allocation in the ICU and suggests that autonomy cannot be the only consideration in these circumstances. In addition to *autonomy*, law, and ethics recognize a *communitarian* value in which the interests of other people also become relevant. Thus, there may be circumstances in which it would be acceptable to refuse a patient admission to an ICU simply because all the existing beds were occupied. Similarly, it may be permissible to transfer a patient from intensive care in order to accommodate a new patient. While everyone would acknowledge that this could not *promote* their best interests, such a course may be lawful provided it does not present unacceptable danger to their best interests and follows reasonable system of risk assessment in their case.

If this is correct, the consent of the patient to this course of action is not crucial. Ultimately, in these most stark and difficult cases, we return to the various observations of the courts in connection with the duties of PCTs and hospitals in circumstances of scarce resources. As the Court of Appeal said in *R v Cambridge DHA, ex p B*

> I have no doubt in a perfect world any treatment which a patient, or a patient's family, sought would be provided if doctors were willing to give it, no matter how much it cost, particularly when a life was potentially at stake. It would however be shutting one's eyes to the real world if the court were to proceed on the basis that we do live in such a word... Difficult and agonizing judgements have to be made as to how a limited budget is best allocated to the maximum advantage of the maximum number of patients. That is not a judgement the court can make.[23]

So much for the broad principle. This leaves unanswered, however, the precise circumstances in which such a decision would be permissible. The courts cannot stand in the doctors' shoes and make *substantive*, patient-level, decisions of this complexity.[24] Equally, they can insist upon good, logical *reasons* that justify such a decision. As the Court of Appeal said in *R v NW Lancashire HA, ex p A, D & G*

> ...the more important the interests of the citizen that the decision effects, the greater will be the degree of consideration that is required of the decision-maker. A decision that, as is the evidence in this case, seriously affects the citizen's health will require substantial consideration, and be subject to careful scrutiny by the court as to its rationality. That will particularly be the case in respect of decisions...which involve the refusing of any, or any significant, treatment...[25]

The issue, then, is not so much *whether* priority setting occurs in intensive care, but *how* it occurs. The distinction is made clear in two cases. First, in the infamous case of *Collier*,[26] a young boy urgently required a hole in the heart operation and was placed top of his consultant's list of clinical priorities. However, he was repeatedly refused access to paediatric intensive care facilities because of a shortage of intensive care nurses. Other than by an imprecise reference to resource shortages, no explanation was offered as to why the boy could not have been transferred to another hospital for his care. Nevertheless, in 1988 his claim for access to the NHS care failed and he died without having the operation. Over 20 years later, such a conclusion is inconceivable. Today, the hospital, or health authority would be required to explain why such an outcome could not reasonably be avoided. On the other hand, as the case of *Girl B*[27] shows, good reasons may explain why beneficial treatment cannot be offered; for example, if it is unlikely to be effective, will cause more harm than good, and divert disproportionate resource from other patients. In cases involving competing claims for scarce IC resources, doctors should be capable of explaining their clinical decisions. Equally, the courts should also be sensitive to the fact that decisions often have to be made rapidly, sometimes in emergency circumstances and without time for agonized reflection. Courts should remember that in litigation, they have a luxury, in terms of the time for calm and detached analysis, which is often not available to doctors in the heat of a clinical crisis.

Withdrawing care and the risks of *transferring* patients

Let us explore this question further by testing the limits of the proposition that rationing in intensive care may be acceptable: Is it acceptable to *withdraw*, rather to withhold care from patients who need intensive care treatment, in order, for example, to transfer them to another hospital? At its most extreme, let us assume that such a transfer to another hospital is impossible because none have spare IC capacity. Would it be justifiable simply to withdraw treatment from patient A in order to admit patient B who has better clinical prospects? The distinction between withholding and withdrawing care is likely to be extremely sensitive in practice. How much more acceptable must it be to withhold care that has not commenced in the first place, than to *withdraw* care once it has been started. Although the evidence is anecdotal, there are at least two views. Some intensivists consider that

> We have a duty of care for patients whose referral we have accepted. Ethically, once we have accepted responsibility for a patient, we should only do what is in the patient's best interests. Logically, transferring an existing critical care patient to make room for a new one is not in the existing patient's best interests, so ethically we cannot do it. Thus, when our unit is full, logically and ethically we must not think about which of our patients is fittest for transfer, we have to transfer the new patent.[28]

By contrast, others reject this view and insist that an assessment must be made as to which patient (including the new one) can be transferred with least risk. 'They are all equal. We cannot discriminate between them except on the basis of need, which means that we must consider all the risks, not just the risks to patients who happened to get sick earlier.'[29] This presents the argument we call 'reverse triage'.

Which view is preferable? As *Girl B* case suggests above, a decision *not* to treat at all may be legitimate on grounds of finite resources, but does this also apply equally to *withdrawing* care from a patient already benefitting from intensive care? Take the case of patient, A, whose best interests are to continue their treatment in intensive care. He is transferred from the unit to make space for another patient in even greater clinical need. His condition deteriorates and he suffers damage that, but for his removal, would have been avoided. Would the law recognize any grounds of complaint? Let us add: (a) that the reasons for removing A were well considered and he was chosen on the ground that his condition was the 'least worst' in the unit and the consultant thought he was likely to suffer the least serious harm as a result and (b) but for his removal, another patient, patient B, could not have been admitted to intensive care and her condition was so serious that she would probably have died without admission.

Are legal arguments available to support patient A's right not to be removed from intensive care, notwithstanding the interests of patient B? Should A have a *prior* right to care over B because they are already in hospital? Such a claim would arise in the law of medical negligence and be based on the duty of care owed to the patient. For example, in *Tony Bland's* case, it was said that '...it would not be lawful for a medical practitioner who assumed responsibility for the care of an unconscious patient simply to give up treatment where continuance of it would confer some benefit on the patient.'[30] But this statement was addressed to the different context of *futile* care in which there were no competing 'macro' interests from other patients. It was not intended to deal with the rights and duties of patients in the ICU. However, there are other negligence cases in which a distinction has been made between *failing* to make things better, and actively making them *worse*. Thus, emergency services have been held not liable for *failing* to respond adequately to emergencies on the ground that their statutory duty is only a 'target' duty, which does not confer rights to claim damages on claimants.[31] However, if for example, the fire services arrive on the scene and actively make things worse, then liability may arise.[32] By analogy with these cases, could it be argued that there is no duty to *admit* a patient to intensive, but that to remove a patient from intensive care when it is not in their best interests, could be actionable under the 'making things worse' rule?

We consider this argument is mistaken. We know of no case that has dealt with precisely this distinction in the IC context and the point appears to be undecided. However, it is surely wrong to imply, as does the first view, that doctors have no duty to those not yet been admitted to the ICU; surely the *hospital* to which the patient has been admitted owes a duty to respond reasonably to the patent's needs.[33] If resource constraints restrict the level of care available, the duty remains to take reasonable steps to respond to the patient's needs. To this extent, therefore, the hospital is under a duty to have *systems* in place which consider whether admission is impossible, whether the patient can be transferred to another hospital, or whether another patient is sufficiently robust to tolerate transfer so that the new patient can be admitted.

Further, the emergency services are not wholly analogous to IC for a number of reasons. First, in the fire brigade cases, unintended *mistakes* were made in the way they responded to the emergencies before them. This would not be the case in respect of deliberate, reasonable, and proportionate transfer decisions in respect of intensive care. Second, as we have seen, it is not accurate to say that *hospitals* do not owe a duty of care to patients admitted for care. They are subject to an enforceable duty of care (not merely an unenforceable 'target' duty).[34] Third, even in the fire-brigade case, it was said that the duty owed to one property owner could not be considered in isolation from the needs of others.

> The fire-brigade's duty is owed to the public at large to prevent the spread of fire and that this may involve a conflict between the various owners of premises. It may be necessary to enter and cause damage to A's premises in order to tackle a fire which has started in B's. During the Great Fire of London the Duke of York had to blow up a number of houses not yet affected by fire, in order to make a fire break.[35]

By analogy with the fire brigade, a doctor too 'owes a duty to the individual patient. But he also owes a duty to his other patients, which may prevent him from giving one patient the treatment or resources he would ideally prefer'.[36] This supports the view that duties can be owed to more than one person at a time.[37] Provided the 'compromise' in responding to competing demands is rational and proportionate, it is unlikely to give rise to a breach of the duty of care. If this is correct, it suggests that even though a party is reliant upon the care of another, and the other takes steps that do not promote the best interests of that party alone, those steps may be justified by public interests, or the needs of other people. Support for this approach is contained in (what is called) the 'policy-operational' distinction, which separates 'public' decisions taken in respect of, for example, public interests and the allocation of scarce resources from matters of a wholly 'private' nature (such as medical negligence) concerning the operation of day-to-day decisions. Decisions at the 'policy' end of the spectrum are said to be 'polycentric' in the sense that changes in one area have inevitable consequences elsewhere (what health economists sometimes call 'opportunity costs'). For this reason, the courts are unlikely to interfere with them unless they are so outrageous that they defy logic and common sense.[38] For example, in a case involving priority setting within a finite local authority budget, the court said

> ...there is a spectrum at one end of which lie decisions which are heavily influenced by policy and which come close to being non-justiciable. In relation to such decisions, the court is unlikely to find negligence proved unless they are ones

which no reasonable education authority could have made. At the other end of the spectrum are decisions involving professional judgement and expertise in relation to individual children... In relation to these decisions, the court will only find negligence on the part of the person (for which the authority may be vicariously liable) if he or she failed to act in accordance with a practice accepted at the time as proper by a responsible body of persons of the same profession and skill: see *Bolam v Friern Hospital Management Committee*.[39]

On this basis, *withdrawing* care from patients for proportionate reasons to do with the overwhelming clinical need of others may be justified under the 'policy' approach over which the judges are so reluctant to adjudicate.

A related argument for the same conclusion can be put another way. One of the central principles of the modern law of negligence is that a duty of care should not be imposed upon a party unless it is 'fair, just and reasonable' to do so.[40] Would this test be satisfied by a patient currently being treated in intensive care, who argued that he was owed a duty of care such that his right to remain in the unit persisted irrespective of the needs of other patients? Arguably, it would not be fair, just, and reasonable to others, perhaps those involved in a serious motorway accident to exclude consideration of their interests in such a way. This is particularly relevant to cases involving sensitive decisions on the allocation of scarce resources. This suggests that, provided the unit works to a reasonable and consistent policy, which responds to individual cases in a proportionate manner, they are unlikely to be in breach of a duty of care to a patient for whom the risk of removal from the unit is acceptable. Equally, were no such policy to exist and decisions were made, which could not be justified, it may be argued that, under the 'policy-operational' distinction, the *operational* judgement in relation to the individual patient was so deficient as to support an allegation of negligence. This strongly suggests that intensivists should agree general transfer guidance in which decisions are not left to single individuals without the support and input of their colleagues.

Institutional negligence

Let us turn finally to the issue of the systems that should exist to enable these unenviable decisions to be made reasonably. As our comments suggest, the right to 'prioritize' intensive care resources exists provided reasonable and proportionate systems are available for doing so. Apart from the duty of care imposed on individual clinicians, the law requires *institutions* to have reasonable systems of management in place to promote proper standards of care and manage risk. Thus, hospitals must ensure effective channels of communication between clinicians,[41] reasonable systems for calling upon consultants working in split site hospitals,[42] and guarantee reasonable supervision for junior staff.[43] How might institutional negligence apply to admitting patients to intensive care? We should start by acknowledging that 'critical care involves uncertainty, variability, nonlinearity, complexity, numerous constraints and expensive resources. It is very difficult, if at all possible, to use randomized trials to obtain the necessary evidence for making good decisions about critical care capacity and organization.'[44] For example, there is no duty to have in place staff and facilities designed to respond to rare events. which are expected very infrequently:

> that the whole system obviously has to be framed to deal with that which is reasonably foreseeable. I do not take the view that the whole system has to be framed to deal with the possibility that a rare occurrence will happen, and by rare the figure mentioned is one in a thousand... The duty to... co-exists with a number of other duties...[45]

If we concede, therefore, that a perfect response to every case will not always be possible, what framework of guidance is available to assist the planning and organization of intensive care services?

The problem of lack of guidance about proper planning of critical care resources arose in the late 1990s. There was an increase in the numbers of critically ill patients transferred between hospitals for non-clinical reasons because of a lack of appropriate critical care beds. The response of the Department of Health was to commission the report: Comprehensive Critical Care.[46] This report, which was accepted in full by the Department of Health in 'HSC 2000/017: Modernising critical care services', redefined the landscape of critical care in the United Kingdom. It defined four levels of support as:

> *Level 0* Patients whose needs can be met through normal ward care in an acute hospital.

Level 1 Patients at risk of their condition deteriorating, or those recently relocated from higher levels of care, whose needs can be met on an acute ward with additional advice and support from the critical care team.

Level 2 Patients requiring more detailed observation or intervention including support for a single failing organ system or post-operative care and those 'stepping down' from higher levels of care.

Level 3 Patients requiring advanced respiratory support alone or basic respiratory support together with support of at least two organ systems. This level includes all complex patients requiring support for multi-organ failure.'[47]

The report recommended planning critical care provision both locally and with further support nationally:

Detailed analysis of the Augmented Care Period (ACP) dataset should be undertaken at Trust level to support assessment of need and service planning, as well as nationally to inform future development. We recommend that necessary modifications to the ACP dataset including its extension to all patients receiving level one care throughout the hospital, should be identified and expedited.[48]

More recently, however, this approach has been criticized for being overly simplistic and alternative models have been proposed.[49] Shahani states, '[i]t is a well-known mathematical fact that required capacities in the face of nonlinearity and considerable variability depend not only on the average values but also the amount of variability.'[50] This mathematical premise is not addressed by the use of the ACP dataset. Shahani et al. argue, 'Within the National Health Service there is a general lack of appreciation of the need for taking complexity, variability, and uncertainty properly into account. The result is that planning decisions are often based on the unsatisfactory approaches such as using average values only.'[51] Never the less, in reply to this paper, Higgs and Goddard[52] illustrate the practical application following a furore about lack of critical care beds during the 2005 General Election[53]. Higgs and Goddard emphasize:

1 Demand is actively managed and coordinated by the provider of care, vs a traditionally uncoordinated, passive, approach.

2 Clinical ownership such that it is a named senior doctor's responsibility to focus on throughput.

3 Perception of fairness by the referring surgical teams, hence the multidisciplinary panel team membership.

4 Authority to make decisions and, in concert with individual surgeons, control operation dates.

5 Clinical credibility—consultant coordination with senior critical care nurse support.[54]

This last example demonstrates what can be achieved by planning and organization. If there are serious concerns about *systematic* under-resourcing, then the clinician is bound by GMC guidance. The GMC says:

> You should make every effort to avoid withholding or stopping treatment when this would involve significant risk for the patient and the only justification for doing so is resource limitation. If you have good reason to think that patient safety is being compromised by inadequate resources, and it is not within your power to put the matter right, you should draw the situation to the attention of the appropriate individual or organisation, following our supplementary guidance on *Raising concerns about patient safety*.[55]

Therefore, some hospitals have initiated systems to monitor and review admissions to ICU. As we have argued, in the absence of such systems that provide for a reasonable and consistent policy about transferring patients, intensivists may leave themselves open to an allegation of negligence. In addition, were a patent to die as a result of a gross failure of management, the managers could be subject to the Corporate Manslaughter and Corporate Homicide Act 2007.[56]

Conclusion

Like so many other specialties, resources in intensive care are constrained. At the best of times, decision-making during these moments is likely to have profound consequences for patients. We should expect, however, that demand for intensive care services will increase both with changes in demography and advances in medical and pharmaceutical technology. We have argued that in both ethics and law, priority setting in intensive care is reasonable. Nevertheless, proper systems must exist as a framework within which these difficult decisions should be addressed. To fail to have systems that are capable of planning for and managing demand exposes both clinicians and hospital trusts to risk, especially if individuals are left to cope alone. Working within this legal framework, the response to the risk presented by the outbreak of H1N1 pandemic influenza forced the government to acknowledge that critical care provision could be swamped. The Department of Health issued guidance on behalf of the H1N1 Critical Care Clinical Group[57] and endorsed some of the approaches that we have discussed. Acknowledging the need for a systematic response to anticipated pressures on intensive care services, it advised that:

4. The topic of triage has been raised in a number of forums. Triage involves managing care where demand is outstripping resources. This is not the same as standard critical care clinical practice where decisions about whether or not an individual will benefit from intensive care are made every day.

5. Triage would involve making choices between patients who would all benefit from intensive care. This does imply however that all other measures (such as stopping elective work, expanding capacity, transfer within networks and transfer between networks)… have been exhausted. This situation has not been reached to date and it is not expected to be, based on the forward modelling of influenza H1N1.

6. The CCCG recommends that if triage has to be undertaken it is done by more than one experienced clinician, is fully documented and such processes are worked through in advance…

7. The intention is that, by robust action now within and between networks, triage will be avoided.…

9. There must be recognition within Trusts (clinical and managerial) of the requirement to cease elective activity when faced with increased demand in line with the guidance on responding to pressures developed by the Department of Health. The following actions are likely:

- ◆ Reducing or stopping elective surgical activity to reduce other calls on critical care;
- ◆ Conversion of level 1 and 2 beds to level 3 beds;
- ◆ Conversion of other areas—such as post operative recovery—to critical care. …

12. The decision to admit a patient into critical care, with or without H1N1 infection, is a clinical one. This takes into consideration many factors but especially the likely benefit (or otherwise) to that individual from critical care. This is not triage—but is standard critical care practice based on clinical prioritisation.

This reinforces the need for a framework for making choices and that, in these difficult circumstances, clinical decisions should normally be made collaboratively and not by individuals working alone. As we have seen from the ICNARC data considered earlier, to the extent that critical care 'need' is predictable, it should be considered in advance by both acute trusts and the wider NHS and responded to with proper planning. To fail to do so exposes individuals and institutions to serious risk.[58]

References

1 Powell E (1966). *A New Look at Medicine*, Pittman Medical Publishing, p. 26.

2 Garrouste-Orgeas M, Montuclard L, Timsit JF, et al. (2005). Predictors of intensive care unit refusal in French intensive care units: a multiple-center study. *Critical Care Medicine* **33**: 750–755.

   Frishmo-Lima P, Gurman G, Schapira A, Porath A (1994). Rationing critical care – what happens to patients who are not admitted? *Theoretical Surgery* **9**: 208–211.

   Sprung CL, Geber D, Eidelman LA, et al. (1999). Evaluation of triage decisions for intensive care admission. *Critical Care Medicine* **27**: 1073–1079.

   Joynt GM, Gomersall CD, Tan P, Lee A, Cheng CA,Wong EL (2001). Prospective evaluation of patients refused admission to an intensive care unit: triage, futility and outcome. *Intensive Care Medicine* **27**: 1459–1465.

   Metcalfe MA, Sloggett A, McPherson K (1997). Mortality among appropriately referred patients refused admission to intensive-care units. *Lancet* **350**: 7–11.

   Garrouste-Orgeas M, Montuclard L, Timsit JF, Misset B, Christias M, Carlet J (2003). Triaging patients to the ICU. A pilot study of factors influencing admission decisions and patient outcomes. *Intensive Care Medicine* **29**: 774–781.

   Simchen E, Sprung CL, Galai N, et al. (2004). Survival of critically ill patients hospitalized in and out of intensive care units under paucity of intensive care unit beds. *Critical Care Medicine* **32**: 1654–1661.

3 Buxton M (1993). Economic appraisal and prescribing choices. *Prescribers Journal* **33**: 133.

4 Syrett K (2007). *Law, Legitimacy and the Rationing of Health Care. A Contextual and Comparative Perspective*. Cambridge University Press, Cambridge, p. 27.

5 DH http://www.dh.gov.uk/en/Publicationsandstatistics/Statistics/Performancedataandstatistics/Beds/DH_077451 (accessed 27 February 2009)

6 Derived Annual reports of Guy's and St Thomas' NHS Foundation Trust and Royal Berkshire NHS Foundation Trust.

7 Personal communication, Dr D Harrison & Prof K Rowan, ICNARC, which we gratefully acknowledge.

8 Fig. 9.2: FOI request from Emergency Bed Service of the London Ambulance Service. May 2009.

9 For example: Duke GJ, Green JV (2001). Outcome of critically ill patients undergoing interhospital transfer. *MJA* **174**: 122–125. Papson, JPN (2007). Unexpected events during the intrahospital transport of critically ill patients. *Academic Emergency Medicine* **14**(6).

Beckmann U, Gillies DM, Berenholtz SM, et al. (2004) Incidents relating to the intra-hospital transfer of critically ill patients. *Intensive Care Medicine* **30**(8): 1579–1585.

10 Sinuff T, Kahnamoui K, Cook DJ, Luce JM, Levy MM. (2004). Rationing critical care beds: a systematic review. For the Values, Ethics & Rationing in Critical Care (VERICC) Task Force. *Critical Care Medicine* **32**: 1588–1597.

11 Ibid, p. 1596. For an earlier consideration of ICU resource management, see Dyson R (1996). *Rational Resource Allocation: Management Perspectives*, in Pace N, McLean SAM (eds). *Ethics and the Law in Intensive Care*. Oxford University Press, Oxford, 1996.

12 Harris J (1985). *The Value of Life*. Routledge, p. 101.

13 Harris J (1999). Justice and equal opportunities in health care. *Bioethics* **13**(5): 392–404, at 392–393.

14 Ibid, p. 393.

15 Ibid, p. 404.

16 See Rescher N (1969). The allocation of exotic medical lifesaving therapy. *Ethics* **79**: 173. See also, McTurk L (1996). Rational resource allocation: ethical perspectives. In Pace N, McLean SAM (eds). *Ethics and the Law in Intensive Care*. Oxford University Press.

17 Hope T, Spirings D, Crisp R (1993). Not clinically indicated: patients interests or resource allocation? *BMJ* **306**: 379.

18 Farrant A (2009). The fair innings argument and increasing life spans. *Journal of Medical Ethics* **35**: 53–56; Shaw AB (1994). In defence of ageism. *Journal of Medical Ethics* **20**: 188.

19 In *Airedale N.H.S. Trust Respondents v. Bland* [1993] AC 789, 883 Lord Browne-Wilkinson said, '… a doctor's decision whether invasive care is in the best interests of the patient falls to be assessed by reference to the test laid down in *Bolam v. Friern Hospital Management Committee* [1957] 1 W.L.R. 582. Note however, that since then the courts have begun to distinguish *Bolam* and "best interests"test. In *Re A (male sterilisation)* (2000) 53 BMLR 66, the Court said that the two duties imposed by *Bolam* and the 'best interests test' have not been conflated into one requirement. "In the case of an application for approval of a sterilisation operation, it is the judge, not the doctor, who makes the decision that it is in the best interests of the patient that the operation be performed." See also In *Re SL (Adult sterilisation)* [2000] Lloyd's Rep Med **339**: 345–446.

20 For instance see:

Himmelstein DU, Woolhandler S, Harnly M, et al. (1984). Patient transfers: Medical practice as social triage. *Am J Public Health* **74**: 494–497.

Waddell G, Scott PDR, Lees NW, et al. (1975). Effects of ambulance transport in critically ill patients. *BMJ* **1**: 386-389.

Karipis H, Scheinkestel CD, Tuxen DV, et al. (1993). Safety of transportation of critically ill patients. *Anaesth Intensive Care* **21**: A7111.

Bristow P, Brown D, Lee A, et al. (1995). Transfer of severely ill patients. *Anaesth Intensive Care* **23**: A399.

21 (2005) 40 EHRR 209. See also *Sentges v Netherlands* (2005). App no 27667/02 (dec inadmissible, DMD case) '… regards must be had to the fair balance that has to be struck between the competing interests of the individual and of the community as a whole and to the wide margin of appreciation enjoyed by States in this respect in determining the steps to be taken to ensure compliance with the Convention… This margin of appreciation is even wider when, as in the present case, the issues involve an assessment of the priorities in the context of the allocation of limited State resources. In view of their familiarity with the demands made on the health care system as well as with the funds available to meet those demands, the national authorities are in a better position to carry out this assessment than an international court.'

22 *End of Life Treatment and Care: Good Practice in Decision-Making* (GMC, draft, 2009), paras 33–34.

23 [1995] 2 All ER 129, 137.

24 Although Lord Mustill said in *Bland*: 'Threaded through the technical arguments addressed to the House were the strands of a much wider position, that it is in the best interests of the community at large that Anthony Bland's life should now end…The large resources of skill, labour and money now being devoted to Anthony Bland might in the opinion of many be more fruitfully employed in improving the condition of other patients, who if treated may have useful, healthy and enjoyable lives for years to come…This argument was never squarely put, although hinted at from time to time. In social terms it has great force, and it will have to be faced in the end. But this is not a task which the courts can possibly undertake. A social cost–benefit analysis of this kind, which would have to embrace 'mercy-killing, to which exactly the same considerations apply, must be for Parliament alone…' (893).

25 [1999] Lloyd's Rep Med 399, 412.

26 *R V Central Birmingham HA, ex parte Collier* (CA, 1988, unreported, discussed in C. Newdick, *Who Should we Treat? Rights, Rationing and Resources in the NHS* (OUP, 2005)), ch.5.

27 *R V Cambridge DHA, ex parte B* [1995] 2 ALL ER 129.

28 Heneghan C (2007). Who to transfer? ethics and morals. *Journal of the Intensive Care Society* (**Spring**): 63.

29 Ibid, p. 64. Dr Heneghan firmly endorses this latter view. 'I know what I will be doing – transferring the fittest even if the longest resident'.

30 *Airedale NHS Trust v Bland* [1993] 1 All ER 821, 861, Lord Keith.

31 See *Capital and Counties plc v Hampshire CC* [1997] 2 All ER 865 (the fire services) and *OLL v Secretary of State* [1997] 3 All ER 897 (the air-sea rescue services).

32 See eg *Capital and Counties plc v Hampshire CC* [1997] 2 All ER 865. In one of these cases, a warehouse fire was being kept under control by a sprinkler system. The fire brigade turned the system off and as a result, the fire spread rapidly and the property was destroyed. In these circumstances, recovery was possible.

33 *Barnett v Chelsea and Kensington Hospital Management Committee* [1969] 1 QB 428, concerning the duty of a doctor to assess and treat a patient admitted to the accident and emergency unit. See also *Kent v Griffiths, Roberts and the LAS* [2000] Lloyds Law Rep 109 on the breach of the duty of care by an ambulance crew who failed to arrive at the scene of emergency within a reasonable time.

34 In *X v Bedfordshire CC* [1995] 3 All ER 353, Lord Jauncey said, at 362: '.... the owners of a National Health Service hospital owe precisely the same duty of care to their patients as do the owners of a private hospital and they owe it because of the common law of negligence and not because they happen to be operating under statutory provisions.'

35 *Capital and Counties plc v Hampshire CC* [1997] 2 All ER 865, 884.

36 Lord Hoffmann in *Hall v Simons* [2002] 1 AC 615, 690.

37 Although the discussion in the fire brigade cases concerned premises which presented a danger to others, so the analogy between fire services and ICU patients is not exact.

38 See *Associated Provincial Picture Houses Ltd v Wednesbury Corporation* [1948] 1KB 223 and *Rowling v Takaro Properties Ltd* [1988] AC 473, 501 per Lord Keith.

39 *Carty v Croydon LBC* [2005] 2 All ER 517, para 26, per Dyson J. The distinction was also discussed in *Anns v Merton LBC* [1978] AC 728. See further the discussion of the evolution of this principle in Newdick C (2005) *Who Should We Treat? – Rights, Rationing and Resources in the NHS*. Oxford University Press, pp. 167–185.

40 In *Caparo Industries v Dickman* [1990] 1 All ER 568, the House of Lords stated that all actions in negligence must satisfy three broad and imprecise tests, namely: (i) foresight of damage, (ii) proximity between claimant and defendant, and (iii) the merits of the case in fair, just and reasonable public policy.

41 *Robertson v Nottingham HA* Bull v Devon AHA [1993] 4 Med LR 117.

42 *Johnstone v Bloomsbury HA* [1991] 2 All ER 293; Bull v Devon AHA [1993] 4 Med LR 117.

43 *R v Prentice and Sullman* [1993] 4 All ER 935.

44 Shahani A, Ridley A, Nielsen M (2008). Modeling patient flows as an aid to decision making for critical care capacities and organisation. *Anaesthesia*, **63**: 1074.

45 *Garcia v St Mary's Hospital NHS Trust* [2006] EWHC 2314, paras 88 and 96.

46 DH. Comprehensive Critical Care. HSC 2000/017.

47 Ibid, p. 16.

48 Ibid, p. 28.

49 Shahani AK, Ridley SA, Nielsen MS (2008). Modelling patient flows as an aid to decision making for critical care capacities and organisation. *Anaesthesia* **63**: 1074–1080.

50 Shahani AK (1981). Reasonable averages that give wrong answers. *Teaching Statistics* **3**: 50–54.

51 Shahani AK, Ridley SA, Nielsen MS. Modelling patient flows as an aid to decision making for critical care capacities and organisation. op. cit., p. 1080.

52 Higgs A, Goddard C (2009). Modelling patient flows to aid decision making for critical care capacities and organisation. *Anaesthesia* **64**: 329–339.

53 Jones G. War of Mrs Dixon's shoulder. *Daily Telegraph*. News 9 March 2005. http://www.telegraph.co.uk/news/uknews/1484884/War-of-Mrs-Dixons-shoulder.html, accessed 21 May 2009.

54 Higgs A, Goddard C. Modelling patient flows to aid decision making for critical care capacities and organisation. Op. cit.

55 GMC. End of Life Care, at Para 35.

56 Note 1(4)(b): 'a breach of a duty of care by an organisation is a "gross" breach if the conduct alleged to amount to a breach of that duty falls far below what can reasonably be expected of the organisation in the circumstances; (c) "senior management"... means the persons who play significant roles in – (i) the making of decisions about how the whole or a substantial part of its activities are to be managed or organized, or (ii) the actual managing or organising of the whole or a substantial part of those activities.'

57 dh_critical care 2-12-09. Advice from the H1N1 Critical Care Clinical Group. http://www.dh.gov.uk/prod-Consum-dh/groups/dh-digitalassets/@dh/@en/documents/digitalasset/dh_109456.pdf accessed on 11 March 2010.

58 The GMC advises in *Treatment and care towards the end of life* (2010): "Decisions about what treatment options can be offered may be complicated by resource constraints – such as funding restrictions on certain treatments in the NHS, or lack of availability of intensive care beds. In such circumstances, you must provide as good a standard of care as you can for the patient, while balancing sometimes competing duties towards the wider population, funding bodies and employers. ...Ideally, decisions about access to treatments should be made on the basis of an agreed local or national policy that takes account of the human rights implications. Decisions made on a case-by-case basis, without reference to agreed policy, risk introducing elements of unfair discrimination or failure to consider properly the patient's legal rights" (para 39).

Chapter 10

Doing what's best: Organ donation and intensive care

John Coggon*

Introduction

This chapter goes to the core of an area of current controversy in the critical care community.[1,2] It examines the effect of the best interests standard on decisions relating to patients in intensive care who physically would be appropriate candidates for organ donation. The particular focus is on controlled non-heart-beating organ donation (NHBOD), where organ retrieval takes place following the planned withdrawal of life support, and thus where the time of cardiac death is controlled.[I] I begin by acknowledging the concerns that health care professionals might feel, before providing an analysis of medical law as it relates to decision-making. Exploration and understanding of legal principle allow me to provide an account of good practice in decision-making in this context. I set aside illusory concerns, and bring to the fore the key matters that the law demands be considered by decision-makers.

* Many thanks to Margaret Brazier, Chris Danbury, and David Price for comments on arguments presented here, to the stimulus provided by the participants of the ESRC seminar series "Transplantation and the Organ Deficit in the UK: Pragmatic Solutions to Ethical Controversy" (Res-451-25-4341), and to the British Academy Postdoctoral Fellowship Scheme. Responsibility for the views expressed in the paper and any errors made is my own.

I The argument in this chapter builds on an earlier work on which I was a co-author (3). Since the chapter's completion and submission, the Department of Health has released welcome guidance on this issue, which essentially conforms with what I argue, and which the reader would do well to consider in light of my position (www.dh.gov.uk/proconsum-dh/groups-dh-digitalassets/documents/digitalasset/dh_109864.pdf). Unfortunately I am unable in the current paper to engage with the guidance, but as will be clear from the argument, I am most pleased about its publication.

I conclude that the law on best interests must not be subjected to the narrow simplification that currently risks besetting it. As best interests demands that due account be given to patients' moral, social, ethical, religious, and other values and beliefs, it is wrong to believe that a treatment decision can be based on an assessment purely of clinical benefits, or on a fictitiously atomized view of the patient. I therefore argue that there will be many situations where controlled NHBOD will be in the best interests of patients in intensive care. Although I am certain of the case I make, recognition of continued concerns from practitioners leads me to repeat a call for the General Medical Council and Department of Health to provide reassurance and clarity in their guidance to practitioners. The chapter ends with a brief consideration of the lack of legal certainty regarding the necessary observation time between the cessation of heart beat and the commencement of organ retrieval.

The apparent minefield

Medical practice, it might be argued, would be a lot easier if there weren't lawyers standing on the sidelines waiting to declare what is right or wrong in a given situation. Health care law and ethics has greatly expanded as an academic field, as well as an area of perennial interest to the press, parliament, and pressure groups. Throughout the literature— public and academic—divergent views abound concerning what is proper practice. It would be no surprise, therefore, if practitioners were to feel that perhaps they would be best off working under an exacting version of the 'precautionary principle'. But even trying to work in accordance with precaution is hard; it is often not clear what the most conservative course of action might be. The practice of so-called 'defensive medicine' is well recognized and easily put down in papers such as this.[II] It can at times be harder, however, to persuade physicians of what is acceptable, lawful practice. This is particularly so in relation to areas of profound social and ethical contention, such as organ retrieval. However, I aim here to explain and explore the correct understanding

[II] See (4), pp. 204–205 for discussion of how much of a problem defensive medicine is in practice.

of law as it has been settled both in the courts and by Parliament, and thus provide some real reassurance to intensive care specialists about the propriety of what might seem to be a legal and ethical minefield. My focus is on modest—but to some minds contentious—measures that may be taken in intensive care for patients who might become organ donors. I consider the prolongation of life-support following a decision that *from a purely clinical perspective* continued provision of treatment is futile; controlled NHBOD. Can it be lawful to allow ventilation to persist in order that the surgical retrieval team have time to coordinate itself and be prepared to have optimal chances of a successful transplantation? I will demonstrate that the answer to this question is yes.

Given the well known scandals relating to posthumous organ retrieval,[5,6] whose aftermath is still felt, the current position of health care practitioners attracts some sympathy: there are radically competing views that proliferate in the literature, both regarding the law and the ethics of organ donation. Bell, a clinician who has published repeatedly on the subject, states that:

> [T]here are salient ethical, legal and logistical hurdles to defensible introduction of either controlled or uncontrolled NHBOD, and it should be noted that in promoting this procurement strategy, neither UK Transplant nor the Department of Health acknowledged these problems or offered solutions[7]... (p. 825).

What, then, are physicians to do? On the one hand, many will be acutely aware of the mismatch between the numbers of people who say they would be willing to donate organs after death and those who actually do[8] (pp. 812–813). On the other hand, many practitioners will be afraid of potential legal ramifications (not to mention ethical criticism or even scandal) if they appear to harm a patient's autonomy in order to optimize the opportunities for donation. The English legal position has not based itself on a presumption that a person would wish to donate. So what is a doctor to do when a patient may be a suitable donor? Is there a clash in duties, and, if so, which duty prevails? Can it be lawful to base treatment options for the patient on potential benefit to a third party? In what follows, I explore these and related questions. By understanding the law's demands regarding medical decision-making, it will become clear that decisions can be made to treat a patient in a way that will benefit a third party. In other words, for a patient who lacks capacity to consent, it can be lawful to undertake harmless acts that enhance the chances of successful organ retrieval, even when these acts confer no *clinical* benefit to the patient who will become a posthumous donor.

The good, the bad, and the clinical

If we could all agree on what is good and what is bad, decision-making would be a great deal less contentious. But life is not so simple, and the law is not either. A liberal social system recognizes that a plurality of views exists, and in many circumstances the default position at law is that the views on what is best should be left to the individual. However, this position is necessarily qualified in various ways. As is familiar in a health care context, medical expertise will only be deferred to if it is supported by a responsible body of medical opinion.[9,10] And if we take the paradigm case of a competent, adult patient, the decision-making capacity given to him is tempered by limits on his positive freedoms. The freedom from interference—sometimes called the 'right to bodily integrity'—is absolute: the patient can say 'no' to any interference proposed as being to his benefit. The strength of this right is often emphasized through expression of Lord Donaldson MR's celebrated dictum in the case of *Re T* that a person is free to refuse a medical intervention for any reason, be it 'rational, irrational, unknown or even non-existent'. (11, p. 102). And it is reinforced by the principle found in the Mental Capacity Act 2005, Section 1(4):

> A person is not to be treated as unable to make a decision merely because he makes an unwise decision.

I shall consider this further in the next section, but should note here that one interpretation of the legal position is that the law is indifferent to the well-being of competent patients: the law demands that you leave alone a competent adult who refuses treatment, even if she appears to be harming herself by doing this. She could tell you she has no reason to be harming herself, or even that her reason is that Tuesday begins with a W, and still you would have to leave her alone. Were she without capacity, you would treat her in her best interests, but when she is competent you have to watch her suffer. Thus, are we to be unconcerned by the best interests of the competent? Arguably, the answer to this is no; that we are not disregarding her best interests by accepting her refusal of consent. The law's emphasis on not questioning a decision because of its apparent lack of wisdom is a means of avoiding value despotism. As an individual is sovereign, at least of her negative freedom, the law cannot allow government to be transferred to a third party. Thus, the respect demanded by law for an adult's right to refuse rests on a need for due deference to the individual's self-government rather than a need to endorse (or approve of, or agree with) the individual's conclusions on what best serves her.[III] As the law works to preserve value pluralism, a strong, overarching conception of the good cannot trump every arguably bad choice a person makes. As such a system is conducive to the well-being of individuals, and recognizes that opinions validly differ,[IV] the law's apparent indifference to a patient's irrational or baseless refusal in itself serves her interests, rather than harms them.[V]

If we move to consider positive freedom—'freedom *to*' as opposed to 'freedom *from*'[15]—the individual's powers of self-government can not be described as absolute. Here the law has a more defensible role in defining benefit and harm. Once people are involved in social interactions, especially those involving state actors (such as doctors working for the National Health Service), it would be unsustainable for individuals to have absolute rights to demand whatever treatment they thought was suitable. In situations where positive demands are made, standards imposed by value systems external to the patient's own come into play. So, while a competent adult does not need his doctor to agree that he should *refuse* treatment for some reason, he cannot expect his doctor to agree that he should *receive* any treatment for any reason.

The crux of this is not on an overall 'life view', or an all-things-considered assessment of good and bad. Rather, it swings on the issue

---

III For an application of this, consider the case of *Ms B* (12).

IV For an account of such liberalism, see (13).

V For application of this in the context of competent decisions concerning posthumous organ donation, see (14).

of clinical interests, or what may be labelled the '*Bolam* aspect' of the decision. The law recognizes a patient's right to health care, and thus a duty on the state to provide it, but *exercise* of the right is not founded (purely, at least) on the patient's assessment of need. It is tempered necessarily by (in principle) just processes of allocation in a system supported by finite resources, and also by clinical expertise.[VI] Therefore, in the Court of Appeal decision in *Burke*, Lord Phillips MR held that:

> The proposition that the patient has a paramount right to refuse treatment is amply demonstrated by the authorities cited by Munby J in paragraphs 54 to 56 of his [first instance] judgement [of this case] under the heading '*Autonomy and self-determination*'. The corollary does not, however, follow, at least as a general proposition. Autonomy and the right of self-determination do not entitle the patient to insist on receiving a particular medical treatment regardless of the nature of the treatment. Insofar as a doctor has a legal obligation to provide treatment this cannot be founded simply upon the fact that the patient demands it. The source of the duty lies elsewhere.[20] (para. 31)

As the jurisprudence on best interests and patient choice has developed, most pronouncedly in that relating to best interests, it has become clear that the law divides health care decision-making into questions about what is clinically indicated—or at times what is clinically defensible—and what is indicated overall given all the relevant values. The resultant position is that, as Dame Elizabeth Butler-Sloss put it in *Re S*, the right decision depends not solely on an assessment defensible by reference to the *Bolam* test, but must 'incorporate broader ethical, social, moral and welfare considerations'[21] (p. 28). Patients are in a position to define what is good and bad, but not what is clinically necessary. And where serving the concepts of good and bad involves the exercise of a positive right, the state also has a legitimate role in defining what is good and what is bad.

Having provided this brief theoretical overview, I will now explore the application of best interests at law, and consider the relevance of capacity and consent in medical decision-making. This involves analysis of the question of whether we care less about those who have capacity than those who do not, a question answered by consideration

---

[VI] For discussion and exploration of the complicated theoretical issues buried in the two sentences leading to this footnote, see (**16–19**).

of how we come to assess the interests of those who are without capacity.

Is there anything special about losing capacity?— Informed consent and best interests

In the section 'The good, the bad, and the clinical', I asked whether the law is indifferent to the well-being of competent adults while simultaneously caring only for the best interests of adults who lack competence. To consider the legal effect of losing capacity, and the interests that then present themselves, let us flip the question on its head: would the law allow an incompetent patient to have her right to health care waived (or qualified in any way) to accord with peculiar values? The short answer is yes. When taking a legal approach, we may only *think about* best interests when we are considering patients without capacity. But best interests must not be taken to represent some sort of objective, one-size-fits-all values-yardstick that can be appealed to when we can not ask someone for consent. The law's recognition of, and respect for, diversity in values extends far beyond those of people who can make a contemporaneous decision. It is for this reason that you cannot wait for a patient who is making an apparently foolish refusal of consent to lose capacity and then overrule her previously expressed will 'using' best interests. That would be *abusing* best interests. While it may be true that our evaluations of incompetent patients' interests are more careful than a competent patient's assessment of her own interests need be,[VII] there is no reason (or freedom) to treat the values of those without capacity differently than we would the values of a competent patient. The patient's values are still crucial to an understanding of what is best in the circumstances. Section 4(6) of the Mental Capacity Act obliges decision-makers to consider in a best interests assessment:

so far as is reasonably ascertainable –

a the person's past and present wishes and feelings (and, in particular, any relevant written statement made by him when he had capacity),

---

[VII] That is to say, the Mental Capacity Act requires decision-makers who are deciding for the patient to follow specific criteria in the process of coming to the decision. The law does not impose such exacting demands on people with capacity when they are deciding for themselves.

  b the beliefs and values that would be likely to influence his decision if he had capacity, and

  c the other factors that he would be likely to consider if her were able to do so.

This statutory understanding of best interests leaves little—if anything—practically different to the common law situation that preceded it. As best interests has developed through the case law, it has become clear that a decision is neither justified simply by, nor necessarily contingent upon, there being a clinical benefit to the patient.[21,22] The same is true for decisions concerning competent patients. Where there are viable options available (including doing nothing), these will be assessed in the light of the patient's preferences and values. In each case, the legal presumption is that the patient's best interests, as permitted within the scheme of rationing and provision, are being served.[VIII] Although commentators may choose to describe this as an 'expanded interpretation' of best interests, it should be noted that applying it in this way is not a question of *expanding* the interpretation afforded by law. It is expanded by contrast with a narrow perspective that considers only the *Bolam* aspect of the decision. It is not, however, an expansion of the law or of legal principle. Without controversy or complication, best interests is a necessarily broad standard, which demands accommodation of the patient's values broadly understood. This all means that, in some sense, there is nothing special about losing capacity. You are still to be treated as an individual whose interests are your own, and whose values affect the importance and desirability of any proposed option. Furthermore, this is well settled law, has been for some time, and is now bolstered by Parliament in the Mental Capacity Act. The principle can be demonstrated by brief reference to the case law.

The cases of *In Re F*[24] and *Re Y*[25] both provide examples of clinical benefit not being a necessary condition for lawful procedure to take place. In *In Re F*, the courts were asked to decide whether it would be lawful to perform a non-therapeutic sterilization on a seriously

---

[VIII] For development of this argument, see (23).

mentally disabled woman, in order that the limited freedom she enjoyed be no further narrowed for fear of her becoming pregnant. *Re Y* concerned the question of allowing an adult who had never had decision-making capacity to be a donor of bone marrow to her sister, whom she could not be said to know in any meaningful sense. In both cases, it was found that the non-therapeutic interventions were in the best interests of the patients as *overall* they would be of benefit.

Ahsan[26] provides an example of a decision where clinical benefit is not the contingent factor in a best interests assessment. Here, the patient who had lived as a devout Muslim had fallen into a persistent vegetative state. It was argued that her best interests would be served by her receiving treatment at home, rather than in a hospital setting. The treatment she was receiving raised no clinical concerns, and it was also clear that the patient would not be aware of the move. Even so, given the patient's values, it was held that her best interests required that she be taken home.

Equally, for competent patients, clinical benefit is neither a necessary nor a sufficient condition of lawful medical intervention. So, for example, the Human Tissue Act (2004) allows live organ donation to take place. That we could choose to donate a kidney is a manifest example of our being permitted (in principle) to perform an act that confers no clinical benefit on us. Other examples of non-therapeutic interventions that competent adults may nonetheless receive include assisted reproduction, sterilization, and cosmetic surgery. And it is well established common law that a health care team is not justified in providing unwanted treatment to a patient with capacity, even if it does so with the very best of intentions.[12] Again the Mental Capacity Act bolsters the situation, making clear that the patient who has capacity is not to be doubted for appearing to make an unwise decision.

Thus, to the extent illustrated, we can say that in-principle welfare concerns in any health care setting where we see a patient who lacks capacity in contrast with one who has capacity are illusory. In both cases, the processes that the law establishes—best interests and consent—are designed to allow the decision that is best accommodated within the value systems of the particular patient, necessarily qualified by the discussion of positive and negative freedoms. Thus, even when we are making non-clinical decisions for an incompetent patient, we do not need (from a legal perspective) to be concerned by the patient's lack of capacity to provide informed consent. Although a decision maker must be careful in assessing the patient's values, by following the principles developed at common law, galvanized in the Mental Capacity Act, and detailed in the Act's Code of Practice, she can make *any* decision regarding an incompetent patient's welfare without fear that she is 'overstepping the mark' simply by virtue of the fact that the decision is not based purely on medical factors, or that the decision takes account of the altruistic, or other-affecting values, of the patient. We are not atomized, completely separate individuals.[4] (pp. 153–154, 27) Although best interests must not be used to make incompetent patients simply a means to a further end, it is wrong to falsely accredit the incompetent with selfish, self-centred, miserly values when these do not accord with their own values. According to law, spiritual, familial, moral, social, and ethical values that we have survive our capacity to understand or communicate them, and the law, as I have shown, demands that decision-makers for those who have lost capacity take account of these values when deciding what would be best for the patient.

Is there anything special about dying?

As I am considering the application of the best interests standard in intensive care, it might strike some that I ought to ask if there is anything special about dying that might render treatment of dying patients a 'special case'. For intuitive, emotional, or deep-seated ethical reasons, people might argue that an extraordinary level and standard of care ought to apply when we are dealing with a patient at the end of life. Simon Woods argues in favour of enhanced protection being given to an individual's perceptions of his interests as he dies, in essence suggesting that we ought to enhance the freedom to act in accordance with the interests of the patient as he sees them as life comes to an end.[28,29] It is likely that Munby J. was driven by some similar type of concern when handing down his (subsequently overruled) judgement in the

Burke case.[30] Here, Munby J. found that a human 'right to die with dignity' formed the basis of a state duty to treat patients as *they* saw fit, notwithstanding objections from clinicians about whatever the proposed course of treatment was.

Inasmuch as a patient may be especially vulnerable in an intensive care setting (or in any end-of-life situation), special diligence is required of decision-makers. But this is not because of something intrinsic to dying. From a legal perspective, there is nothing special about dying. This chapter is not the place to offer a full analysis of whether dying *should* affect legal freedoms, but I would urge serious consideration of the way the full scheme of the law would be affected before a proposal such as Woods' or Munby J.'s were adopted.[IX] The point to make here, however, is that best interests is what the law provides decision-makers who are caring for those who lack capacity. Although best interests cannot be boiled down to a single test (or concept),[32] there is a wealth of guidance and principle provided in the case law, the Mental Capacity Act, and the Act's Code of Practice. This principle pervades all medical decision-making where consent is unobtainable. Whether you are deciding if you ought to provide a blood transfusion to an unconscious Jehovah's Witness, if you ought to provide antibiotics to treat an infection in a permanently comatose 23-year-old, or if you ought to pump the stomach of an apparent suicide attempt, you are governed by the constraints and freedoms afforded by best interests. Equally, when you are asked whether it would be lawful to continue medically futile but physically harmless ventilation of a patient in intensive care, in order that the patient's organs may be donated posthumously with a greater chance of success, you are governed by best interests. The balancing exercise involved in decision-making will necessarily differ from case to case. But the principles run throughout. Thus, it is appropriate to consider how the patient's values would weigh on the decision. That continued ventilation would confer no clinical benefit of itself does not provide compelling reason to withdraw treatment. In the following section, I

[IX] I would suggest to the interested reader to consider the analysis in (31).

will demonstrate with three practical examples how the assessments might be made in practice.

Marrying principle and practice: Difficult decisions explored

Consider the following scenarios involving patients in intensive care. Each patient is in a position where the medical team justifiably thinks further treatment is clinically futile. Thus, if a decision regarding the patients were to be made purely on medical grounds, withdrawal of treatment would be the indicated course of action.

1 George is 48 years old. He has an Organ Donor card. He has also told members of his family that he would consent to 'any of my body parts being used if they can be helpful, after I'm dead'.

2 Rubinda is 20 years old. She has not got round to getting an Organ Donor card because she thought it would be 'tempting fate'. However, her family and friends understand clearly that she viewed posthumous organ donation as a 'strong social duty'.

3 Siobhan is 25 years old. She has never had any profound decision-making capacity, and has never been able to communicate any but the most basic of messages.

Each of the patients could become a donor after death. However, in each case it would take a few hours for the surgical retrieval team to prepare itself. To optimize the chance of successful retrieval and transplantation, it is suggested that the patients be kept on life support following the futility declaration, until the surgical team is ready. When the team is ready, cardiac arrest would be allowed to happen, and following cardiac death organ retrieval could take place.

Would it be lawful to prolong life support to allow donation to take place in these cases? Let us consider them one by one.

Drawing the line between consent and best interests

In George's case, we are told that he 'would consent' to body parts being retrieved after his death, and that he carries an organ donor card. For many, the act of joining the organ donor register may represent the starkest example of consent to donation, especially given the language that abounds in discussions of these matters, such as 'opt-in' and 'opt-out'. We ought, however, to acknowledge the complications with this simplification, and the example provided by George gives a helpful opportunity to do so. Consent is a fairly loose term when it applies to matters that happen after we lose capacity: thinking more broadly, one only has to consider the well-rehearsed problems that apply to the applicability or otherwise of advance directives. This chapter is not, and does not pretend to be, a philosophical critique of the alignment of previously expressed wishes by beings whose connectedness to the now extinguished will is corporeal rather than psychological. From a legal perspective, however, we might well question whether the processes involved in obtaining a donor card fulfil the requirements expected for sufficiently informed consent to a procedure. It takes little reflection to notice that a person need hardly—perhaps *can* hardly—be aware of the nature of the processes that might befall his body in order to retrieve his organs, beyond an understanding in the broadest possible terms. Recent jurisprudence, most notably the case of *Chester* v *Afshar*,[33] has made it established law that for consent to be 'real' a high level of information that the patient might consider relevant must be provided. Mere possession of a donor card, and even a broad expression of will such as that given by George, can hardly be taken as qualifying as informed consent in the sense that medical lawyers have grown to understand it.

This is not a problem. Let us assume—as is almost certainly proper to do—that George has not *consented* to being kept alive for a couple of hours more than would otherwise be the case in order that he might be a better donor. It does not follow that he has *refused* consent. We can still take his expressions as indications of his values in this situation. And his values must bear directly on the decision-maker's assessment of what would be in George's best interests. In other words, George is a willing donor. There must, of course, be limits to his willingness. We could not brutalize him, or harm him in some other way, in order to retrieve his organs while hiding behind the pretence of consent. We can, however, recognize that his values regarding donation are altruistic. By losing competence, he does not suddenly have to be treated as a selfish individual. Both the case law and now the Mental Capacity Act require that *his* past and present wishes and feelings, and *his* beliefs and values be considered. The donor card and statement he made may not provide a consent, but they do provide a strong indication that it would be in George's best interests to be kept alive while the organ retrieval team assembled itself. They are evidence that, were he told of this situation, he would consent. In the absence of evidence to the contrary, I would suggest that this is an example where best interests would demand that the patient be kept alive, albeit that the principal beneficiaries of the action *appear* not to be him.

Straightforward best interests

Given what we have said about George, there is little of principle to add in the case of Rubinda. From the facts given, we have no reason to believe that there is even an argument that she consents. It seems that she has tried to put her mind away from consideration of this situation. Nevertheless, we once more have an expression of values. In a case such as this, we might be more extensive in our search for the views of family and others who know the patient, to be sure about the extent of her values. If the evidence is that Rubinda would prefer that she be kept alive in order to optimize the chances of successful donation, were she able to reflect on the situation, it would be perfectly compatible with law that this course of action were pursued. As in the case of George, it would be wrong to infer from lack of consent a refusal of consent. A refusal of consent would be binding. In the absence of consent and refusal, best interests applies. If careful, good faith application of best interests recommends that Rubinda be kept alive, this will be the lawful course of action.

Complex best interests

It is only Siobhan's case that raises significant theoretical difficulties. In contrast with the cases of George and Rubinda, it is possible here to argue that Siobhan has *never* had a sufficiently established scheme of values that she can truly be said to be a willing donor, or that *she* would be benefitted by being kept alive. With regard just to posthumous donation, provided 'appropriate consent' were given in accordance with the Human Tissue Act 2004, the organ retrieval itself could lawfully be undertaken. However, there is no system of 'appropriate consent' applicable while Siobhan is still alive. Patients who never have had capacity are much less easily argued to have a will, or value system, that supports donation.

Even so, consideration of the case law may support donation. The reasoning in *Re Y*[25] supported donation, notwithstanding that the patient could not be said to want it. What seemed to be the main benefit— treatment of her sister—was not something the patient would be aware of. Even if we find the reasoning of Connell J. to have been excessively stretched, it is possible to see an arguable benefit to Y: she would benefit from a continued relationship with her mother following her sister's treatment. Siobhan will derive no such benefit. Nor can 'family values' come into this. As she will be a posthumous donor, there is no significant chance of her organs being given to family members or others close to her.[X] For a patient who cannot be said ever to have had values that would support donation, it will be very difficult to argue that there will be a significant benefit in being kept alive—even painlessly—for a brief period for the good of others. Some theorists may find this an ugly default position: perhaps the law should not presume that a person's interests are best served by exclusively self-regarding matters.[XI] However, I would argue that in Siobhan's case, at least from the limited facts given, her best interests require withdrawal of treatment immediately following the futility decision. I accept that there might be an argument if she were from a family or community whose shared values strongly supported donation, but in the absence of such knowledge I would find it difficult to interpret her best interests as including this act of altruism.

Contention for contention's sake?

I do not for a moment underestimate the difficulties for those working in intensive care, who I appreciate will carry the burden of decision-making, and may feel justified in a view that the law—and lawyers—can

---

[X] Directed donation, though permissible for living donors, is not permissible for donation made post-mortem.

[XI] See the reasoning in (34).

be of little help in areas of serious moral, political, and social contention. Thus I do not believe that disputes in this area amount simply to contention for the sake of it. However, I am absolutely clear that the principle discussed in this chapter is based on the law as it exists and is to be interpreted. As there may be misgivings among practitioners, I would repeat a call made by me and others in the *British Medical Journal* for the General Medical Council to incorporate the conclusions of the arguments advanced here in its guidance, in order that reassurance may be provided to practitioners.[3] I would also be pleased to see the Department of Health publish guidance on this.

On timing

One further area of contention, on which the law is unfortunately silent, relates to the timing of NHBOD after cardiac death. Current practice is generally to wait for 5–10 minutes before beginning organ retrieval.[35] This accords with the Academy of Medical Royal Colleges' code of practice[36] (p. 12) and the British Transplantation Society's guidelines[37] (p. 11). Clearly neither of these amounts to comprehensive *legal* guidance, and a potentially significant issue is raised as situations exist in which the chances of optimizing transplant success would require a shorter period. A paper from the United States discusses three cases where hearts were transplanted from donors who had suffered cardiac death; one was observed for three minutes following the cessation of cardiocirculatory function, the other two for just 75 seconds.[38] If performed in England, it is unclear whether such measures would be lawful or not. On the one hand, it might be argued that if a 'responsible body of medical men skilled in that particular art'[9] (p. 587) supported such practice, the courts would likely find it acceptable, provided there had also been support from family members of the deceased. On the other hand, without a statutory definition of death, and on such a politically and ethically contentious matter, it may be that strict accordance with the guidance is the most sensible approach to this matter, notwithstanding that the guidance itself states that it may not apply in every case.[36] (p. 6). This, of course, leaves the health care practitioners in the invidious position of either facing the risk of falling foul of the law, or of less than optimizing their transplant efforts. Clarity may be found when the Human Tissue Authority issues guidance on the definition of death. It is not possible in a chapter with the generality that this has to offer reassurance beyond stating that there is an argument that could be made for the lawfulness of having an observation period of under 5 minutes following cardiac arrest.

Conclusion

Notwithstanding my sympathy with practitioners working on the front line, I would urge the following two points. First, what I am advocating is not an 'expanded interpretation' of best interests. Best interests, as presented here, is how it exists at law. It is neither expanded nor compounded nor selectively interpreted. Best interests does not under law represent solely an individual patient's clinical needs. The law, both as it developed in the courts, and now as it exists in the Mental Capacity Act, makes this clear. Considering the understanding as 'expanded' will unnerve clinicians for no good reason, and will skew how best interests is rightly understood at law. Second, I caution against an excessive preoccupation with informed consent as it relates to the donor register. As ought to be clear, best interests judgements are necessarily made *absent* consent of the patient, and thus no one would claim that the conditions necessary for lawful consent are (or ought to be) present in the situations considered in this chapter. Nor, as I have demonstrated, should it be assumed that signing onto the donor register serves as informed consent: it is an indication of a willingness to donate given the propitious conditions, which of necessity will be unknown at the time of joining the register. Just as many people are not on the organ donor register, many people have not, for example, made 'living wills', yet practitioners find themselves equipped to make decisions regarding proper treatment of this latter group of patients. It is a cliché, though not necessarily wrong, to observe that doing what is best is not always the same as doing what is easiest. I nevertheless suggest that a proper understanding and application of best interests should pervade *all* decision-making for those without capacity. A decision to prolong medically futile ventilation for the reasons considered in this chapter should be subject to no less complete an evaluation than any other decision. Where the patient's values require a modest, harmless prolongation of life for the great potential benefit to others, good practice requires respect for this.

References

1 Bell MDD (2005). Non-heartbeating organ donation: clinical process and fundamental issues. *British Journal of Anaesthesia* **94**(4): 474–478.

2 Gardiner D, Riley B (2007). Non-heart-beating organ donation – solution or a step too far? *Anaesthesia* **62**: 431–433.

3 Coggon J, Brazier M, Murphy P, Price D, Quigley M (2008). Best interests and potential organ donors. *British Medical Journal* **336**: 1346–1347.

4 Brazier M, Cave E (2007). *Medicine, Patients and the Law*, 4th edn. Penguin, London.

5 *Learning from Bristol: The Report of the Public Inquiry into Children's Heart Surgery at the Bristol Royal Infirmary 1984–1995* (2001) Cm 5270(1).

6 *The Royal Children's Inquiry Report* (2001) HC 12-11.

7 Bell MDD (2006). Emergency medicine, organ donation and the Human Tissue Act. *Emerg Med J* **23**: 824–827.

8 Price D (2005). The Human Tissue Act 2004. *Modern Law Review*, **68**(5), 798–821.

9 *Bolam v. Friern Hospital Management Committee* [1957] 1 WLR 582.

10 *Bolitho v. City and Hackney Health Authority* [1998] AC 232.

11 *In Re T (Adult: Refusal of Treatment)* [1993] Fam 95.

12 *Ms B v An NHS Hospital Trust* [2002] 2 All ER 449.

13 Gray J (1996). *Isaiah Berlin* Princeton University Press, Princeton, NJ.

14 McGuinness S, Brazier M (2008). Respecting the living means respecting the dead too. *Oxford Journal of Legal Studies*, **28**(2): 297–316.

15 Berlin I (1969). Two concepts of liberty, in *Four Essays on Liberty*, Oxford University Press, Oxford.

16 Newdick C, Derrett S (2006). Access, equity and the role of rights in health care. *Health Care Analysis*, **14**: 157–168.

17 Newdick C (2008). Preserving social citizenship in health care markets: there may be trouble ahead. *McGill Journal of Law and Health*, **2**: 93–108.

18 Newdick C (2005). *Who Should We Treat?: Rights, Rationing and Resources*, 2nd ed. Oxford University Press, Oxford.

19 Syrett K (2007). *Law, Legitimacy and the Rationing of Health Care*. Cambridge University Press, Cambridge.

20 *R (On the Application of Oliver Leslie Burke) vs. The General Medical Council* [2005] EWCA Civ 1003.

21 *In Re S (Adult Patient: Sterilisation)* [2001] Fam 15.

22 *In Re A (Medical Treatment: Male Sterilisation)* [2000] 1 FCR 193.

23 Coggon J (2008). Best interests, public interest, and the power of the medical profession. *Health Care Analysis* **16**(3): 219–232.

24 *In Re F (Mental Patient: Sterilisation)* [1990] 2 AC 1.

25 *Re Y (Mental Patient: Bone Marrow Donation)* [1997] 2 WLR 556.

26 *Ahsan* v *University Hospitals Leicester NHS Trust* [2007] PIQR P19.

27 Brazier M (2006). Do no harm – do patients have responsibilities too? *Cambridge Law Journal,* **65**(2): 397–422.

28 Woods S (2008). Best interests: Puzzles and plausible solutions at the end of life. *Health Care Analysis,* **16**(3): 279–287.

29 Woods S (2007). *Death's Dominion: Ethics and the End of Life.* Open University Press, Berkshire.

30 *R (on the application of Burke) v. General Medical Council* [2005] 2 WLR 431.

31 Huxtable R (2008). Whatever you want? beyond the patient in medical law. *Health Care Analysis,* **16**(3): 288–301.

32 Kopelman LM (1997). The best-interests standard as threshold, ideal, and standard of reasonableness. *Journal of Medicine and Philosophy,* **22**(3): 271–289.

33 *Chester v. Afshar* [2005] 1 AC 134.

34 Harris J, Holm S (2003). Should we presume moral turpitude in our children? – Small children and consent to medical research. *Theoretical Medicine and Bioethics,* **24**(2): 121–129.

35 Personal communication from Chris Danbury, 7 December 2008.

36 Academy of Royal Colleges (2008). A Code of Practice for the Diagnosis and Confirmation of Death. Available at http://www.aomrc.org.uk/aomrc/admin/reports/docs/DofD-final.pdf (accessed 19 January 2009).

37 British Transplantation Society (2004). Guidelines relating to solid organ transplants from non-heart beating donors. Available at http://www.bts.org.uk/Forms/Guidelines_Nov_2004.pdf (accessed 19 January 2009).

38 Boucek MM, Mashburn C, Dunn SM, et al. (2008). Pediatric Heart Transplantation after Declaration of Cardiocirculatory Death. *New England Journal of Medicine,* **359**: 709–714.

Chapter 11

Conflicts of interest

Carl Waldmann, Neil Soni, and
Andrew Lawson

Introduction

Conflicts of interest appear in all walks of life and indeed may be a
normative aspect of society as institutions and individuals may have
conflicting obligations, which they have to reconcile. In the medical
world, relationships between physicians and industry have always been
important and are possibly increasingly important in the current
economic climate. The positive side of the liaison has been seen in
impressive medical advances, new products for patient care, increased
research, and improved education. However, it can create opportunities for bias, unfavorable public perceptions, and over-consumption
and misuse of public funds. In the 1980s, the large cash payments and
lavish gifts doctors received from drug companies captured public
attention and caused concern that physician integrity was falling victim
to commercial influences.[1]

That the clash of agendas of the principal players in the health care
setting may produce a conflict of interest is hardly surprising. On the
one hand, industry works principally for shareholders, not patients,
and survival or success depends on sales, which in turn depends on
doctors who prescribe or use its products. However, on the other hand,
the industry has a vested interest in being seen to be benefactor and to
contribute meaningfully to patient well being from which they derive
their income. Commercial interest does not necessarily preclude altruism or doing good; however, without profit companies cannot fund
ongoing research as well as pay shareholders. The physician's primary
role or duty is acting for the benefit of the patients,[2] but they also have

a personal agenda to provide an adequate lifestyle for their families, capability for their research programmes, and the ability to facilitate education within their specialties. Patients have a primary aim in the maintenance of health or life and governments have interests in cost containment, patient welfare, and political survival.

Industry sponsorship of research and guidelines

At the opening of the European Society of Intensive Care Medicine's congress in Berlin in 2007, Dr Professor Jukka Takala made some very pertinent comments on the issue of 'conflicts of interest'. He emphasized that a gap has developed in how research is conducted compared to how it ought to be carried out, focusing on the concerns that occur when industry partners clinicians for the purpose of research. How can we, as physicians be sure that results are not biased, and therefore be sure that patients do not suffer unnecessarily as a result?[3,4] He pointed out that trials sponsored by pharmaceutical companies were more likely to be published when results had a favourable outcome for their product. This observation has been made by others.[5-8] if trials, which show no benefit, were similarly publicised, then it would be easier to provide a balanced opinion to readers.

Marcia Angell, a former editor of the *New England Journal of Medicine*, was interviewed by the *New York Times* on 14 September 2004 prior to the publication of her book *The Truth About the Drug Companies: How They Deceive Us and What to Do About It*. She commented:

> As a journal editor, I witnessed a disturbing trend in pharmaceutical research. Twenty years ago, most drug trials were conducted at academic medical centers and the pharmaceutical companies tended to stand back during the testing period. However, in recent years, the companies have succeeded in attaching strings to research contracts, often designing the studies themselves, keeping the data in-house and deciding whether or not to publish the results. They also began to contract with private research companies for testing. Moreover, the medical schools and even individual researchers began to enter into entrepreneurial arrangements with the drug companies.

The forces acting on Western medicine are immense. The demands for medical advances for research output and for higher educational standards are only exceeded by the demands by governments to contain health care costs and in particular overheads on delivering medical care.

Research and education overheads are part of the cost structure. In the absence of complete government funding, collaboration between physicians and industry is and will be increasingly essential as physicians are end users of the products. In a free market economy, collaboration entails 'financial linkage' without which the prospect of impressive medical advances, new products for patient care, increased research, and improved education may not be possible. It seems that conflicts of interest are inevitable. The promotion of drugs by medical professionals with financial stakes in the drugs' success has already badly eroded public trust in medicine and industry in some quarters. However, there have been phenomenal advances in many areas of medical practice that have resulted from this collaboration with clear translation into improved medical care.

Professor Takala made several recommendations:

◆ Practice guidelines should be developed by experts who do not have conflicts; Source data from completed clinical trials should be made available to an external academic coordinating centre for systematic analysis.

◆ Journals should require statistical confirmation of clinical trial results by external academic sources for all industry-sponsored studies.

◆ Research institutes should require unrestricted access to the trial database and unlimited rights to publish the results.

These recommendations are both sensible and pragmatic but there is a risk that the bureaucracy may make such systems unworkable, obstructive, or financially unacceptable. This has already been seen in both the European and British approach to streamlining ethics approvals which has done almost exactly the reverse.[9]

The *XIGRIS* story

A critical juncture in the history of this issue in Critical Care was the development, the research and the marketing underpinning *activated protein C* (*Xigris* the result of 40 years of research), which was heralded as a major advance. The whole issue of conflicts of interest in critical care was brought to the fore when Eli Lilly successfully brought activated protein-C onto the market place.

The PROWESS trial coordinated by Bernard from Vanderbilt University showed a reduced mortality in patients with severe sepsis.[10] As one of the first trials to show a therapeutic benefit from a new drug in the critically ill with sepsis, it marked the end of a dismal era of repeated failure in clinical trials in this field and heralded the prospect of successful active intervention. It was exciting but expensive, a course of the drug costs £4500, three times the usual daily cost of providing intensive care for a patient. In 2002 during the annual congress of the European Society of Intensive Care Medicine (ESICM) in Barcelona, several hundred participants signed a declaration producing *Surviving Sepsis Campaign or SSC*.[11] It called on health care professionals and their organizations, governments, health agencies, and public to support an initiative to reduce the mortality from sepsis by 25% within 5 years. This process involved a number of leading international societies coming together to develop an evidenced-based set of guidelines (*Sepsis Care Initiative*) that could then be implemented into clinical practice. The SCI was strongly criticized by some authors[12] who suggested that the sponsors of the SSC were too closely aligned with the process leading the integrity of the guidelines to be questioned. To some what was contentious was that part of the SSC initially had three sponsors one of which provided 90% of the financial support.[11] It was felt that there was an obvious conflict of interest as it would appear that the guidelines might well confer benefit on the sponsors. The issue is not whether this was the intent, but rather the perception of inappropriate influence. If a drug works beyond all reasonable doubt, then marketing and clinical practice should and would have some degree of confluence but in any situation less ideal than this there will inevitably be suspicion as to the role of that conflict of interest. This is important at a time when guidelines are increasingly popular as a means of translating, and by default enforcing, evidence-based medicine to clinical practice.

Guidelines

Developing a guideline combines evidence-based medicine and consensus opinion. It costs money. In the formation of any guideline, there are vested interests, which include a government trying to contain cost while looking for cost-effectiveness, industry trying to market products, enthusiasts trying to drive their own ideas, and patients trying to get a fair and safe deal. Whatever the funding, there will almost always be secondary interests among those involved. The key assumption about guidelines is that with opinion leaders using an evidence based approach quality and hence reliability will be assured.[13,14] There is only one study looking at the quality of guidelines in critical care medicine and that suggests it is low.[15]

Key questions about a proposed guideline might include the following:

- Is this enterprise primarily in the patients' best interests?
- Are those involved, individual clinician, Institution, academic body, industry, and government all primarily focused on patient benefit? If not what are the other areas of interest/conflict?
- Are there specific gains, which are not patient based which might accrue to any of the interested parties?
- How significant is the issue of cost containment for the state or other funding body, in the synthesis of the guideline and how does it impact on the benefit of the guidelines to the individual?

Gifts

Gift giving has always been a key part of marketing. In 2000 the pharmaceutical industry spent $13.2 billion on advertising and promotions directed at professionals, which amounted to 12% of all sales revenues.[16] The relevant guidelines from the DoH in the UK state that staff should 'refuse gifts, benefits, hospitality or sponsorship of any kind which might be seen to compromise their personal judgement or integrity and to avoid seeking to exert influence to obtain preferential consideration'.

The EC Directive 2001/83 Art. 94 says:

> Where medicinal products are being promoted to persons qualified to prescribe or supply them, no gifts, pecuniary advantages or benefits in kind may be supplied, offered or promised to such persons, unless they are inexpensive and relevant to the practice of medicine or pharmacy.

The most obvious way that conflicts of interest is manifested are in the form of a gift from the company to a doctor. These can be small such as pens or paperweights or they can be more substantial such as luxurious accommodation for a congress.[17] Gifts may be more in the form of sponsorship for attending meetings or an honorarium for talking at a meeting. The basic concept of providing 'something' for the recipient supposedly divorced from any obligation induces a feeling of obligation for the future. It does engender goodwill.[18] However, a gift invokes a favour—reciprocity. The cost is passed on to the public with higher priced drugs, which has been described as the misuse of public money with patients, or taxpayers, paying for a benefit captured by their physicians.[19,20] Some physicians meet industry representatives several times a month and often cite gifts as the sole reason.[1] Gifts often purchase *access* but to extrapolate that to purchasing changes in *practice* may be unfair. Interposed between the two is professional integrity but what price professional integrity among physicians? The American Medical Association adopted voluntary guidelines prohibiting cash or gifts but inexpensive gifts such as pens and notepads were allowed providing they were related to medical practice.[1] Washlick and Coyle have written a position paper, which recognizes the potential for small gifts to compromise clinical judgement.[21,22] This can be taken further. If the review by Wazana is correct, then even a meeting with a pharmaceutical representative might influence practice change and so simple company or flattery or both may be the real price for some.[23,24] Other forms of gift may also influence activity. In a review of 538 studies of industry–physician relations sponsored CME events with funding for travel or lodging for educational symposia were associated with increased prescription rates of the sponsor's medication. Incumbent in this is the observation that drug company sponsored CME frequently preferentially highlighted the sponsor's drug compared with other CME programs.

Patients may have views as to the probity of gift giving and taking. In a family practice patient survey, 48% disapproved of doctors receiving free dinners and 18% disapproved of physicians receiving ballpoint pens; 54% believed drug company gifts influence physician prescribing and 16% believed the influence was frequent.[25] Ideally patients need to have the correct, unbiased medical information when there are treatment choices so that informed decisions can be made without external influence. Transparent and consistent dealings between physicians and industry will provide some reassurance that the advice they receive is unbiased.

In summary, it is as naïve to think that any gift is dangerous as it is that all gifts are dangerous. We still depend on the integrity of physicians to not be persuaded because of gifts.

Innovation and research

Innovation poses some interesting dilemmas. Innovation will require time, manpower, and hence money to bring forward. While ideas may translate into patient benefit at some time the up front costs are rarely publicly supported. Hospitals with tight budgets rarely have money for innovation, competition for charitable funds is tight, and so the major source is industry. Such investment is key to future activity. Tensions are prone to develop if the immediate goals of the innovator and industry diverge. Compromise in direction may occur or there may need to be a trade-off between the immediate needs of industry and the financial needs of the research facility developing the program. This is fertile ground for conflict. In pharmaceuticals, the innovator is often industry with a need to test its developments. In a 'win–win' situation a great drug will bring financial reward to the company and kudos to the clinicians involved. Shareholders will be happy and patients will benefit. The world is rarely like that and *most developments have marginal or negligible benefits.* Financial success depends on advantage and clinical or research kudos needs positive results.[26] This is a key area for conflict.

Universities are now being run along business lines and are becoming centres of innovation.[27] The benefits are obvious. It circumvents industry and shareholders and reduces the external conflicts of interest and returns profits to the university. As academic posts also depend on successful bids for research income, it raises a further issue of whether this new direction of university entrepreneurship is in itself a potent source of conflict of interest. One of the most difficult aspects of research and industry is that the clinicians and institutions seem to need funding to do industry work. When carrying out research on behalf of a company, rewarding the doctors per patient recruited helps ensure adequate numbers for the trial but inevitably leads to concerns about a conflict of interest in the recruiting personnel. Without an incentive, the trial may fail and the incentive itself is often providing surplus money that can help fund other projects. As both the primary trial and the spin off research are all for patient benefit then it would seem ideal. The problems are many. The incentive may be the only reason for involvement so that the secondary projects can be done and hence are just a source of income.[28] This may then encourage activity that may be inappropriate and or reduce the quality of the work. The driving forces can identify the conflicts. There are two: money and kudos. The former is at corporate and personal level but has linkages to assessment exercises and other activities masquerading as being quality measures but underpinned by income. The latter phenomenon is organizational or personal kudos inevitably tied to ambition at whatever level it is partially dependent on financial linkage.

Education

The situation can become more complicated when industry is involved in the organization of educational meetings. Industry needs physicians to know about its products. Pamphlets are rarely read and directly run industry meetings relatively unsuccessful as they almost always favour their own product and are obvious. Indirect sponsorship is seen as a way to get information across. There is some evidence to suggest that in some environments a change of practice has been seen.[29] More useful are educational events where a secondary effect is that products are discussed, hopefully in a positive light.

Industry facilitates education by sponsorship. The quid pro quo is exposure of physicians to their advertising and to their product information. Mechanisms that increase the likelihood of the products being discussed whether by related topics on the program or using speakers who are likely to speak favourably will 'enhance' the product's profile. Paradoxically blatant pushing of a product by a speaker sponsored by industry is usually counter-productive. Surreptitious use of respected opinion leaders likely to speak favourably is far more effective especially at large meetings run by respected organizations where the assumption is that such activity cannot happen. Further goodwill can be engendered by generous provision of travel and accommodation. In all of these circumstances, professionals with integrity and intelligence are expected to use discretion in how they assimilate information and follow professional guidelines.

Share dealing and consultancy

An area that has been highlighted is the potential for involvement of physicians in share trading. It has been noted that physicians in research often have early access to information about their own projects or others. Premature disclosure of results or even probable results based on research could constitute 'insider trading' as could share trading using that information. Consultancy advice to investors either individually or through advisers could also constitute criminal activity.[30] Clearly there is a fine line between direct and indirect disclosure of information but ignorance is no defence with this kind of activity.

What the medical profession needs

Table 11.1 summarizes what the profession might reasonably expect from industry.

Table 11.1 Industry involvement

Developing new drugs—phenomenally expensive and almost entirely industry driven
New equipment—ideas from medicine and industry but development usually requires industry
Providing information about specific products
Grants for unrelated activities—educational grants
Setting up and running development programs
Funding research projects
Funding Fellows
Assisting running studies
Individual and local education support
Infrastructure and support for international meetings and forum
Assisting with national projects
Supporting national bodies

The Achilles heel of medicine is continuing medical education, which is required but is expensive. Many countries, if not most, owe a significant portion of their postgraduate education to industry funding by one route or another. The magnitude of industry involvement would become very clear if it was removed and it would be disastrous in the opinion of the authors.

What does industry need?

Industry needs to sell its products. In order to know what products to manufacture and to run clinical trials it needs an effective interface with clinicians. The stringent requirements to bring a product to market through licensing necessitate a close liaison with medicine. A spin-off of these endeavours has been a rising standard and cost of research, which paradoxically imposes financial restraint on research activity. They need to advertise the existence of the product through legitimate promotion and this may involve both product or brand identification activities.

Information of the efficacy of products can only be promulgated through discussion and debate so although studies and publications are useful, personal opinion and unsolicited recommendation are a far more powerful tool. The ultimate recommendation in the United Kingdom now would presumably be NICE, which can circumvent the need for advertising and could be considered, if successful, the ultimate advertising tool. Industry needs to get products to market and they need doctors not only as that market but also potentially to influence that market.

Opinion research and industry

In the United States, 28% of faculty with significant NIH funding also had industry research funds.[29,31] and 43% of faculty received gifts defined as discretionary funds, biomaterials, equipment educational support, and travel.[32] Many trials are fully supported by industry. A significant proportion of research fellows are dependent on industry although the exact number is unknown. These figures illustrate not just the potential for conflicts but more importantly the involvement of industry in medical research.

The role of sales representatives includes increasing awareness of the drug or product, so they may provide education and information but may also influence practice. In 2001 the budget for representatives in one part of the United States was a remarkable $100,000 for 11 doctors, which reputedly led to non-rational prescribing and increased costs of medications.[33] This would be very atypical of the United Kingdom at least in critical care. Junior doctors are perceived to be vulnerable with some suggestion of a link between company access and independent funding streams.[34,35] Although perceived to be highly effective, the reduction in numbers and access of representatives in the UK implies that they may be less effective than previously thought, or it may simply be that in the critical care environment central purchasing is a more worthwhile target. Work experience with doctors for which the doctor might receive a fee, has been criticized.[36]

Education has significant funding issues and it is inevitable that government commitment will fall as other priorities impose on budgets and that industry will be expected to make good the deficiencies.[37] Single company sponsorships have been criticized for the use of misleading titles, prominent brand names association, a lack of peer review, and are often highly promotional.[38] Yet most are considered good value and high quality.[39] Publication of symposia proceedings is also a potential area of conflict and are often heavily focused on single drugs.[38] In the United States the EU and the UK regulations abound to control potential abuses.[40] The expert opinion from a convincing and renowned speaker will carry an audience. They may 'owe' a company in one of many ways whether it be financial, travel and expenses, departmental support, fellowships, grants, or just a longstanding relationship. They are effectively compromised and may not even know it. Usually some of the audience will. The line between independent expert and company spokesperson appears grey.[39,41]

There are legitimate concerns as to industry-sponsored trials. Between 1997 and 2000 industry-sponsored trials increased by 62%. Author–industry affiliation increased to 66% and industry employees are increasingly appearing as authors.[42] This may reflect greater industry engagement and transparency but other influences may be less benign. For example, in sponsored studies, SSRI are far better than tricyclics than in non-sponsored studies. In one superb example, 45 of 45 industry sponsored rheumatology RCTs the results favoured the sponsor.[43] These problems abound to the extent where in some fields if you know the sponsor you know the outcome.[43] The odds ratio for an industry-sponsored paper to be favourable was 3.6 (CI 2.6–4.9) and if it was only assessing RCTs the number was 4.13 (CI 2.72–6.32).[44,45] The reader should of course be aware that these are all peer-reviewed papers usually in highly respected journals. Dubious research techniques should be eliminated. Classic tricks such as testing the trial drug against placebo or an ineffective dose or altered route of administration should be identified.[45] Likewise recruitment selectivity, drop out rates, late exclusions or inclusions, or altering the outcome measures.[46] It is interesting that in a survey of review articles details of techniques used in trials were rarely reported nor were potential conflicts of interest highlighting yet another area of potential problems.[47] The issue of how this can be controlled is complex. Journals try and enforce codes of practice in publication, reviewers look for deviation from acceptable practice, and most researchers do adhere to what they consider good practice. It is clearly not enough but how this can be improved without draconian regulations is unclear.

UK codes and regulation

In spite of the concerns and perceptions of medicine/ industry interactions, in reality there is a highly successful and symbiotic relationship. In the United Kingdom, the pharmaceutical industry has developed robust guidelines acknowledging both the need to foster relationships and defining clear rules of engagement.[48–50] There are specific guidelines for industry involvement in publication.[51] The Royal College of Physicians has a code of conduct that is representative of the central thrust of most other codes.[40] A key statement is that 'doctors should avoid accepting any pecuniary or material inducement that might compromise, or be regarded by others as likely to compromise, the independent exercise of their professional judgement and practice'.

In Good Medical Practice, the phrase 'you must not ask for or accept any inducement, gift or hospitality which may affect or be seen to affect your judgement' was added. It covers gifts prizes and samples. Only the company logo is allowed on the gift and it should be clear that it is entirely educational. Gifts should not exceed a very modest figure, which at one stage was £6.00. Industry-sponsored prizes for competitions should not exceed £100.00 and the competition should be serious in nature and relevant to the competitors.

In meetings purporting to be educational, the speakers cannot be chosen solely by the company and sponsorship should be openly declared at the beginning. Hospitality for speakers is acceptable but should be commensurate with what they themselves or their employer might provide. Any honoraria and expenses should be handled through an independent scientific body. Support to attend meetings, whether registration, travel, or accommodation, should again be acceptable but should not exceed that which they or their employer might reasonably supply. The attendance at the meeting should be in the interests of the service, be free of commercial pressure, and not be touristic in nature. There are clear guidelines on accompanying persons. Local meetings should be educational with only modest support and again clear guidelines exist. Grant scholarships are acceptable but the funds must rest with the institution.

The guidelines regarding research are more complex. Financial matters should bypass the involved clinicians and there should be no financial interest for either clinicians or patients. Indemnity must be provided. With regards to gag clauses, there should be free access to data, independent analysis, and no restraint on publication.[14] It is imperative that academic institutions adopt and uniformly enforce these standards despite potential short-term financial losses. Delays for patent application are approved but should be short. There must be clear declaration of interest. The rules of engagement for clinicians working with or advising companies are clearly stated. Indeed this document should be mandatory reading for all doctors.

Industry also has guidelines and the interface between the medical profession and industry are far more rigid than one might imagine. In the United Kingdom, the ABPI is very active and has an impressive

50-page Code of Practice (2008), which is currently being updated. Industry is well informed of the rules by which doctors must operate but there is a curious lack of information for doctors about the rules under which industry operates.

Conclusions

Despite the bad press, significant conflicts of interest with potentially damaging outcomes are relatively rare, but highly publicized when detected. Medicine and industry need to be symbiotic and government should act as an enabler of such a relationship. Strong regulatory authorities need to establish clear and obvious behaviour boundaries to inhibit abuse without being so draconian as to make co-operation impossible. A pragmatic approach requires the involvement of those active in research and engaging with industry rather than disengaged bureaucrats. In any situation where the interests of multiple institutions and individuals coalesce there are necessarily bound to be conflicts. In health care, it is the interests of the patients that are paramount and while there have been a number of episodes where individuals and companies have profited, given the size of the industry and the complexity of modern health care the incidence of patient harm following on conflict of interests remains low. Excessive and over intrusive regulation may produce an example of the law of unintended consequences where patients suffer through stifling of innovation. Recognizing the problem is in itself a form of solution.

Some useful addresses

+ Code of Practice for the Pharmaceutical Industry: www.abpi.org.uk
+ Joint Declaration on the Cooperation between the Medical Profession and the Pharmaceutical Industry: www.efpia.org.
+ The Code of Ethics and Standards 2004: www.rpsgb.org.uk/members/ethics/
+ ISPOR(76): http://www.ispor.org/workpaper/healthscience/TFCodeEthics.pdf.

- The pharmaceutical industry and the clinical professions. Royal College of Physicians:

- http://www.rcplondon.ac.uk/pubs/journal/journ_34_mar_ed4.htm

- Research ethics, UK: http://www.corec.org.uk/

- *EC Directive 2001/83 Art.*

- Biomedial ethics: bioethicsweb.ac.uk/browse/

- Prescription Medicines Code of Practice Authority. Code of practice for the pharmaceutical industry. PMCPA, London, 1998.

References

1 Katz D, Caplan AL, Merz JF (2003). All gifts large and small: toward an understanding of the ethics of pharmaceutical industry gift-giving. *Am J Bioeth.* 3(3): 39–46.

2 Gale EA (2003). Between two cultures: the expert clinician and the pharmaceutical industry. *Clin Med.* 3(6): 538–541.

3 Lexchin J, Bero LA, Djulbegovic B, Clark O (2003). Pharmaceutical industry sponsorship and research outcome and quality: systematic review. *BMJ* 326(7400): 1167–1170.

4 Kjaergard LL, Als-Nielsen B (2002). Association between competing interests and authors' conclusions: epidemiological study of randomized clinical trials published in the BMJ. *BMJ.* 325(7358): 249.

5 Als-Nielsen B, Chen W, Gluud C, Kjaergard LL (2003). Association of funding and conclusions in randomized drug trials: a reflection of treatment effect or adverse Events? *J Am Med Assoc* 290(7): 921–928.

6 Brown A, Kraft D, Schmitz SM, Sharpless V, Martin C, Shah R, et al. (2006). Association of industry sponsorship to published outcomes in gastrointestinal clinical research. *Clin Gastroenterol Hepatol.* 4(12): 1445–1451.

7 Felson DT, Glantz L. (2004). A surplus of positive trials: Weighing biases and reconsidering equipoise. *Arthritis Research & Therapy.* 6(3): 117–119.

8 Hartmann M, Knoth H, Schulz D, Knoth S (2003). Industry-sponsored economic studies in oncology vs studies sponsored by nonprofit organisations. *Br J Cancer* 89(8): 1405–1408.

9 Stewart PM, Stears A, Tomlinson JW, Brown MJ (2008). Regulation – the real threat to clinical research. *BMJ* 337:a1732.

10 Bernard GR, Vincent JL, Laterre PF, LaRosa SP, Dhainaut JF, Lopez-Rodriguez A, et al. (2001). Efficacy and safety of recombinant human activated protein C for severe sepsis. *N Engl J Med.* 344(10): 699–709.

11 Dellinger RP, Carlet JM, Masur H, Gerlach H, Calandra T, Cohen J, et al. (2004). Surviving Sepsis Campaign guidelines for management of severe sepsis and septic shock. *Intensive Care Med.* **30**(4): 536–555.

12 Eichacker PQ, Natanson C, Danner RL (2006). Surviving sepsis – practice guidelines, marketing campaigns, and Eli Lilly. *N Engl J Med.* **355**(16): 1640–1642.

13 Penston J (2007). Patients' preferences shed light on the murky world of guideline-based medicine. *J Eval Clin Pract.***13**(1): 154–159.

14 Rashidian A, Eccles MP, Russell I (2008). Falling on stony ground? A qualitative study of implementation of clinical guidelines' prescribing recommendations in primary care. *Health Policy.* **85**(2): 148–161.

15 Sinuff T, Patel RV, Adhikari NK, Meade MO, Schunemann HJ, Cook DJ (2008). Quality of professional society guidelines and consensus conference statements in critical care. *Crit Care Med.* **36**(4): 1049–1058.

16 Rosenthal MB, Berndt ER, Donohue JM, Frank RG, Epstein AM (2002). Promotion of prescription drugs to consumers. *N Engl J Med.* **346**(7): 498–505.

17 Desmet C (2003). Pharmaceutical firms' generosity and physicians: legal aspects in Belgium. *Med Law.* **22**(3): 473–487.

18 Sandberg WS, Carlos R, Sandberg EH, Roizen MF (1997). The effect of educational gifts from pharmaceutical firms on medical students' recall of company names or products. *Acad Med.* **72**(10): 916–918.

19 DeMaria AN (2007). Your soul for a pen? *J Am Coll Cardiol.* **49**(11): 1220–1222.

20 Iserson KV, Cerfolio RJ, Sade RM (2007). Politely refuse the pen and note pad: gifts from industry to physicians harm patients. *Ann Thorac Surg.* **84**(4): 1077–1084.

21 Washlick JR, Welch SS (2008). Physician–vendor marketing and financial relationships under attack. *J Health Life Sci Law.* **2**(1): 151, 153–228.

22 Coyle SL (2002). Physician–industry relations. Part 2: organizational issues. *Ann Intern Med.* **136**(5): 403–406.

23 Blumenthal D, Causino N, Campbell E, Louis KS. Relationships between academic institutions and industry in the life sciences – an industry survey. *N Engl J Med.* **334**(6): 368–373.

24 Wazana A (2000). Gifts to physicians from the pharmaceutical industry. *JAMA.* **283**(20): 2655–2658.

25 Blake RL, Jr., Early EK (1995). Patients' attitudes about gifts to physicians from pharmaceutical companies. *J Am Board Fam Pract.* **8**(6): 457–464.

26 Friedberg M, Saffran B, Stinson TJ, Nelson W, Bennett CL (1999). Evaluation of conflict of interest in economic analyses of new drugs used in oncology. *Jama.* **282**(15): 1453–1457.

27 Evans GR, Packham DE (2003). Ethical issues at the university-industry interface: a way forward? *Sci Eng Ethics.* **9**(1): 3–16.

28 Ashar BH, Miller RG, Getz KJ, Powe NR (2004). Prevalence and determinants of physician participation in conducting pharmaceutical-sponsored clinical trials and lectures. *J Gen Intern Med.* **19**(11): 1140–1145.

29 Blumenthal D, Campbell EG, Causino N, Louis KS (1996). Participation of life-science faculty in research relationships with industry. *N Engl J Med.* **335**(23): 1734–1749.

30 Freestone DS, Mitchell H (1993). Inappropriate publication of trial results and potential for allegations of illegal share dealing. *BMJ.* **306**(6885): 1112–1114.

31 Campbell EG, Weissman JS, Ehringhaus S, Rao SR, Moy B, Feibelmann S, et al. (2007). Institutional academic industry relationships. *JAMA.***298**(15): 1779–1786.

32 Campbell EG, Louis KS, Blumenthal D (1998). Looking a gift horse in the mouth: corporate gifts supporting life sciences research. *JAMA.* **279**(13): 995–999.

33 Whiteway DE (2001). Physicians and the pharmaceutical industry: a growing embarrassment and liability. *WMJ.* **100**(9): 39–44, 57.

34 Lichstein PR, Turner RC, O'Brien K (1992). Impact of pharmaceutical company representatives on internal medicine residency programs. A survey of residency program directors. *Arch Intern Med.* **152**(5): 1009–1013.

35 Wazana A (2000). Physicians and the pharmaceutical industry: is a gift ever just a gift? *JAMA.* **283**(3): 373–380.

36 Wall LL, Brown D (2002). Pharmaceutical sales representatives and the doctor/patient relationship. *Obstet Gynecol.* **100**(3): 594–599.

37 Drack G, Kuhn HP, Haller U (2003). Is continuing medical education under suspicion of corruption? Contribution to the discussion by the committee for quality preservation of the swiss society of gynaecology and obstetrics. [German]. *Gynakologisch Geburtshilfliche Rundschau.* **43**(2): 111–117.

38 Bero LA, Galbraith A, Rennie D (1992). The publication of sponsored symposiums in medical journals. *N Engl J Med.* **327**(16): 1135–1140.

39 Carney SL, Nair KR, Sales MA, Walsh J (2001). Pharmaceutical industry-sponsored meetings: Good value or just a free meal? *Intern. Med. J.* **31**(8): 488–491.

40 Bennett J, Collins J (2002). The relationship between physicians and the biomedical industries: advice from the Royal College of Physicians. *Clin Med.* **2**(4): 320–322.

41 Wilson FS (2003). Continuing medical education: Ethical collaboration between sponsor and industry. *Clinical Orthopaed Related Res Issue.* **412**: 33–37.

42 Buchkowsky SS, Jewesson PJ (2004). Industry sponsorship and authorship of clinical trials over 20 years. *Ann Pharmacother.* **38**(4): 579–585.

43 Fries JF, Krishnan E (2004). Equipoise, design bias, and randomized controlled trials: the elusive ethics of new drug development. *Arthritis Res Ther.* **6**(3): R250–R255.

44 Bekelman JE, Li Y, Gross CP (2003). Scope and impact of financial conflicts of interest in biomedical research: a systematic review. *JAMA.* **289**(4): 454–465.

45 Kjaergard LL, Nikolova D, Gluud C (1999). Randomized clinical trials in hepatology: Predictors of quality. *Hepatology.* **30**(5): 1134–1138.

46 Peloso PM, Riley ML (1998). Controlled clinical trials and clinical patient-care: sometimes in conflict. *Ann R Coll Physicians Surg Can.* **31**(8): 372–374.

47 Roundtree AK, Kallen MA, Lopez-Olivo MA, Kimmel B, Skidmore B, Ortiz Z, et al. (2009). Poor reporting of search strategy and conflict of interest in over 250 narrative and systematic reviews of two biologic agents in arthritis: a systematic review. *J Clin Epidemiol.* **62**(2): 128–137.

48 Simmonds HJ (2004). Association of British Pharmaceutical Industry's code of practice needs to be clarified. *BMJ.* **329**(7462): 404.

49 Palumbo FB, Barnes R, Deverka P, McGhan W, Mullany L, Wertheimer A (2004). ISPOR Code of Ethics for Researchers background article–report of the ISPOR Task Force on Code of Ethics for Researchers. *Value Health.* **7**(2): 111–117.

50 Milne RJ (2004). ISPOR's "Code of Ethics for Researchers": is it ethical? *Value Health.* **7**(2): 107–110.

51 Wager E, Field EA, Grossman L (2003). Good publication practice for pharmaceutical companies. *Curr Med Res Opin.* **19**(3): 149–154.

Index